THE REAL
GERMAN WAR PLAN
1904-14

Terence Zuber

The
History
Press

For LTC Eldon K. Schroeder
Commander 2nd Battalion 2nd Infantry

Cover illustrations: front, top: Schlieffen Plan map drawn by Glad Stockdale; the younger Moltke; front, below: machine-gunners in firing position; back: the Kaiser and the younger Moltke, as the trumpeters play *General Halt* at the end of the last *Kaisermanoever* in 1913.

First published 2011

The History Press
The Mill, Brimscombe Port
Stroud, Gloucestershire, GL5 2QG
www.thehistorypress.co.uk

© Terence Zuber, 2011

The right of Terence Zuber to be identified as the Author
of this work has been asserted in accordance with the
Copyrights, Designs and Patents Act 1988.

British Library Cataloguing in Publication Data.
A catalogue record for this book is available from the British Library.

ISBN 978 0 7524 5664 5

Typesetting and origination by The History Press
Printed in Great Britain
Manufacturing managed by Jellyfish Print Solutions Ltd

THE REAL GERMAN WAR PLAN, 1904–14

The Schlieffen Plan

From 1920 until 1999 very little was known concerning German war planning prior to the Great War. It was, however, 'common knowledge' that in 1914 the Germans had been following the 'Schlieffen plan', which was presented in a *Denkschrift* (study) written by the German chief of the general staff, Count Alfred von Schlieffen, and dated December 1905. Beginning in 1920, semi-official histories, written by retired First World War German army officers such as Lieutenant-Colonel Wolfgang Foerster, General Hermann von Kuhl and General Wilhelm Groener, as well as the first volume of the official history of the war produced by the Reichsarchiv in 1925,[1] first revealed the Schlieffen plan, not as the complete document but as a very general paraphrase. The intent of the Schlieffen plan was to annihilate the French army in one quick enormous battle (*Vernichtungsschlacht*). The concept was to deploy seven-eighths of the German army between Metz and Aachen, on the right wing of the German front, leaving one-eighth of the army to guard the left flank in Lorraine against a French attack. No forces would be sent to protect East Prussia against the Russians. The right wing would sweep through Belgium and northern France, if necessary swinging to the west of Paris, continually turning the French left flank, and eventually pushing the French army into Switzerland.

If the French attacked the German left, in Lorraine, they would be doing the Germans a favour, for the attack would accomplish nothing and the French forces in the north would be that much weaker. Groener et al. (the 'Schlieffen School') maintained that this *Denkschrift* represented the culmination of Schlieffen's military thought and provided Germany with a nearly infallible war plan; all that Schlieffen's successor, Helmuth von Moltke, needed to do was to execute the Schlieffen plan, and Germany would have been practically assured of victory in

August 1914.They contended that Moltke did not understand the concept of the Schlieffen plan and modified it – 'watered it down' – by strengthening the forces on the left wing at the expense of the main attack on the right. For this reason, the German army failed to destroy the French army in the initial campaign in the west in 1914.

The original war plans of both Schlieffen and Moltke were kept under tight control in the Reichsarchiv on the Brauhausberg in Potsdam and treated as secret documents, made available only to reliable officer-historians and then strictly on a 'need to know' basis. The details of Schlieffen's planning were never revealed. Moreover, nothing was known of the war planning from 1906 to 1914 of Schlieffen's successor, the younger Moltke, aside from the fact that he had 'watered down' the Schlieffen plan. The German army archive was then destroyed by British bombers on the night of 14 April 1945.

It seemed that only the original text of the famous Schlieffen plan *Denkschrift* had survived the bombing, because it had been transferred out of Potsdam. It had been seized by the American army and in the early 1950s was stored in the American National Archives, where Gerhard Ritter found it. He published the text in German in 1956 (in English in 1958).[2] In preparing the plan for publication, Ritter learned from Foerster that the *Denkschrift* had actually been written in January and February 1906, after Schlieffen had retired (and no longer had any authority to write war plans), and backdated to make it appear that it was written while he was still chief of the general staff.

Ritter did not submit the *Denkschrift* to a thorough analysis, nor did he explain the many inconsistencies it contained. Instead, he concluded that the *Denkschrift* confirmed that the Schlieffen plan was the template for the German war plan in 1914. Ritter further deduced that the Germans had an aggressive war plan, which was the proximate cause of the Great War. Ritter's opinions became 'common knowledge', so much so that the Schlieffen plan is a question in British A-level school-leaving examinations and the topic of commercially available term papers.

The Schlieffen Plan's Ghost Divisions

During the tenure of both Schlieffen and Moltke, the German army conscripted only 55 per cent of each year group. Both Schlieffen and Moltke argued that this was insufficient and that Germany needed to implement genuine universal conscription. This was never accomplished in peacetime for two reasons: the expense of the High Seas Fleet and the fundamental opposition of the German Socialist Party (SPD) to the German army. The SPD was doctrinaire Marxist, opposed to 'militarism' and convinced that the European proletariat would make war impossible by paralysing mobilisation with a general strike. The SPD's motto was 'not one man, not one penny' for the army, and any attempt by the German government to increase the size of the army would bring on a domestic political crisis that was best avoided.

The Reichsarchiv history freely acknowledged that Schlieffen did not have enough divisions to execute the plan outlined in the *Denkschrift*: 'a number of the reserve corps which were employed [in the Schlieffen plan] as complete [two-division] corps, did not have the second division. The mobilization plan [also] did not provide for the immediate creation of the [eight] ersatz corps.'[3] The Schlieffen plan also included the 43rd Infantry Division, which never existed. It employed ninety-six divisions, including twenty-four imaginary divisions. Ludendorff said outright that even in a one-front war against France alone, Schlieffen was twenty-four divisions short of the total force required. The *Denkschrift* also expressly said that in a one-front war even ninety-six divisions were not adequate and more – non-existent – manoeuvre units needed to be raised.[4] The Reichsarchiv said that the need to raise these units was an integral part of the plan and Schlieffen's legacy to Moltke. Most of these divisions were never established.

Inventing the Schlieffen Plan

Unknown to all but a few East German and Soviet archivists, several documents had survived the Potsdam bombing because they were in a nearby undamaged office building. They had been seized by the Red Army and returned to the East German military archive, but not made available to historians. With the fall of the Wall these documents came into the possession of the unified German military archives at Freiburg, and therefore were accessible for historical research. Foremost among these documents were two Reichsarchiv studies: Wilhelm Dieckmann's *Der Schlieffenplan*, a summary of Schlieffen's planning until 1904, and Hellmuth Greiner's analysis of the German west front intelligence estimate from 1885 to 1914.

I utilised these documents, along with several of Schlieffen's war games in the Bavarian army archive in Munich, to produce a fundamental reappraisal of Schlieffen's planning in 'The Schlieffen Plan Reconsidered' in *War in History*,[5] and in *Inventing the Schlieffen Plan: German War Planning 1871–1914* in 2002.[6] I pointed out that the Schlieffen plan was for a one-front war against France only, which was unlikely in 1906 and impossible in 1914. Even in this one-front war, the plan required twenty-four divisions that existed neither in 1906 nor in 1914. Schlieffen's purpose was not to write a war plan using 'ghost divisions' but as one more proposal to realise full conscription. He wanted to show that even a one-front war against France, and even with twenty-four non-existent 'ghost divisions', the German army was going to have its hands full.

Incongruously, in August 1914 the original text of the great plan was the property of Schlieffen's daughters and was being stored with the family photos. None of Schlieffen's surviving war games tested the Schlieffen plan. In fact, Schlieffen's actual war plans and war games were based on using Germany's interior position and rail mobility to counter-attack against the expected French and Russian offensives, and was not a desperate attempt to invade France.

My conclusion, that there never was a Schlieffen plan, met with considerable hostility. The existence of a Schlieffen plan had become dogma. An enormous body of historical explanation, including German war guilt, was based on the Schlieffen plan. Many in the historical establishment were on the record confirming the importance of the Schlieffen plan and were outraged that their sacred cow had been slaughtered.

More German Planning Documents Appear

In the autumn of 2004 the German army historical section (*Militärgeschichtliches Forschungsamt* – MGFA) held a conference titled *Der Schlieffenplan*. In preparation for this conference the Bundesarchiv-Militärarchiv (BA-MA), the German army archives at Freiburg, made available to the MGFA document BA-MA RH 61/v.96, a summary of German deployment plans from 1893/94 to 1914/15.[7] This document had been in the Potsdam army archive but was not accessible to researchers between 1996 and 2002. It provides, for the first time, a look at Schlieffen's deployment plans in 1904/05, 1905/06 and 1906/07, as well as those of the younger Moltke from 1907/08 to 1914/15. This document is presented here in English for the first time and is given the first critical analysis in any language.

Subsequent to the Schlieffen plan conference, a summary of Schlieffen's 1905 *Generalstabsreise West* (west front general staff ride) was discovered in the Freiburg archive by a MGFA historian.[8] This exercise is significant because members of the Schlieffen School contended since the 1930s that in this war game Schlieffen had tested the Schlieffen plan, but revealed the conduct of the exercise only in a sketchy outline. Nevertheless, the MGFA historian failed to discuss the details of this document, saying that it was 'obviously' the predecessor of the Schlieffen plan; a full summary and analysis of it is presented here for the first time.

These two documents are problematic because they are not the original war game after-action reports or war plan; they are only summaries written post-war by official German army historians who had a stake in fostering the

CONTENTS

ACKNOWLEDGEMENTS

I am deeply indebted to the History Department of the University of Würzburg, and especially my *Doktorvater*, Professor Wolfgang Altgeld, and Professor Rainer Schmidt for their insistence on the central importance of primary sources in the study of history. I conducted research for this book at the Kriegsarchiv in Munich, the Militärarchiv in Freiburg, the Hauptsstaatsarchiv in Stuttgart and in Dresden and the Generallandesarchiv in Karlsruhe, of which I have nothing but the fondest memories.

Publishing with The History Press is a pleasure. I want in particular to thank my editors, Simon Hamlet and Abbie Wood. Heather Wetzel and Herr Klaus Schinagl prepared the maps. West Virginia Northern Community College has given me invaluable administrative support, and the Dean, Larry Tackett, has assisted with his computer expertise.

Schlieffen plan dogma. Nevertheless, with careful analysis they add considerably to our knowledge of German army planning prior to the Great War. These new documents also confirm my initial thesis: there never was a Schlieffen plan.

In addition, this book utilises other operational documents that I have found since *Inventing the Schlieffen Plan* was published in 2002, as well as hitherto unused German intelligence estimates. The result is the first detailed and credible picture of German war planning from 1904 to 1914.[9]

Notes

1 H. von Kuhl, *Der deutsche Generalstab in Vorbereitung und Durchführung des Weltkrieges* (Berlin, 1920). Reichsarchiv, *Der Weltkrieg* (Berlin, 1925), especially pp. 49–65.

2 Original documents: Bundesarchiv-Militärarchiv (BA-MA) Freiburg im Breisgau, *Nachlass* Schlieffen N138 (Schlieffen plan *Denkschrift*) N141K (map). G. Ritter, *Der Schlieffenplan. Kritik eines Mythos* (Munich, 1956); *The Schlieffen Plan: Critique of a Myth* (London, 1958).

3 Reichsarchiv, *Der Weltkrieg* I (Berlin, 1925) p. 55. The ersatz divisions were to be made up of excess trained reservists. Until 1913 there was no equipment or cadres available to form these units.

4 Having discussed the movement of the right wing around Paris, which included the employment of the eight non-existent ersatz corps and the eight non-existent active and reserve divisions, Schlieffen wrote (Zuber, *German War Planning*, p. 195): '*it will soon become clear that we will be too weak to continue the operation in this direction* [author's italics]. We will have the same experience as that of all previous conquerors, that offensive warfare both requires and uses up very strong forces, that these forces continually become weaker even as those of the defender become stronger, and that this is especially true in a land that bristles with fortresses.'

5 T. Zuber, 'The Schlieffen Plan Reconsidered' in *War in History*, 1999; 3: pp. 262–305.

6 T. Zuber, *Inventing the Schlieffen Plan: German War Planning 1871–1914* (Oxford, 2002). I translated these documents in: T. Zuber, *German War Planning, 1891–1914: Sources and Interpretations* (Boydell and Brewer, 2004).

7 The text of this document is reproduced in German in *Der Schlieffenplan*, Hans Ehlert, Michael Epkenhans & Gerhard Groß (eds) (Paderborn, Munich, Vienna, Zurich, 2006) pp. 341–484.

8 Also in German in *Der Schlieffenplan*, Ehlert/Epkenhans/Gross (Paderborn, 2006) pp. 138–40.

9 While 85 per cent of this book consists of new material, it has been necessary to reprint some of my previously published work.

SCHLIEFFEN'S LAST WAR PLANS, 1891–1904

French Plan XIV (1898–1903)

The French field army included thirty-eight active and twelve divisions – fifty infantry divisions in total. Plan XIV concentrated the French army on its border with Germany in a tight diamond formation from St Dizier to Nancy to Epinal.[1] It pushed forward an advance guard 1st Army (three corps) in front of Nancy. There were three armies grouped behind it: the 4th (four corps) on the left, east of St Dizier; the 3rd (four corps) in the centre, south of Neufchâteau; and the 2nd (five corps) on the right, at Epinal. Behind the 3rd and 4th was the 5th, reserve army (three corps). There were three groups of four reserve divisions, one each behind the French left, centre and right. The French operational concept was based on the theories of Bonnal, who called this formation a *bataillon carrée*, which he said was the same one used by Napoleon. The strategy was defensive-offensive: advanced guard army would engage the enemy, forming a base of manoeuvre for the 2nd, 3rd and 4th Armies. The 5th Army would deliver the decisive attack.

German Intelligence Estimate in West 1885–1903

From 1885 to 1894 the Germans had an agent in place in the French eastern railway system who provided them with abstracts of the French rail-march tables, and even the actual march tables. After 1894 the agent material dried up and German intelligence was limited to evaluating 'open source' material, such as improvements to the French rail net or changes in French peacetime force structure. The Germans were reduced to guesses concerning the French deployment, and were painfully aware of this fact.

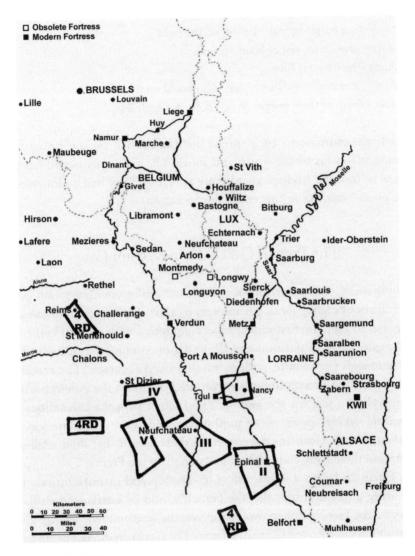

French Plan XIV (1898–1903)

The Germans were always completely in the dark concerning French operational intentions, that is, the course of action the French intended to adopt when deployment was completed. In general, the French could conduct an immediate attack into German Lorraine between Metz and Strasbourg or, based on their border fortifications, they could conduct a defensive-offensive operation.

Another major problem for German intelligence was determining how many reserve divisions the French would raise, how they would deploy, and how far the French would trust them in combat. From 1899/1900 to 1903 the Germans believed that the French would deploy with four armies on line:

1st Army (four corps) Epinal – Belfort on the right
2nd Army (five corps) east of Neufchâteau
3rd Army (three corps) Toul
4th Army (four corps) St Dizier – Ste Ménehould on the left
and four groups of three reserve divisions, one for each army.[2]

The German estimate to 1903 spread out the French on too broad a front, extending it too far to the north and south. The Germans would have been surprised to find the advance guard army at Nancy. They had no knowledge of Bonnal's neo-Napoleonic concept of the operation.

The French Quick-Firing 75mm Gun

Beginning in 1896, the Germans rearmed their artillery with a 77mm gun that could fire about eight rounds per minute. In 1897 the French introduced their famous 75mm gun, the first artillery piece equipped with a recoil brake, which kept the gun stable in position and allowed a maximum rate of fire of twenty to thirty rounds per minute, with much improved accuracy.[3] The recoil brake also permitted the French to put an armoured shield on the gun to protect the crew, as well as a seat for the gunner. The French kept the capabilities of the *mademoiselle soixante-quinze* secret until it was used against the Boxers in China in 1901, when the Germans discovered to their horror that their artillery was obsolete and their army completely out-gunned by the French.

The Germans began a frantic effort to develop and manufacture their own quick-firing gun. Until they did, the French would be guaranteed artillery fire superiority; the French artillery would suppress the unarmoured German guns and then crush the unprotected German infantry. The Germans did not begin to rearm with the improved '1896 n/A' until 1905. Fielding was not completed until 1908. Attacking France before 1908 was tantamount to German national suicide. The argument advanced so often that Schlieffen intended the Schlieffen plan for a war in 1906 is, therefore, unlikely: Schlieffen knew full well that Germany could not conduct an offensive war until the new artillery had been fully fielded, the crews were trained and tactical doctrine modified to accommodate the new weapon.

Schlieffen's Planning to 1903/04

When Schlieffen became chief of the general staff in 1891 it was clear that Germany faced the prospect of a two-front war: the Germans had allowed the

Reinsurance Treaty with Russia to lapse and Franco-Russian rapprochement was clearly under way. The most dangerous – and most likely – Franco-Russian course of action was to conduct simultaneous offensives. This would ensure that the Germans would be outnumbered on both fronts and would not be able to use their interior position to mass against one opponent.

Until 1900/01 Schlieffen usually deployed about two-thirds of the German army against France and one-third against Russia. Little of Schlieffen's west front planning survives, but it is clear that with such a division of forces, the German army was too weak to conduct an offensive against France. A *Denkschrift*, written by one of Schlieffen's senior staff officers in 1895, stated that an attack against the French border fortifications could not be decisive. Schlieffen's first *Denkschrift* concerning an attack through Belgium, in 1897, concluded that the German army was too weak for such an operation. The only *Denkschrift* for an offensive in the west was written not by Schlieffen but by General von Beseler in 1900. It provided for an advance by half the army through the Ardennes and across the Meuse while the other half advanced from Lorraine to fix the French in place. The intent was to break the French border fortifications by attacking them from the front and rear.[4] The disadvantage of this plan was that the French would be on an interior position between the two halves of the German army. They would probably hold off the German forces in Lorraine with the aid of their border fortifications and mass against the German right wing.

Beginning in 1899/1900 Schlieffen used two deployment plans (*Aufmärsche*). *Aufmarsch* I was for a war against France, though usually a force was left to defend East Prussia against the Russians. *Aufmarsch* II involved a stronger concentration in the east.

In 1900/01 and 1901/02 Schlieffen radically changed the war plan, deploying forty-four divisions in the east and only twenty-four in the west. This was called the *Grosser Ostaufmarsch* (Great Eastern Deployment). It appears that his intent was to maul the Russians, forcing the French to advance forward of their border fortifications and attack in order to rescue their Russian ally, at which point Schlieffen would utilise rail mobility to counter-attack against the French offensive. By the 1902/03 *Aufmarschplan* he returned the ratio of forces to forty-four divisions in the west, twenty-four in the east.[5]

All of Schlieffen's *Generalstabsreisen Ost*, his general staff rides in the east, played a Russian offensive, with the Germans using rail mobility to counter-attack. The 1894 *Generalstabsreise Ost* was the template for the Battle of Tannenberg in August 1914: the Germans exploited the fact that the Russians would be forced to deploy two armies, one attacking from Lithuania to the east, one from Warsaw to the south, which were divided by the Masurian Lakes. The Germans used rail mobility and interior lines to mass against the southern army and destroy it. The 1902 *Generalstabsreise Ost* played an *Ostaufmarsch* in which Schlieffen deployed nearly half the German army in the east, consistent with his deployment plans at that time. Nevertheless, the exercise still played a German counter-attack. In 1903 Schlieffen played a massive Russian attack down the Vistula, which was met by an equally massive German transfer of eleven corps by rail from the west to the east for a counter-attack.[6]

In 1903/04 Schlieffen planned only for *Aufmarsch* I, with sixty-five divisions in the west and ten divisions in the east. *Aufmarsch* II was written only as a 'study', not a formal war plan.

In the west, the Germans were spread evenly from St Vith in the Ardennes to Freiburg in south Germany. In Lorraine, the Germans were deployed well to the east, along the Saar. This formation was suited for a defence along the Saar against a French attack, followed by a German counter-attack with the 1st and 2nd Armies. This is somewhat surprising since the Germans probably expected to be opposed by thirty-two active and twelve reserve divisions – forty-four infantry divisions in total. It may be explained by the fact that, given the French border fortifications and the superiority of the French 75mm gun, Schlieffen did not feel that the German army was strong enough to conduct an outright offensive.

French 1900/01 Intelligence Estimate[7]

The 1900/01 French intelligence estimate said that the Germans had twenty-three corps (forty-six divisions) and twenty-four reserve divisions, seventy divisions in total, which was essentially correct. Five active corps and eight reserve divisions, eighteen divisions in total, would be deployed against the Russians, leaving fifty-two divisions against the French. The French based their estimate of the German deployment on the density and location of the German rail net. The Germans would deploy on line, without an advance guard or reserve, with a maximum density of one corps leading and a second following. The Germans active corps would deploy on a front from Metz–Diedenhofen (Thionville) to Sarrebourg. The German reserve divisions would deploy in three groups behind the left, centre and right.

The French 1899 hypothesis, that the Germans would attack with four corps from Alsace to turn the French right to the east of Epinal, had been rejected: the German forces in Alsace would be on the defensive. The German concept would be to launch immediately a violent offensive from Diedenhofen to turn the French left, while the German centre at Sarrebourg attacked towards the *trouée de Charmes* between Toul and Epinal to fix the French forces there in place.

The Germans would attack twenty-four hours after they had finished their deployment. If they attacked solely with their active army units, they could cross the border on the fifteenth day of mobilisation. If they waited until the reserve

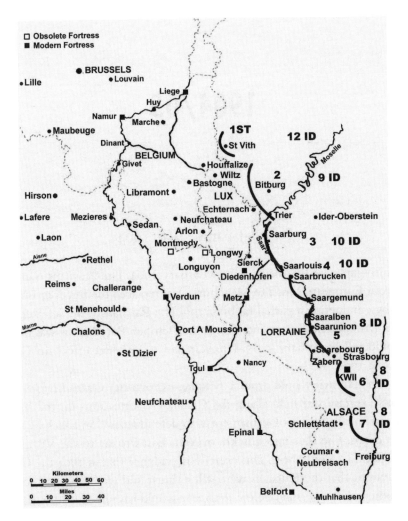

1903/04 *Aufmarsch* I *West*

divisions and the supply units of the active army corps deployed, then they could not attack until the eighteenth day, in which case the French would have completed their deployment first. According to the French estimate, the most important point of difference between the French and German plans was that the German was 'purely offensive'.

The French estimate was apparently still applicable in 1903. If compared with the German 1903/04 deployment, it is clear that the French would have had some surprises too. The Germans employed sixty-five divisions in the west, not fifty-two. But even if the Germans did launch an offensive, it would have come much later than anticipated; they were not densely concentrated in Lorraine and the right wing extended further to the north than predicted.

1904/05

Russo-Japanese War, 1904

The Russo-Japanese War began on 8 February 1904. The Russians transferred forces from European Russia to Manchuria, but replaced the forces in European Russia by conducting a partial mobilisation. The Russians were defeated at the Battle of Mukden in August and Sha-ho in October. Port Arthur was besieged and would fall in January 1905. The war had no evident effect on German planning in 1904.

The German army held annual *Festungs-* (Fortress) *Generalstabsreisen*. In 1904 this exercise was held along the German fortifications on the Vistula.[8] The scenario called for six German corps to defend against an attack by sixteen Russian corps. The Russians quickly overran East Prussia to the Vistula with the exception of Königsberg. This exercise is evidence that in 1904 the German army thought that the Russians were still a threat and would remain so in the future, otherwise the *Festungs-Generalstabsreise* would have been held in the west.

1904 International Affairs

On 8 April the Anglo-French Entente was concluded, settling all outstanding differences and paving the way for British military assistance to France in case of a war with Germany. Between 27 October and 23 November Russia and Germany conducted negotiations for an alliance, but these broke down over Russian unwillingness to compromise the alliance with France.

Document RH 61/v.96
(Summary of German War Plans 1893–1914)[9]

This document, in the Bundesarchiv-Militärarchiv, the German army archive, was probably compiled after the Great War by either a Reichsarchiv historian or a historian from the Wehrmacht historical section (*Kriegsgeschichtliche Forschungsanstalt*). There are numerous indications in internal Reichsarchiv documents that it was intended to publish a second, revised edition of at least the first, third and fourth volumes of the German army official history of the Great War, which covers the Marne campaign. RH 61/v.96 was probably written in the late 1930s and early 1940s in preparation for this second edition.

It survived the destruction of the Potsdam archive in 1945 most likely because it was not being stored in the archive proper but was being used in a nearby office building. It was confiscated by the Red Army and returned to the East Germans sometime after 1955 and was kept in the East German army archives in Potsdam until the fall of the Wall. It remained in Potsdam until this archive was closed in January 1996. The document was again available to researchers in Freiburg only in 2002.[10] It is listed in the Bundesarchiv-Militärarchiv index (*Findbuch*) RH 61, titled *Kriegsgeschichtliche Forschungsanstalt des Heeres* (Army Military History Research Agency).

Based on guidance from the chief of the general staff, the imperial German army revised its war plan each winter and the new plan went into effect on 1 April of that year. Therefore, the plans were designated by two years, such as 1904/05; that is, effective from 1 April 1904 to 31 March 1905. The preceding year's plans and most of the supporting planning documents were usually destroyed. It was therefore difficult for German army official historians working both before and after the Great War to reconstruct the German war plans.

The summary of each deployment plan begins with a list of the planning materials that were available. Sometimes general map sketches are included. Occasionally there is an enemy estimate. Border security is often discussed in great detail.

The documents and maps available to the author(s) of RH 61/v.96 were not reproduced but only summarised. None of these original planning documents survived and were probably destroyed when the Reichsarchiv was bombed. The author of RH 61/v.96 influenced the nature of the summary by his choice and description of the original documents. The compiler was both aware of the Schlieffen plan dogma and worked for the organisation that was the origin of that dogma. The author's selection and interpretation of the material available to him would have been influenced by a desire to emphasise the importance of the Schlieffen plan. Nevertheless, like the rest of the Schlieffen School, there is no evidence that the author actually falsified documents. RH 61/v.96 must therefore be considered a secondary, not primary, source material. However, when evaluated professionally this is an invaluable document.

These are, as the name expressly states, deployment plans, not operations orders. The commander's overall intent and concept of the whole operation was almost never given. The deployment was described, and sometimes the initial advance as well. As of the 1906/07 year the *Aufmarschanweisungen* – the opening instructions to the army commanders – were generally available. The initial German actions were contingent on enemy behaviour. Subsequent actions were dependent on the results of the first battles. The war plan seldom stipulated any actions after initial contact was made with the enemy.

RH 61/v.96 deals separately with each mobilisation year from 1893/94 to 1914/15. To the 1902/03 plan the notes are handwritten in German Standard script; from 1903/04 they are typed. This would seem to indicate that the handwritten notes were in preparation for Wilhelm Dieckmann's *Schlieffenplan* manuscript. Dieckmann's text covers the period to 1903/04 thoroughly: perhaps Dieckmann's successor started the typed notes with the last year that Dieckmann described. There are only three pages of stenographic notes available concerning the 1912/13 plan[11] and only five pages concerning the 1914/15 deployment plan, which was the plan actually used in 1914.

RH 61/v.96 adds valuable detail to Dieckmann's manuscript, which tells us about Schlieffen's planning to 1903/04. It gives the first detailed view of Schlieffen's 1904/05, 1905/06 and 1906/07 plans, which are not in Dieckmann. It shows that Schlieffen did not implement the Schlieffen plan in any of his real war plans, and particularly not in the 1906/07 plan.

More importantly, for the first time this document gives us detailed information concerning the development of Moltke's planning from 1907/08 to 1913/14. It shows that Moltke did not slavishly follow the Schlieffen plan but developed his own plans in order to meet the changes in the European military and diplomatic situation.

Aufmarsch 1904/05

The author of RH 61/v.96 had eight original documents available concerning the 1904/05 *Aufmarsch*: the *Mobilmachungskalendar* (mobilisation schedule); two maps of the covering force deployment in the west (one with an enemy estimate); two covering force deployment maps in the east; an order of battle for *Aufmarsch* I; and the *Aufmarschanweisungen* (deployment orders), without annexes, for *Aufmarsch* I *West*, *Aufmarsch* I *Ost* and *Aufmarsch* II *Ost*.

The summaries of these documents comprise eight typewritten pages with generous spacing, which allowed handwritten annotations, plus a page of

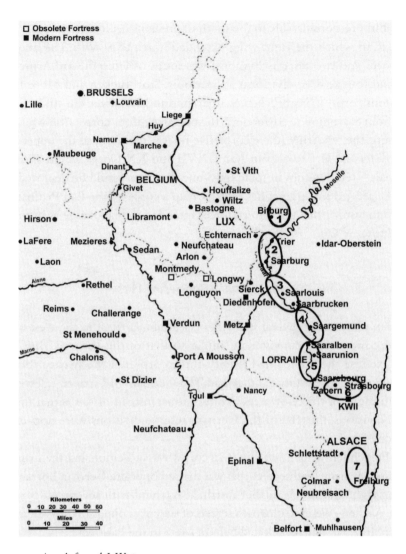

1904/05 *Aufmarsch* I *West*

handwritten notes giving the German order of battle. There are no maps of the deployment, only a general sketch for the east and west fronts.

Aufmarsch I in 1904/05 was for a war with France alone; twenty-five corps and fifteen reserve divisions (probably sixty-seven divisions in total) were deployed against France, and four reserve divisions were left in the east 'in order that the province [may] not be completely denuded of troops from the outset'.[12] The great majority of the available information was concerned with border security. However, the bare outlines of the deployments were also described. The centre of mass of the 1st Army on the right (four corps, four reserve divisions) was now at Bitburg, considerably to the south of previous deployments (1902/03 and 1903/04), in which the right wing extended north to St Vith. The 2nd Army (four corps and two reserve divisions) was south of Trier; the 3rd Army (three corps and four reserve divisions) at Saarlouis, Saarbrücken and Metz; the 4th Army (four corps) at Saarbrücken, Saargemünd and Saaralben; the 5th Army (four corps) from Saarunion to Sarrebourg; the 6th Army (four corps) near Mutzig and Strasbourg; the 7th Army (three corps, five reserve divisions) in the upper Alsace.

For *Aufmarsch* II, a two-front war, I, XVII and XX Corps would also be left in the east – ten divisions in total; sixty-one divisions would be deployed in the west. The 1st, 3rd and 4th Armies each gave up a corps for the East Prussian army. It is safe to assume that the eastern forces intended to manoeuvre as in the 1894 *Generalstabsreise Ost.*

1904 *Generalstabsreisen West*

Schlieffen played two general staff rides (*Generalstabsreisen*) in the west in 1904. Neither concerned a deployment similar to that of the 1904/05 *Aufmarsch.*[13] In the exercise the French had twenty-three corps, not the twenty corps that German intelligence estimated they had. The Germans had sixteen reserve corps, the equivalent of thirty-two reserve divisions, instead of the actual nineteen reserve divisions: thirteen of the German reserve divisions were non-existent 'ghost divisions'.

The French left wing 4th Army (five corps) was at Verdun, but the main body of the French army (eighteen corps) was massed opposite German Lorraine. The German right was much further north, at Aachen, with seventeen corps in a triangle Aachen–Wesel–Cologne, a screen of six corps opposite the Ardennes, six more at Metz and nine echeloned behind Metz in the Palatinate.

In the exercise critique (*Schlussbesprechung*) Schlieffen said that the possibility of a German attack through Belgium was no secret: everybody in Europe (and even in America) foresaw such a German operation. The problem was that an attack through the Ardennes crossed the Meuse and divided the German army: the French would mass against the German right wing and defeat it in detail. If the Germans extended their right to march through the Belgian plain north of the Meuse, the approach march would take so long that the French could break through in Lorraine.

Given a German right-wing advance through the north Belgian plain, Schlieffen's French 'school solution' was to launch just such an offensive into Lorraine. In response, the German 1st Army (seven corps), followed by six reserve divisions, marched into Belgium between Brussels and Namur, which

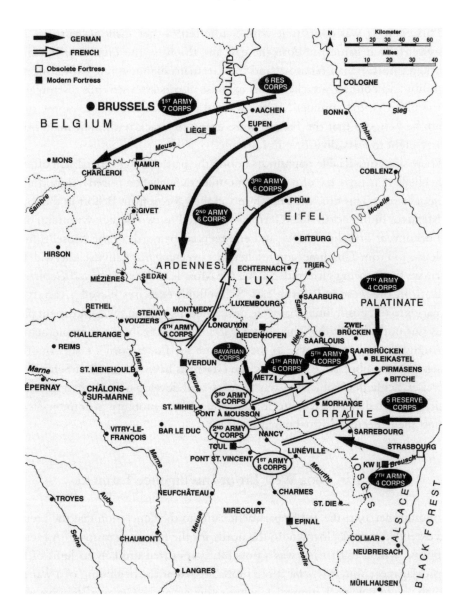

1st General Staff Ride West

found no enemy forces and accomplished nothing. The 2nd Army swung south into the Ardennes and the 3rd also moved south into Luxembourg. The French 4th Army (eighteen divisions) turned north to meet them. But this was a sideshow. The French mass of manoeuvre (forty divisions) penetrated deeply into Lorraine, at which point the German main force counter-attacked from Metz and Strasbourg, enveloping the French.

This exercise was consistent with Schlieffen's other *Generalstabsreisen* and *Kriegsspiele* (war games) in both the east and the west: the French or Russians attacked into German territory and the Germans manoeuvred, exploiting rail mobility, and counter-attacked. This exercise also bears a striking resemblance to the plan that the younger Moltke wanted to implement on 15 August 1914, when he believed that the French were going to attack with their main body (thirty-eight to forty divisions) in Lorraine.[14]

There was considerable opposition among the participating general staff officers to Schlieffen's massive use of non-existent units, so Schlieffen played a second 1904 *Generalstabsreise*. This time the French spread their forces from Belfort in the south to Mézières in the north. The Germans deployed in two bodies, with ten corps in Lorraine, at or behind Metz, and eighteen corps north of the Moselle, from Cologne to Prüm. This dispersion resulted in a sweeping manoeuvre battle, with the Germans finally being surrounded along the Moselle between Trier and Coblenz.

Both in the west and in the east, Schlieffen's exercises played a variety of scenarios to test possibilities that were never incorporated in the deployment plan. This was not wasted time. The 1903 *Generalstabsreise Ost* was not implemented in August 1914, but did serve as the template for Ludendorff's *Lodz* counter-attack in November 1914.[15] Nor did the Germans have to win all of Schlieffen's exercises. Schlieffen's objective was to teach and develop a 'Schlieffen doctrine' which exploited Germany's interior position and rail mobility to counter-attack against the expected Russo-French offensive.

German 1904 West Front Intelligence Estimate

In midsummer 1904 the 3rd Department came to the conclusion that the French had extended their deployment to the north, for the following reasons.[16] A French offensive, which until 1904 was a possibility, appeared unlikely in light of the Russo-Japanese War. It was far more probable that at the beginning of a war the French would not attack immediately, but rather await the German offensive in an assembly area behind their fortifications. A French defensive deployment which extended their left flank to the north, opposite the Belgian Ardennes, seemed more likely than the previous offensive concentration opposite German Lorraine.

The August 1904 estimate said that the French would deploy with:

1st Army (right flank, VII Corps – three divisions – on Vosges from Belfort to St Die, with four corps behind it at Belfort – Epinal)[17]

2nd Army (centre, five corps, Toul)

3rd Army (reserve, five corps, west of Toul)

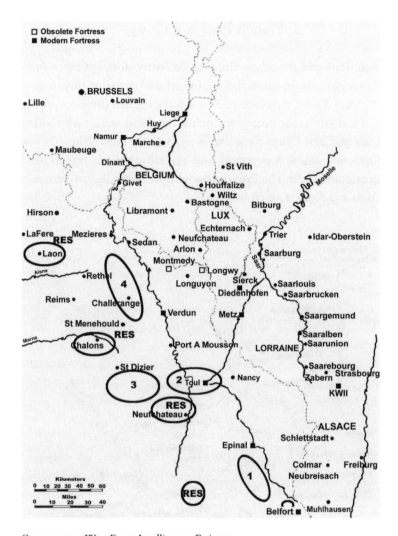

German 1904 West Front Intelligence Estimate

4th Army (left flank, five corps, west of Verdun – Sedan)
1st Group of Reserve Divisions (four reserve divisions, behind right wing)
2nd Group (three reserve divisions, Neufchâteau)
3rd Group (three reserve divisions, Châlons sur Marne)
4th Group (four reserve divisions, Laon)

This probably came to fifty-five divisions in total (forty-one active and fourteen reserve). The French actually had twenty-two corps (probably forty-four divisions) and twelve reserve divisions for use with the field army – fifty-six divisions in total.[18]

French Plan XV (1903)[19]

The French deployed the advance guard 1st Army (four corps) at Nancy, with the 2nd Army (five corps) on its right at Epinal, and the 4th Army (four corps) on its left at Verdun. There were two reserve armies: the 4th (four corps) was behind the 1st, and the 5th (three corps) was behind the 2nd, with 19th Corps arriving from Algeria and 21st Corps from excess units in the Alps. When they would be available was not stated. A group of four reserve divisions was located behind the left, centre and right. The French thought the most likely German course of action was to attack the French left.

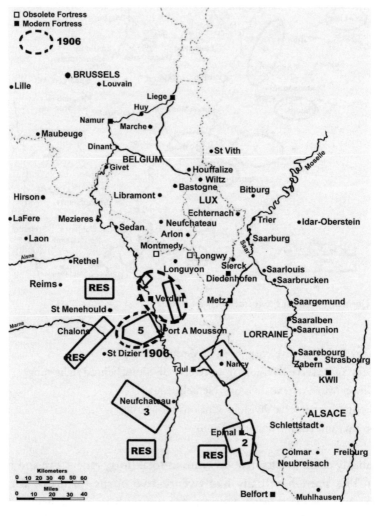

French Plan XV 1903 (with 1906 modification)

If the German estimate is compared with the actual French deployment in Plan XV (1903), the Germans made several major errors. Most important, the French did not change their plan in 1905. The Germans made the French left too strong and put it too far to the north. The Germans still did not recognise that the French would deploy an advance guard army at Nancy. The Germans did not understand the importance of the neo-Napoleonic theories of Bonnal, according to which the Germans would be fixed in place by the advanced guard while the flank and reserve armies manoeuvred. The French advanced guard 1st Army in the centre (at Nancy) was assumed to be further to the west, at and south-west of Toul. The 4th Army, on the left flank, was further south than the German estimate. The centre of mass of the reserve 3rd and 5th Armies was north of where the German estimate thought it would be. The French did not intend to leave significant active army forces in the Alps: whatever the Germans may have thought of Italian loyalty to the Triple Alliance, the French did not rate it highly.

Plan XV was, however, strikingly similar to the French deployment played by Schlieffen in the 1st 1904 *Generalstabsreise West*. It was a flexible formation, allowing a shift to block a German attack against the French left or a commitment of the reserve army to the left or right of the centre army for an offensive into German Lorraine. In the 1st 1904 *Generalstabsreise West* Schlieffen said that, given this French deployment and a German main effort in Belgium, the best French course of action was an offensive into Lorraine.

1905/06

Russo-Japanese War, 1905

In Russia, 22 January was Bloody Sunday, as troops fired on a procession of workers, killing seventy. The Russians lost the Battle of Mukden, which was fought between 23 February and 10 March, and the last Russian fleet was destroyed at Tsushima on 27 May. On 5 September the Treaty of Portsmouth ended the war, and the Russian army began redeploying from Manchuria to European Russia. Between June and August there was an epidemic of industrial strikes, agrarian disorder and mutiny on the battleship *Potemkin*, culminating in the great general strike from 20–30 October. On 30 October the Tsar issued the October Manifesto and appointed Sergei Witte prime minister, rallying the Octobrist party behind him. On 16 December Witte ordered the St Petersburg Soviet, which had directed the general strike there, to be arrested. This led to a worker's insurrection in Moscow from 22 December to 1 January, which was put down by the army with much bloodshed. During the winter the army took action to restore order in the countryside.

1905 International Affairs

On 31 March Emperor Wilhelm visited Tangier, setting off the first Morocco crisis, which was a German attempt to test the Anglo-French Entente. The British responded in May by offering to conduct talks with the French concerning military co-operation. Emperor Wilhelm and the Tsar signed the Treaty of Björkö on 24 July, an attempt on Wilhelm's part to test the Russo-French alliance. The treaty collapsed in October due to French objections. At this time Britain and Russia began entente negotiations.

German 1905 Intelligence Summary for Russia

At the end of each year the German army compiled an intelligence summary for each of the major powers. The Russian estimate for 1905 was sixty-two pages long and showed that German intelligence had a detailed and accurate picture of all aspects of the Russian Army.[20]

It is commonly assumed that Schlieffen could send the entire German army against France because the Russian army was fully committed to the war in Manchuria. The 1905 intelligence summary shows that this was far from being true. The authorised strength of the Russian army in Europe in 1905 was 1,089 infantry battalions, 700 cavalry squadrons and 525 artillery batteries; 397 battalions, 42 squadrons and 201 batteries had been sent to the east, or 39 per cent of the European infantry and 37 per cent of the artillery. The rest of the Manchurian army consisted of units that had been stationed there in peacetime or new formations.

To compensate for this deployment from European Russia, the Russian army mobilised 219 battalions, 213 squadrons and 96 batteries. This meant that the Russian army in Europe was only weaker than before the war by 178 battalions (16 per cent) and 105 batteries (20 per cent), and actually stronger by 169 squadrons (24 per cent). Moreover, with the signing of the peace of Portsmouth on 5 September 1905 the Russian army had immediately begun redeploying from Manchuria to European Russia. Because of the war, the Russian army had also modernised; for example, every Russian infantry division or light infantry brigade now had a machine gun company, which made the Russian army far better equipped with MGs than any army in Europe.

In addition, the Russian troops were still disciplined and loyal. There were isolated mutinies in south Russia and the Caucasus in July, and 'coarse riots' in November and December following the proclamation of the constitution. Indiscipline was always of short duration: the intelligence estimate cited the example of the Brest infantry regiment at Sevastopol, which initially sided with the mutinous sailors, but returned to the control of their officers after a few hours and fought effectively against the mutineers. The troops' real complaint was not political, but bad food and low pay, and the desire of the Manchurian army to go home, all of which were being remedied. The troops, especially the Cossacks, were completely reliable while suppressing the December revolutions in Moscow and south Russia.

The idea that the Russian army had collapsed in 1905 finds no support in the German 1905 intelligence summary.

East Front *Operationsstudie* (Operational Study)
January 1905

In January 1905, that is, in the middle of the Russo-Japanese War, Schlieffen conducted an *Operationsstudie* concerning a Russian attack on East Prussia.[21] The General Situation stated that France and Russia had declared war on Germany. Austria supported Germany but had to deploy part of her forces to secure her southern border (presumably Italian, or Serbian, or both). France and Russia had agreed to attack Germany simultaneously, unless the Germans attacked beforehand. The Russians still had twenty divisions (fifteen active and five reserve) to commit against Germany, plus three reserve divisions in the Warsaw garrison. By the twenty-third day of mobilisation the Russians had adopted their normal deployment: a Niemen army with three corps and three reserve divisions and a Narew army with four corps, the 3rd Guard Infantry Division and two reserve divisions. The Russians thought that the mass of the German army had deployed in the west, leaving only those forces in the east that had their home stations in East or West Prussia (three corps and three or four reserve divisions). The Russian mission was to occupy the German territory east of the Vistula and then advance on Berlin. The first requirement was to write an operations plan for the Russians.

Both the intent and the conduct of this exercise would be nonsensical if Schlieffen believed, as it is so often contended, that the Russian army was incapable of offensive operations in 1905.

War with France & England, 1905

Both Saxony and Bavaria had their own semi-independent armies, with their own general staffs, and maintained military representatives in Berlin. On 6 September 1905 the Saxon military representative reported to his government in Dresden that he had received highly confidential information from a Great General Staff officer concerning a conference that Emperor Wilhelm had held sometime that spring with the chief of the general staff, Schlieffen, and the chief of the naval staff, Büchsel, concerning a war with France and Britain.[22] Schlieffen said that in such a case he would commit the entire army against France; coastal defence against the British fleet was the navy's problem. The naval staff was clearly horrified by the prospect of a war against Britain. Büchsel objected that the combined British and French fleets would blockade the German coast and the British would land 50,000 troops in Denmark and march them into Schleswig. It was therefore necessary to leave 50,000 German troops to defend Schleswig. Schlieffen replied that the war would be decided in France and those 50,000 troops might be the margin of speedy victory. The naval staff countered that the decision on land might not come until the British had seized the canal from the North Sea to the Baltic (which would have cut off the High Seas Fleet's escape route to the Baltic and could potentially have led to its destruction).

The conference resulted only in a decision to conduct some amateur espionage. Two officers, one from each staff, posing as businessmen, were sent to Denmark to observe the visit of the British fleet to see if any preparations for a landing were being made. None were seen, much to Schlieffen's satisfaction. Here the matter ended. It is no surprise that Schlieffen would have liked to fight a one-front war against France and Britain. On the other hand, if war is, as Clausewitz says, an extension of national policy, then a one-front war against France and Britain was a dead letter. German grand strategy aimed at attaining World Power: creation of a High Seas battle fleet, colonies and a say in world affairs. The naval staff was convinced that military success against France would probably be paid for with the destruction of the High Seas Fleet by the British, and the end of Germany's overseas ambitions. There is no evidence – indeed, in light of the navy's opposition, it is highly unlikely – that the joint war plan the Kaiser wanted was ever drawn up.

In spite of Schlieffen's protests, in his 1906/07 *Aufmarschplan*, his last, IX RK (*Reservekorps* – reserve corps), which had only one division, would be given the mission of protecting the North Sea coast.

1905 *Generalstabsreise West*

The Schlieffen School always maintained that Schlieffen had tested the concept of the Schlieffen plan *Denkschrift* in his 1905 *Generalstabsreise West*. Generalleutnant Eugen Zoellner made this assertion and gave a description of this exercise in 1938. Schlieffen 'laid his cards on the table'.[23] However, no matter how much the Schlieffen School was willing to spin the facts to prove there was a Schlieffen plan, they stopped short of lying or inventing facts, so Zoellner's description of the exercise has no resemblance to the concept of the Schlieffen plan.[24]

Zoellner says that Schlieffen, who was also the exercise director, played the German side against three French scenarios. The French were told that the Germans had deployed all along the Rhine. In his discussion of the German deployment, Schlieffen went to great lengths to describe the disadvantages of the German attack through Belgium. The approach march was long, the fortresses of Liège, Namur and Antwerp would have to be bypassed, and the French could fall back on successive defensive lines along the rivers and fortresses of northern France. This was anything but a ringing endorsement of the right-wing attack. In all three cases the French response to the German advance through Belgium was to attack.

In the first scenario, the French, played by Hugo Freiherr von Freytag-Loringhoven, attacked into Belgium. Schlieffen counter-attacked from Metz against the French right and pushed in the French reserve divisions defending the French left. The French were defeated in Belgium. In the second scenario, the French, played by Colonel Steuben, attacked in Lorraine between Metz and Strasbourg. Schlieffen shifted forces by rail from the right wing to the left and swung the remainder of the right wing due south, to counter-attack from Metz and Strasbourg against the French flanks and defeat this advance too. In the third scenario, Hermann von Kuhl attacked on both sides of Metz. The French attack in Lorraine was stopped and Schlieffen counter-attacked against the French right from Strasbourg. Friedrich von Boetticher had given a similar summary of the exercise in 1933.[25]

In the 1905 *Generalstabsreise West* the French are attacking. In the Schlieffen plan the French are defending and a French attack is a *Liebesdienst* (a great favour). In the 1905 *Generalstabsreise West* Schlieffen counter-attacks to defeat the French in Belgium and Lorraine. In the Schlieffen plan the right wing pushes the French into Switzerland, advancing to the west of Paris in order to do so. The 1905 *Generalstabsreise West* is an isolated Franco-German war. In February 1906 Schlieffen was forced to modify the Schlieffen plan to account for British intervention on the continent. Aside from the fact that in both the 1905 *Generalstabsreise West* and the Schlieffen plan the German right wing extends to Belgium, the two have nothing in common. Zoellner and Boetticher were vitally interested in proving that Schlieffen tested the Schlieffen plan in a war game, but this was the best they could do.

In Boetticher's papers at the Militärarchiv in Freiburg, Gerhard Gross, a lieutenant-colonel working for the *Militärgeschichtliches Forschungsamt*, the German army's historical section, found some of the materials on which Boetticher and Zoellner had based their articles. In making his analysis of these documents public, Gross did not mention the fact that the 1905 *Generalstabsreise West* was discussed in the articles written in the 1930s by Boetticher and Zoellner. Instead, he proclaimed that he had found the war game that Schlieffen used to develop the Schlieffen plan, as though he had made a spectacular discovery which proved that there was a Schlieffen plan.[26]

I cited Zoellner's article extensively in 1999 in 'The Schlieffen Plan Reconsidered'[27] and in 2002 in *Inventing the Schlieffen Plan*.[28] Boetticher's notes add only details to what has been widely known for seventy years.

Gross gave only a cursory description of Boetticher's notes, saying that a complete description of them was unnecessary as it was 'obvious' that 1905 *Generalstabsreise West* was the basis of the Schlieffen plan.[29] It is curious that in a forty-three-page article defending the Schlieffen plan, Gross couldn't find the space to describe one of his principal pieces of evidence. The first useful description of Boetticher's notes is presented below. The reason why Gross was suddenly so uncharacteristically laconic becomes clear.

It is important to note that Boetticher's papers did not include any primary source documents, not even the 1905 *Generalstabsreise West* exercise critique. We are dealing with a secondary source, which requires additional evaluation, caution and attention to detail, none of which Gross provides.

From the published articles by Boetticher and Zoellner we know that Schlieffen replayed all three scenarios of the 1905 *Generalstabsreise West*, but neither treat this as being important or give any specifics. Now Boetticher's notes for these articles tell us that, after the 1905 *Generalstabsreise West* had been concluded, Schlieffen replayed these scenarios not as part of the *Generalstabsreise* proper, but as a 'study', a far less extensive format than the *Generalstabsreise*.

Boetticher's notes for the 1905 *Generalstabsreise West* consist of four separate documents.[30] Document 1 is titled 'Great [General Staff] Ride 1905. Initial Situation for all three scenarios Freytag – Kuhl – Steuben. May 1905', and is thirty-eight pages long. It was written by Wilhelm von Hahnke, Schlieffen's son-in-law and adjutant, who was personally present. It describes only the *Generalstabsreise* proper and not the study which followed. Document 2 is titled 'Exercise Critique', but it is really only the stenographic notes for the exercise critique Schlieffen gave at Freiburg on 17 July 1905, not the written critique itself. It is nineteen pages long, including a cover letter by Hahnke. Hahnke's letter describes the original situation. He cites three original documents – the individual critiques for Freytag, Kuhl and Steuben – all of which have been lost. Document 2 concerns only the *Generalstabsreise* proper, and not the subsequent operational study. Document 3 is titled 'Great General Staff Ride 1905', is thirteen pages long and describes both the *Generalstabsreise* and the subsequent operational study. The author of this document had only the exercise critique and the working papers of one player available (which one isn't specified). These original documents have been lost. He attached twelve sketches and three maps. Document 4 is titled 'Great General Staff Ride 1905', is seven pages long, was probably written by Boetticher and describes both the *Generalstabsreise* and the operational study.

Document 1 gives the initial French situation, including border security, fortress garrisons and French deployment, which was the same as the current 3rd Department intelligence estimate: the 1st Army on the right with centre of mass at Epinal; the 2nd in the centre at Toul; the 3rd in reserve south of St Dizier; the 4th on the left at Challerange. The French deployment would be complete by the eighteenth day of mobilisation. The strength of the French armies was not given, other than the fact that they had ten Territorial divisions available for field operations. Document 4 says that the French had to leave two corps and two reserve divisions on the Italian border. There is every reason to believe that the exercise was also based on the size of the French army in the German 1905 intelligence estimate: thirty-seven active divisions, twelve reserve divisions, forty-nine divisions in total.[31]

Document 4 says the situation was 'particularly favourable for the Germans due to the assumption that all forces could be employed against France and that it was unnecessary to leave forces in the east'. On page 21 of Document 1 Hahnke gives us the German order of battle: twenty-six corps, nineteen reserve divisions, seventy-two divisions in total (I Corps had three divisions), which was the actual strength for the entire German army at that time. The Germans also had twenty Landwehr divisions, which did not exist (in the 1905/06 *Aufmarsch* I there were twenty-six Landwehr *brigades*). Schlieffen's imaginary 1905 Landwehr divisions also had twice as much artillery as comparable Landwehr units would have in 1914. Document 3 concludes by expressly calling attention to the fact that Schlieffen used twenty Landwehr divisions in these exercises, but the German army in the west in 1914 had only twenty Landwehr brigades. Gross fails to give the German and French force structures – a serious lack of attention to detail.

In the 1905 *Generalstabsreise West* Schlieffen employed ninety-two divisions, twenty of which did not actually exist. Twenty divisions are equal to the strength of two entire armies. The 1905 *Generalstabsreise West* has this much in common with the Schlieffen plan, which employed ninety-six divisions, including twenty-four divisions that did not exist.

Small wonder that in the 1905 *Generalstabsreise West* the Germans always won: in the August 1905 west front intelligence estimate the French had forty-nine active and reserve divisions (which was essentially correct), against seventy-two German divisions – the Germans were twenty-three divisions stronger. If the ten French Territorial and twenty German Landwehr divisions are added, that makes fifty-nine French divisions against ninety-two German. The Germans now had thirty-five more divisions than the French did.

Once again it is clear that in Schlieffen's opinion, even in a one-front war against France alone, Germany needed more divisions than she actually possessed.

The Germans began the 1914 campaign in the west not with ninety-two divisions, but sixty-eight divisions. The Germans thought they would be opposed by seventy-five French, Belgian and British divisions. In 1914 it was the Germans that were outnumbered.

There is no possibility that the 1905 *Generalstabsreise West*, which employed twenty divisions that did not exist, and which gave the Germans considerable numerical superiority, could have any relevance to the 1914 war plan. As we will see, Gross denies that this is a problem – Gross thinks that it is perfectly acceptable to write war plans which employ masses of imaginary units.[32]

Document 1 says that the French solution was worked out by eleven officers. Hahnke shows us that there was a French solution, in addition to those of Freytag, Kuhl and Steuben, which was not mentioned in the articles by Boetticher and Zoellner. It was presented by Colonel Matthias, and in Hahnke's opinion it was 'masterful'. Upon completion of the French deployment Matthias conducted a redeployment. A 5th Army with six corps was sent to Lille–Maubeuge (Hahnke emphasised this with an exclamation mark). The 4th Army, with two corps and four reserve divisions, was moved to the north of Mézières; the 3rd Army, with five corps, was between Mézières and Verdun; the 2nd Army (three corps, three reserve divisions) was between Verdun and Toul; and the 1st Army (two corps, seven reserve divisions) was between Toul and Epinal, with one corps between Epinal and Belfort. Matthias had thirteen corps to oppose the German right wing. The three corps in the centre, at Verdun–Toul, were positioned to attack against the left flank of the German right wing, a French manoeuvre that was the constant bugbear of German planning. Only three corps and eight reserve divisions held the front opposite Alsace and Lorraine. The French front from Toul to Namur would be covered by the Meuse River, which is perhaps the most significant natural defensive line in Europe, being not only deep and wide, but lined with cliffs and dense woods. Most important, Matthias intended to remain on the defensive and allow the Germans to conduct their march through Belgium.

Schlieffen not only refused to play Matthias' solution, he refused to comment on it. Gross' description of Matthias' solution is so cursory as to be nearly incomprehensible, perhaps intentionally so. The reason is not far to seek. Using the terrain and border fortresses as force multipliers and by standing on the defensive, Matthias, outnumbered as he was, might still have been able to bring the great right-wing attack to a screeching halt. Moreover, there was a chance that the French might actually have adopted this solution in wartime, which Hahnke expressly noted looked very much like the war plan proposed by General Michel in 1911. (This comment proves that the notes were made not in 1905 but after the publication of the French official history in 1923.)

Document 2 is a transcript of stenographic notes of Schlieffen's exercise critique given at Freiburg on 17 July 1905. At the top, under the title 1. *Grosse Generalstabsreise 1905*, is a heading which says 'From his Excellency to the 1st Adjutant. For the Collection W. Ha. [Wilhelm Hahnke] 31 December 1905'. The next line is 'Exercise Critique'. The line below that says: 'From the original stenographic notes of Captain Hellfeld. A copy was apparently not made.' A comment by Hahnke on the first page says that Schlieffen did not subsequently rework and polish these notes. A second comment by Hahnke says that while cleaning out his desk, preparatory to his retirement on 1 January 1906, Schlieffen gave the transcript to Hahnke with instructions that Hahnke should give it to his successor, Moltke's adjutant, Major Dommes. Dommes (or perhaps Hahnke) apparently had it typed.

So, all we have of the exercise critique, which Gross says is the sole exercise in which Schlieffen tested a war plan, and the sole test of the Schlieffen plan to boot, is a copy of some stenographic notes taken by a captain, which Schlieffen did not even bother to read, and which was passed along as an afterthought from the outgoing to the incoming adjutant. Schlieffen himself did not keep a copy of it.

Document 2 adds interesting details to what we already know from Zoellner's and Boetticher's published articles. Schlieffen said that the only way the French border fortifications could be avoided is if the neutrality of Luxembourg, Belgium and Holland were violated. He says that this may be forbidden politically, but could be considered as an academic exercise without any harm being done! This is a fascinating statement, which of course Gross does not mention. In the exercise that Gross says was the centrepiece of Schlieffen's war planning, Schlieffen could be considered as disavowing aggression against Belgium.

This was consistent with Schlieffen's counter-attack doctrine. Four months later, in the 1905 *Kriegsspiel*, the German army remained on the defensive and it was the French who entered Belgium first.

Schlieffen also said that the advance through Belgium and France was a difficult undertaking. It was necessary to get past Antwerp. The French had fortified lines at Lille–Maubeuge and behind that at La Fère–Laon–Reims. It must be anticipated that the attack would face the entire French army, reinforced by the Dutch and Belgians. It was therefore necessary to deploy all the active German corps between Diedenhofen and Brussels, but that was not easy to do due to insufficient rail lines and roads.

Schlieffen assigned additional officers to assist the French commanders. Steuben got a general officer to command the 1st and 2nd Armies, another to command the 3rd, 4th and 5th Armies, and two colonels to command the 6th and 7th Armies. Freytag was assisted by three generals and a colonel; Kuhl by two generals and two colonels.

In Boetticher's notes there are crude sketches showing the general course of the Freytag, Kuhl and Steuben scenarios of the 1905 *Generalstabsreise West* (see sketches 1–6).[33] According to Gross, these sketches were not the original maps but were prepared by Boetticher. They are nowhere near as detailed or professional as the maps that accompanied a real exercise critique. They also do not look like the Schlieffen plan, so Gross did not reproduce them.

In Freytag's scenario the French redeployed in order to attempt to catch the Germans as they moved through the Brussels–Namur defile. Schlieffen approved of the concept but faulted the execution, which relied on the inadequate offensive power of an army of reserve units. The French should also have shifted

1905 Generalstabsreise West

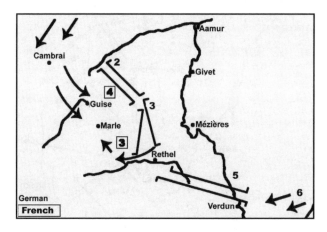

1 Freytag
22nd day

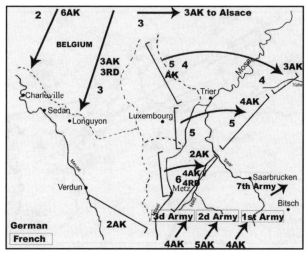

2 Steuben
15th day

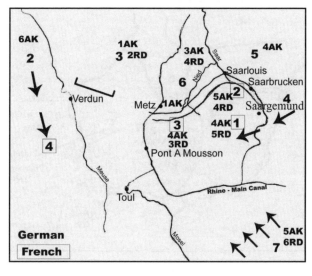

3 Steuben
22nd day

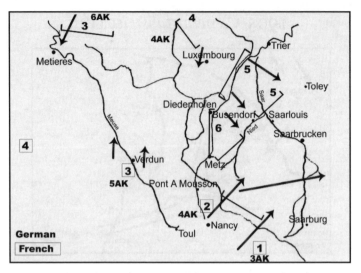

4 Kuhl
15th day

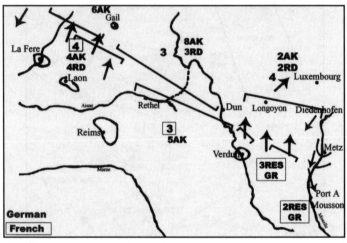

5 Kuhl
23rd day
west

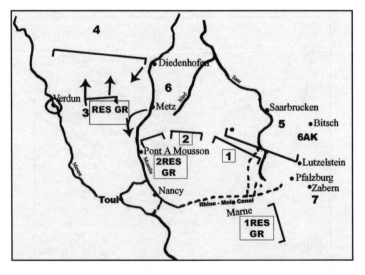

6 Kuhl
23rd day
east

more to the left, which was the decisive error. Schlieffen spent another five pages criticising French errors in movement and co-ordination. By the twenty-second day the Germans had broken through the French centre at Rethel and surrounded the French 4th and 3rd Armies north-west of Rethel. The French made the mistake of not breaking contact and withdrawing in time. The French intended to withdraw to the south-west, anchoring their left flank on Paris in the hopes of being able to attack the German left flank, but the exercise was terminated on about the twenty-second day of mobilisation.

In Steuben's scenario the French attacked between Metz and Strasbourg. Schlieffen gave this plan little chance of success because it would run into the field fortifications on the Nied. When the French attacked into Lorraine, the German right-wing 4th, 5th and 6th Armies began to swing back to the east to form an immense 110km-long line in German territory from Metz to Idar-Oberstein. Three corps from the 3rd Army were moved by rail to Strasbourg, Schlettstadt and Colmar in Alsace. The German 6th Army held the Nied, the 5th the Saar from Saarlouis to Saarbrücken, while the 4th achieved a breakthrough at Saargemünd and the 7th Army crossed the Vosges in the French rear. The 2nd Army from the German right wing was chasing the French left flank to the west of Verdun. The 1st Army was following the 2nd Army and could accomplish nothing. Schlieffen said that the French would have been unable to withdraw such masses out of Lorraine and across the Meuse. This exercise was also terminated on about the twenty-second mobilisation day.

In Kuhl's scenario the French attacked on both sides of Metz. Schlieffen said that Kuhl didn't really believe in the effectiveness of this plan himself, for he only attacked with two armies in Lorraine while two armies stayed on the defensive 'on an enormous front' from Verdun to the Aisne to La Fère. As in Steuben's scenario, the 5th and 6th German Armies moved from the right wing to Lorraine, while three corps were moved from the German right wing to the left by rail. As the situation in Lorraine stabilised, Kuhl attacked with the French left wing. This attack failed, principally because the French missed an opportunity for a breakthrough at Mézières, while the Germans broke through the French centre at Pont à Mousson. The French left fell back to their start line on the Aisne to La Fère. The German mission was now to turn the French left. The exercise was ended at this point, on about the twenty-third day.

For Gross, in common with the rest of the Schlieffen School, the essential elements of the Schlieffen plan are the attack with the strong right wing through Belgium and north France to produce a quick battle of annihilation. It is therefore not surprising that Gross refuses to discuss these exercises in detail, for this is the only way that he can avoid recognising that they have little to do with the Schlieffen plan.

The only thing these exercises have in common with the Schlieffen plan is that they are both based on unrealistic assumptions: a one-front war in which the Germans have upwards of twenty non-existent divisions and massive numerical superiority. In two scenarios in the *Generalstabsreise* (Kuhl and Steuben) the mass of the German right wing moves back east into Germany, not west into France. In Freytag's scenario the French suffer a partial defeat not because the Germans turn their left, but because they break through the French centre. In his closing comments, Schlieffen said that the same elements were repeated in all three exercises: withdrawal, breakthrough and pursuit; there is no mention of 'making the right wing strong'.

This was the end of the 1905 *Generalstabsreise West*. Document 4 says expressly that 'on the day of the exercise critique Schlieffen began the operation again and conducted it as a study'. There is no mention of this study in Documents 1 and 2, which concern the 1905 *Generalstabsreise West* proper. A study would have been far quicker and much less formal than a *Generalstabsreise*. There is no mention of the involvement of anyone in the study other than Kuhl, Freytag, Steuben and Schlieffen. There is no evidence that the orders were written down at army level, as in the *Generalstabsreise*. Gross failed to mention all of this, while attempting to portray the 'study' as a *Generalstabsreise*.

Gross does not mention Steuben's scenario in the 'study' because this time Steuben was not just attacking into Lorraine, he was also attacking into Alsace. As in the 1905 *Generalstabsreise West*, Schlieffen moved the right wing south-east into Lorraine. There is no resemblance to the Schlieffen plan here.

Gross says that the other two 'study' scenarios, Kuhl's and Freytag's (but not Steuben's), are the direct predecessors of the Schlieffen plan; indeed, these are the only times that Schlieffen tested the Schlieffen plan, or any other war plan. According to Gross, in no other exercise did Schlieffen test war planning: all the other *Generalstabsreisen*, war games and the like were held for 'staff training'.[34] Why are the Kuhl and Freytag scenarios the only exception? Because Gross thinks they look like the Schlieffen plan. Gross' 'proof' is based on circular reasoning.

Gross has said it is unnecessary to describe the Kuhl and Freytag scenarios in detail. True to his word, he does not provide a description of the forces involved, the enemy estimate, the decisions taken or the results of combat.

In the German version of Gross' article – but not the English version – there are two very general sketch maps from the Boetticher file (sketches 7 and 9, also sketch 8 which was not reproduced in Gross' article) which show the Kuhl and Freytag 'studies'. Once again, they were not originals but copies drawn by Boetticher. Compared to the large number of excellent maps that accompanied real exercise critiques of *Generalstabsreisen*, these maps of the Kuhl and Freytag 'studies' are poor.

Kuhl and Freytag's 1905 'Studies'

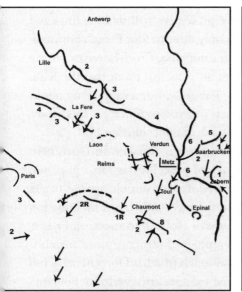

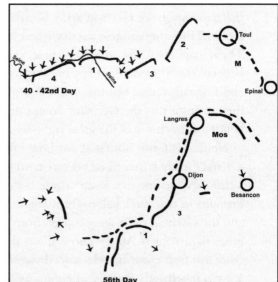

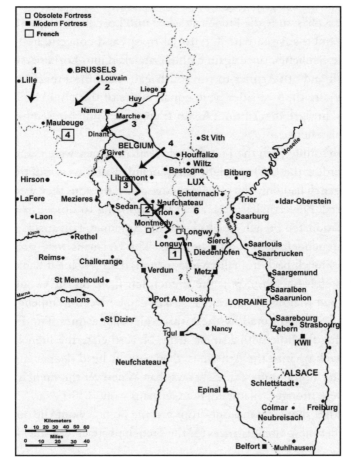

7 *Top left* Kuhl

8 *Left* Freytag
20th day

9 *Top right*
Freytag
40th–56th days

The maps cover all of eastern France. The French units are only designated at the army level; the German army is usually represented by little blue lines and arrows. The entire campaign is described with only three or four French positions. These maps are so vague as to be practically meaningless. Gross, however, clearly believes that these 'little maps, big arrows' are his principal proof that the Kuhl and Freytag studies test the Schlieffen plan. The most interesting thing about these maps is that the Germans do not go west of Paris: so much for this 'study' being the precursor of the great right-wing attack of the Schlieffen plan.

Neither is Gross honest about how little evidence is available. In Document 4, Kuhl's study is described on one double-spaced page; Freytag's in a page and a half. In Document 3, Kuhl's study is described on two double-spaced pages; Freytag's in two and a half pages: it lasted until the fifty-sixth day of mobilisation and the German right wing moved from southern Holland to southern France, more than 800km. All we know about the conduct of this enormous march is what can fit on four double-spaced pages, and much of what Documents 3 and 4 say is repetitious. By way of comparison, the exercise critique for Schlieffen's 1905 *Kriegsspiel* is thirty-six pages long.

In fact, in Kuhl's study, the French attacked into Lorraine with two armies, held the Meuse and the Aisne with Territorial troops and concentrated nine corps near La Fère. Schlieffen once again counter-attacked into Lorraine, swinging the German 5th and 6th Armies to the south-east. Half the French army was in Lorraine, where the two sides were equal. None of this could be determined from Gross' meagre description. Again there is not much resemblance to the Schlieffen plan here.

In Freytag's study both the French and German armies were assembled north of Metz–Verdun: the German right wing included all fifty-two active divisions. Since the French had only thirty-seven active army divisions they were decisively outnumbered. Nevertheless, instead of withdrawing to hold a front between Paris and Verdun, the French attacked into the Ardennes. This attack ensured that the open French left flank would be weak. The Germans were strong enough to push the French back frontally while turning the French left flank with three armies. A sketch (sketch 9) puts the French left flank on the twentieth day of mobilisation at Maubeuge; there is a 200km gap between Maubeuge and Paris, which was being exploited by these three German armies. The French were trying to plug the hole with a single army. Nevertheless, the French 2nd Army was still attacking into the Ardennes, thrusting its head deeper into the sack. The summary of the study expressly says that 'Wherever the French turned, the Germans were stronger'. Naturally, the Germans won.

Both 'studies' show that in a one-front war the French would be outnumbered, and that under these circumstances for the French to attack was suicide. The mid-

1904 German intelligence estimate did not expect the French to attack anyway. These 'studies' were even less relevant for the German situation in 1914, when the Germans were faced with the certainty of a two-front war and it was they who would be outnumbered.

In the Schlieffen plan the French were on the defensive: Schlieffen expected that they would hold a line between Paris and Verdun, which would force him to circumnavigate Paris. This would require twenty-four divisions that he did not have; indeed, which the German army would never have.

Boetticher and Zoellner both maintain that the three scenarios of the 1905 *Generalstabsreise West* proper were the predecessors of the Schlieffen plan. The study conducted after the *Generalstabsreise* was over was mentioned only in passing. Why? Because if the contention that the Schlieffen plan was actually the template for the German war plan is to be plausible, Schlieffen had to have tested it beforehand, and the 1905 *Generalstabsreise West* was the only exercise that was ever conducted that bore the slightest resemblance to the Schlieffen plan. The Schlieffen School was not willing to invent evidence, although they were more than happy to spin whatever documents were available to suit themselves. The study conducted after the *Generalstabsreise* was over was simply inadequate to bear the load of being Schlieffen's greatest war game.

1905: The Great *Kriegsspiel*

In November and December 1905, about four months after he supposedly tested the Schlieffen plan in the 1905 *Generalstabsreise West*, Schlieffen conducted his last *Kriegsspiel*.[35] This was by far the most ambitious exercise of Schlieffen's career, perhaps the greatest war game in modern military history. In it, Schlieffen played both fronts simultaneously to the forty-second day of mobilisation. For advocates of the Schlieffen plan, as well as for those such as Ritter who saw in Schlieffen only aggressive militarism, this war game is a bitter disappointment, for in this, Schlieffen's last, greatest exercise, he played a radically different concept for the German army: strategic defensive on both the east and west fronts.

Gross' answer to this conundrum is that the 1905 *Kriegsspiel* was held only for 'staff training' and, unlikely as it might seem, had nothing to do with German planning whatsoever.[36] Gross is using the same dubious methods as Foerster, Kuhl and Groener – withholding information and spinning the facts – to prove the existence of a Schlieffen plan. In contrast to the meagre description of the 1905 *Generalstabsreise West*, for the 1905 *Kriegsspiel* we have the complete exercise critique which was distributed to corps-sized units. It was thirty-six typed pages long and included numerous highly detailed maps.

In the exercise critique, Schlieffen said that it was advantageous for Germany to wait until one of her enemies crossed the border and then attack them. Usually the counter-offensive should be made to the east, because there the Germans had the greater prospects of not just throwing back their opponent, but of decisively defeating him. He said the disadvantage of this plan was that Germany might be attacked on both fronts simultaneously. His concept for the operation was to conduct a strong initial *Aufmarsch* in East Prussia with sixteen divisions (five corps and six reserve divisions). When the Russians had committed themselves to attacking, he would reinforce the eastern force with an additional twenty-two divisions (eight corps and six reserve divisions). This total of thirty-eight divisions was all that the East Prussian railway net could support. This was not sufficiently superior to the expected Russian force of thirty-three divisions (eleven and a half corps and ten reserve divisions) to ensure German victory. The German army must exploit the two advantages it possessed in East Prussia: Fortress Königsberg and the Masurian Lakes. As with Metz, Schlieffen advocated building Königsberg into a fortified zone in time of war. He said that in four weeks adequate field fortifications could be built along the Deime, Pregel and Frischung, creating a base for a German counter-attack. The Masurian Lakes forced the Russians to divide their forces.

The Russians crossed the border on the twenty-seventh day of mobilisation. By the thirtieth day they had reached a line, Königsberg–Soldau. With the arrival of their massive reinforcements, the Germans launched surprise counter-offensives on three avenues of approach: out of Fortress Königsberg against the right flank of the Niemen army; out of the Lake district against their inside flanks of both armies; and against the left flank of the Narew army. Both Russian armies were annihilated and by the thirty-fifth day of mobilisation the transfer of troops to the west could begin. There was no pursuit into Russia.

Schlieffen then gave his officers some last thoughts on the character of the next war and the conduct of operations in it. He said that in the future it would be very easy to allow operations to degenerate into positional warfare: the war in Manchuria had demonstrated that. Nevertheless, the German army must always seek to win decisive victories in manoeuvre battles and never allow a war of attrition to drag on indecisively for 'one or two years'. Such a protracted war would produce nothing but mutual exhaustion and economic chaos. But even if positional warfare did set in, long defensive positions might offer weak spots where the attacker could achieve a breakthrough. In mobile operations the German army would generally try to envelop the enemy flank. Schlieffen said that one should never conduct a shallow turning movement but envelop the enemy flank with a strong force while attacking his front to fix him in position.

Returning to the *Kriegsspiel*, Schlieffen said that the French were twice as strong as the Germans and therefore clearly held the initiative. Schlieffen gave the

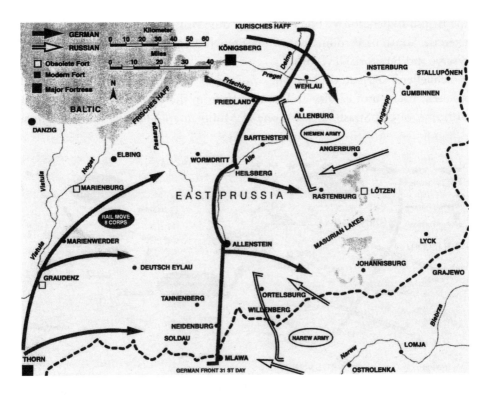

1905 *Kriegsspiel* East

French fifty-eight active and reserve divisions. (Because the French did not leave significant forces to face the Italians, in Plan XV the French initially had fifty-six divisions. The 1904 German intelligence estimate said that the French could initially deploy fifty-five divisions against Germany.) In addition, the French had twelve Territorial divisions, for a grand total of seventy divisions. The Germans had thirty-seven infantry divisions (eleven and a half corps and fourteen reserve divisions). With the thirty-eight divisions in the east, Schlieffen was employing seventy-five German divisions in total – three more than were actually on the German order of battle.

The deployment plan and force structure which Schlieffen gave to the French for this war game is strongly reminiscent of the French general Michel's 1911 war plan. Both the war game and Michel's plan were based on the exhaustive use of trained French manpower. Michel wanted to add more reservists to the active units. Schlieffen utilised French reserve and Territorial divisions in the front line. In both Schlieffen's exercise deployment and in Michel's plan, the French mass of manoeuvre was on the left wing and this left wing extended all the way to the English Channel. On the far left wing of the French forces, Schlieffen deployed the British Expeditionary Force – the first time British units appear in a German exercise. South of Verdun, Schlieffen's French deployment consisted largely of reserve and Territorial divisions.

Schlieffen's German deployment consisted of six corps between Cologne and Aachen, a screen of cavalry and Landwehr from there to Metz, three corps in Lorraine, one at Strasbourg and one at Mühlhausen. The two south German

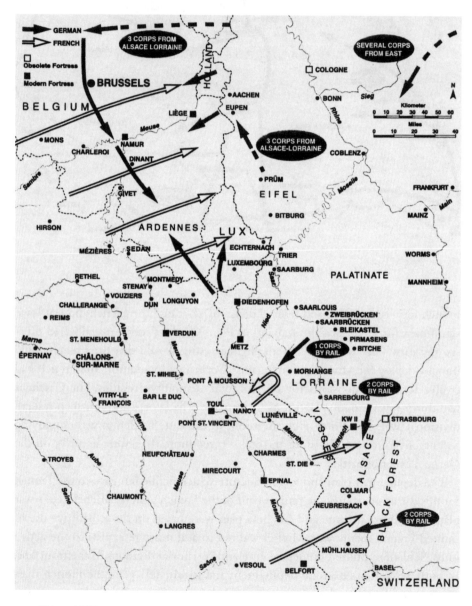

1905 *Kriegsspiel* West

corps and the three Bavarian corps remained in their mobilisation stations. Schlieffen scraped the bottom of the German manpower barrel, employing Landwehr, Landsturm and ersatz units on the front lines, especially in Alsace.

The French crossed the Franco-Belgian border on the twenty-third day of mobilisation, at which point Belgium and Holland allied themselves with Germany. At the same time, the French attacked into Alsace and Lorraine. Schlieffen said that it was essential for the Germans to hold Lorraine and the right bank of the Moselle as a base for a counter-attack against the French left wing, and sent all the Bavarian and south German corps there by rail to counter-attack; by the twenty-sixth day these forces had driven back the French attack in both provinces with heavy losses.

In Schlieffen's opinion a pursuit through the gap in the French fortress line at the *trouée de Charmes* led nowhere and involved considerable risk; therefore, as of the twenty-seventh day, he began to transfer three corps north. By the thirty-first day the French had reached a line Antwerp–Liège and had crossed the Belgian-German border south of Liège. By the thirty-third day the three German corps being transferred from the south had arrived in Antwerp with the prospect of three more arriving from the east by the thirty-seventh day. Schlieffen said that the proper course of action was to attack south from Antwerp with these first three corps against the French flank; such an attack carried with it a considerable element of risk, but no great deeds could be accomplished without risk (a direct quote from Moltke). Such an attack would be unexpected and should achieve surprise. In order to make this outflanking attack from Antwerp effective, however, the French armies had to be fixed by a frontal attack, even if the attacking forces were inferior to the defenders. The French reaction to all these unexpected moves would be hasty and unco-ordinated and this would, to some degree, counterbalance the risk the Germans were taking.

The German envelopment was directed on Namur, which was still in Belgian hands. This gave the envelopment operational depth, but nothing like the strategic depth envisaged by the envelopment around Paris in the 'Schlieffen plan' *Denkschrift*. By the thirty-seventh day the left flank French army had been surrounded inside the triangle Namur–Liège–Antwerp and the German enveloping force had crossed the Meuse at Namur. On the thirty-ninth day the Germans launched an attack from Metz–Diedenhofen to the north-west against the right flank of the French main body. By the forty-second day three French armies were surrounded in the Ardennes and a fourth was surrounded west of Luxembourg. The exercise was then terminated. Concerning the British army, Schlieffen quoted Lord Roberts who had said publicly that it would be the 'height of insanity' to involve the British army in a continental war, for which it was poorly prepared; Schlieffen said that Roberts should know what he was talking about.

In his last and most ambitious war game, Schlieffen tested concepts which had nothing to do with the Schlieffen plan. Given a simultaneous Franco-Russian offensive, Schlieffen replied with a strategic defensive on both fronts. When the Franco-Russian armies approached the German border, Schlieffen used the German rail net to mass uncommitted forces against the two Russian armies in East Prussia and destroy them. At the same time, he conducted an active defence in the west, retaining five corps in their mobilisation stations and then committing them by rail to obtain local superiority against the French forces invading Alsace and Lorraine and crushing them. Finally, he used rail mobility to redeploy forces from the east and from Alsace to attack the flanks of the French main body in the Ardennes and destroy it.

Aufmarsch 1905/06

Seven original documents were available concerning the 1905/06 deployment: the mobilisation schedule, the order of battle for *Aufmarsch* I, maps of the covering force in the east and the west, the *Aufmarschanweisungen* (minus the annexes) for *Aufmarsch* I and for coastal defence, and for *Aufmarsch* II *Ost*. There are no deployment maps, but the author of RH 61/v.96 made very general sketches of the west and east front deployments. The summaries of these documents comprise eight typewritten (with handwritten annotations) and two handwritten pages.

In *Aufmarsch* I the entire German army – seventy-two divisions (fifty-two active army and twenty reserve), eleven cavalry divisions and twenty-six and a half Landwehr brigades – were employed in the west. The order of battle was also given for *Aufmarsch* II, a two-front war, with sixty-two divisions in the west and ten in the east. No concept of the operation was provided.

In *Aufmarsch* I, the 1st Army deployed with three corps and four reserve corps north-west and west of Essen, opposite the Dutch border. The 2nd Army, with four corps and a reserve corps, was deployed north-east of Aachen. Belgium and Holland were only to be entered on order from the *Oberste Heeresleitung* (OHL), the senior German headquarters. The 3rd Army (four corps and two and a half reserve corps) was deployed south-east of Aachen; the 4th Army (three corps) in the area of Bitburg; the 5th Army (three corps) around Trier; the 6th Army (three corps) between Diedenhofen and Saarlouis; the 7th Army (three corps) around Metz; and the 8th Army (three corps and three reserve corps) in Lorraine around Saaralben.

Preparations were to be made to transport the reserve and ersatz troops of five corps areas and one division area to Holstein for coast defence duties as of the tenth day of mobilisation. This is the only reference to ersatz units. There is

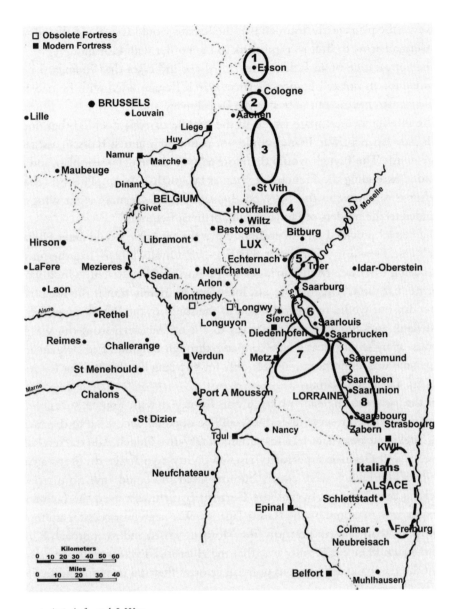

1905/06 *Aufmarsch* I *West*

no mention, as in the Schlieffen plan, of organising sixteen ersatz divisions, or of committing them against France.

No troops were to be deployed in Alsace south of Strasbourg. This was because the plan assumed that an Italian army of five corps (ten infantry divisions) and two cavalry divisions would deploy to Alsace. The plan stated that whether this deployment would take place or not depended on the political situation.

However, the plan clearly assumed that the Italians would arrive, and this allowed the German army to shift its right flank to the border with Holland.

The appearance of an Italian army in Alsace indicates that *Aufmarsch* I was intended for an isolated Franco-German war. If Britain sided with France, Italy would remain neutral out of fear of the British navy.

The intelligence estimate issued in the middle of 1904 decided that due to the Russo-Japanese War, France could not count on as much Russian assistance as previously. The French would therefore adopt a more defensive plan, and this included extending the French left wing as far north as Sedan. This is probably another reason why, in the 1905/06 *Aufmarsch* I, the German right wing was extended to the borders of Holland and northern Belgium.

Aufmarsch I provided for the possibility that the 1st Army would enter Holland. In this case, *Heereskavaalleriekorps* 1 (HKK 1 – 1st Cavalry Corps) had the mission of securing the three Meuse bridges to the north of Maastricht, which would indicate that the Germans were not intending to merely transit the Maastricht Appendix, but would occupy Holland to the south of the Rhine, guarding the right flank and allowing the Germans to cut off Antwerp from the sea. The German army would clearly have to march through Belgium. The Belgian army at this time was insignificant, suitable only for guarding the three major fortresses, Antwerp, Liège and Namur.

In the 1905/06 *Aufmarsch* I, for a one-front war with France, seventy-two German active and reserve divisions would be opposed, according to the August 1904 intelligence estimate, by a maximum of fifty-five French. Add the ten Italian divisions and German superiority rises to eighty-two active divisions against fifty-five. The French were clearly outnumbered and could have no interest in attacking the Germans. In fact, the German government used the favourable situation brought about by the Russo-Japanese War in an unsuccessful attempt to improve its world power position (the Morocco crisis) and to approach Russia, not to attack France. The only way that the *Aufmarsch* I war would come about was if the French made a serious political error, as they did in 1870, and declared war on Germany.

In addition, *Aufmarsch* I assumed that the British would not support the French – another unlikely proposition. If the British did support the French, then the Italians would not support the Germans. German world trade would end and the colonies would be lost. Given the need to guard the North Sea coast, blockade the Belgian fortresses, and with the arrival of the British army, German numerical superiority would disappear.

Due to German *Weltpolitik*, the construction of the German High Seas Fleet (and the fear that the British would 'Copenhagen' the German fleet) and British support of France during the Morocco crisis, a war between Germany and

Britain was as likely as one between Germany and France.[37] As late as February 1911 the French intelligence estimate rated the possibility of a British-German war, which would involve France, then 'most of the European powers', as being high.[38] The best that can be said for *Aufmarsch* I is that, in a war against Britain, the concentration of forces on the Dutch border would be useful to seize the North Sea coast and the ports of Rotterdam and Antwerp, while deploying the rest of the army against French intervention.

The 1905/06 *Aufmarsch* I clearly represents the German 'best case' scenario. It is related to the Schlieffen plan solely because the Schlieffen plan, with its twenty-four non-existent 'ghost divisions', is a 'better than best case' scenario.

In *Aufmarsch* II *Ost*, three corps and four reserve divisions deployed in East Prussia, ten divisions in total. One corps and a reserve division were in the easternmost part of the province, behind the Angerapp River; a corps was in the centre at Allenstein; a corps and a reserve division were at Deutsch Eylau in the western part of the province; a reserve division garrisoned Breslau and another Posen. In the west the Germans would have a slight numerical superiority: sixty-two divisions to forty-nine to fifty-five French.

French 1905 Intelligence Estimate[39]

The French thought that the Germans had created four more active corps, eight divisions, using the third division and fifth brigade excess to some corps. The total German force consisted of twenty-seven active corps (fifty-four divisions) and twenty-four reserve divisions, seventy-eight divisions, which was six divisions too many. The French thought that the Germans could now deploy twenty-four active corps (forty-eight divisions) and fourteen reserve divisions against France, sixty-two divisions in total, which for *Aufmarsch* II was essentially correct.

The French, therefore, thought that the Germans would still have to deploy sixteen divisions in East Prussia: *Aufmarsch* II actually deployed ten. The French, who were vitally concerned with the state of the Russian military, obviously did not believe that the Russian army opposite Germany had been crippled by the Manchurian War.

The French believed the Germans would deploy from Sarrebourg to Metz to the north of Trier in the Eifel. They would refuse their left flank in Alsace and attack on both sides of Verdun with the intent of turning the French left flank. This envelopment would be deeper than previously. If the Germans attacked with their active corps alone they would cross the border on the thirteenth day of mobilisation; if they waited until their army was complete, on the seventeenth day. The construction of new fortifications, by which the French meant Metz–

Thionville, allowed them to move their deployment assembly areas forward, speeding up their attack by two days.

The German right-wing manoeuvre army would deploy in the Eifel with at least six active corps, reinforced by four newly formed divisions or divisions of reserve, some 200,000 men. These forces would need a maximum of four days to march to the French border. The mass of the German army would deploy from Metz to Sarrebourg, two corps (50–60km) deep. These forces would attack on both sides of Metz. To do so, they would have to wait for the arrival of the army from the Eifel, and for that reason the German general offensive would not begin until the nineteenth day. In summary, the Germans would conduct a strategic defensive in Lorraine with 470 battalions (thirty-nine divisions) until the arrival of the right wing from the Eifel with 192 battalions (sixteen divisions) on the nineteenth day, when they would launch a general offensive. If the French attacked beforehand into Lorraine, the Germans would attack from Metz against the French left flank as of the nineteenth or twentieth day of mobilisation.

The French intelligence estimate admitted that this was only one of several hypotheses, but it corresponded to two important German indicators. First, the German rail net behind Metz facilitated concentration of the German army there. Second, and the best proof, was that the Germans had recently built massive new fortifications at Metz–Diedenhofen to protect this rail hub. The French intelligence estimate concluded that the German scheme of manoeuvre was based on the defensive power of the fortified zone at Metz–Diedenhofen. If the French decided to attack first, this was where the French main point of effort must lie.

Strategic Situation, 1905

A comparison of German and French deployments and intelligence estimates at this critical juncture presents a fascinating picture. The German *Aufmarsch* I for an isolated Franco-German war was a dead letter. The French had learned their lesson in 1870/71: fighting the Germans without an eastern ally (which in 1870/71 the French had hoped in vain would be Austria-Hungary) was a non-starter. The French were not going to go to war without Russian help, and they were confident that in a war with Germany they would receive Russian help. The French intelligence estimate shows that the French were counting on the Russians drawing off about 20 per cent of the German army. In spite of the Manchurian War, the French still thought the Russians could accomplish this. As proof of this the French did not, as the Germans had assumed, switch over to a defensive strategy: they did not change their 1903 plan at all until 1907. Had war broken out between France and Germany in 1905, the Germans would have been in for a very nasty surprise: the British would have supported the French. The German navy was aghast at such a prospect.

The French were clearly contemplating using their faster deployment and the isolation of the German right wing to launch an attack on both sides of Metz before the Germans were ready. The French would have been pleasantly surprised. Instead of meeting thirty-nine German divisions in Lorraine, as they expected, they would have met no more than twenty-six. The 1st German Army was lined up on the Dutch border; the 2nd at Aachen; and the 3rd were opposite the Ardennes and out of the fight for weeks. The French would have had a significant superiority and time to use it.

War in 1905 would have been a test of the first 1904 and 1906 *Generalstabsreisen West*. The German response to a French attack into Lorraine was to swing the right wing south to attack through Metz. In 1905 the French anticipated such a manoeuvre.

The French could have looked at war in 1905 with a certain degree of confidence. The French had *mademoiselle soixante-quinze*, the quick-firing 75mm cannon, and at this time she was probably a battle-winning weapon. She was armoured, could fire three times as fast as the German field gun and far more accurately. In 1905 field artillery was the sole source of fire support for the infantry; except for the Russians, European armies had not yet fielded machine guns. War in 1905 would have been a question of French infantry and quick-firing artillery against German infantry and completely obsolete artillery: the outcome would not have been pretty for the Germans.

1906/07

Aufmarsch 1906/07

There were thirteen original documents available to the author of the RH 61/v.96 summary of German war planning: the deployment schedule; order of battle for *Aufmarsch* I, II *West*, II *Ost* and *Nord* (north); covering force maps in the west and east; deployment maps with enemy situation in the west (1:300,000 and 1:200,000), the east (a rail map) and in the north (1:300,000); a coastal defence map; and the initial instructions (*Aufmarschanweisungen*) to the army commanders in the west, including the Italian army, and in the east (without annexes). The summary of these documents comprised ten typed pages with handwritten annotations, a handwritten force structure table and a deployment map (1:2,000,000) for the west only. Only *Aufmarsch* I is discussed, probably because the author wanted to highlight the Schlieffen plan.

Work would have begun on the plan in the winter of 1905/06. Ludendorff says that Schlieffen gave the guidance for the plan in November 1905.[40] Schlieffen was still working on the Schlieffen plan *Denkschrift* in January and February 1906, which means that the November 1905 guidance he gave to Ludendorff was not the Schlieffen plan. The Schlieffen plan was written far too late to allow it to be implemented by 1 April 1906, when the 1906/07 *Aufmarsch* went into effect. In fact, the Schlieffen plan should have been written in the winter of 1904/05 (for the 1905/06 deployment plan), when the Russo-Japanese War began, and not in January and February 1906, by which time the Russo-Japanese War had been over for nearly half a year. With each succeeding month the chances of fighting a one-front war, which were never very good, became less.

Aufmarsch I states that 'Holland's attitude is expected to be friendly rather than hostile, while the Belgian attitude is expected to be hostile'. This estimation of the Dutch was wishful thinking. In 1907/08 the attitude of Holland would be characterised as 'doubtful'.

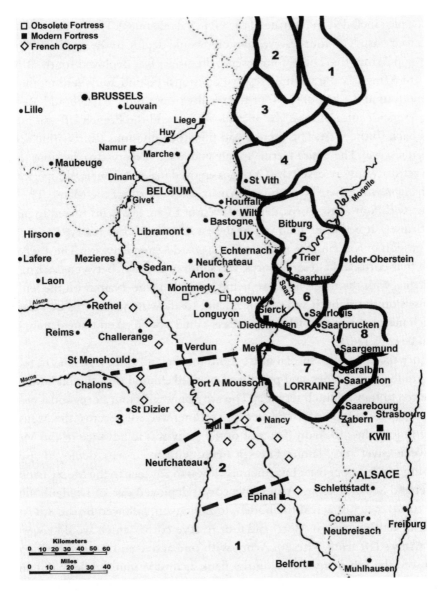

1906/07 West I

Aufmarsch I says: 'It is not out of the question that the British army will support Belgium. The British can land in Antwerp or move through Holland.' IX Reserve Corps was retained to guard against a landing on the North Sea coast. The British minister of war, Haldane, did not institute his reforms of the British army until 1906–07. British intervention in 1906/07 would have been slower and less powerful than it was in 1914.

The plan included an estimate of the French deployment. The French 1st Army, with four corps and four reserve divisions, would deploy to the north of Belfort. The 2nd Army (five corps, four reserve divisions) was deployed south of Toul; the 3rd Army (six corps, three reserve divisions) behind Toul-Verdun; the 4th Army (four and a half corps, four reserve divisions) at Ste Menehould-Rethel. The French centre of mass was at Toul-Verdun and the French left was pulled well back to the west. The French had fifty-four divisions (thirty-nine active, fifteen reserve). The entire German army contained seventy-two divisions (fifty-two active, twenty reserve): the Germans enjoyed massive numerical superiority.

In *Aufmarsch* I there were three German armies north of the Meuse. The 2nd Army, with four active corps, deployed west of Essen. It was instructed to march on Brussels. It was to be followed by the 1st Army, with five reserve corps, with the mission of covering the right flank and guard against Antwerp. The 3rd Army, with four corps and a reserve corps, was south of the 2nd, between Aachen and Cologne, with the mission of advancing between Liège–Namur on the left and Brussels on the right. It was instructed 'not to allow its advance to be delayed', which meant that if the Belgian fortresses could not be taken immediately, they must be bypassed.

Since there were no special instructions for the 2nd and 1st Armies to follow the 3rd through Aachen and past Liège, in all likelihood they would have been required to transit Dutch territory. The 4th Army, with four corps and a reserve corps, had instructions to send a corps and a reserve corps across the Meuse at Huy to join the 3rd Army. The rest of the army was to advance to the Meuse between Givet and Namur. The 5th Army, with five corps, deployed around Bitburg and Trier opposite Luxembourg. It was to advance to the Meuse between Givet and Sedan. The 6th Army (five corps) deployed east of Diedenhofen. It was to advance just across the border, to Longuyon, followed by the 8th Army, with an active corps (at Metz) and four reserve corps, which would cover the 6th Army's left flank. The 8th Army, with one active and four reserve corps, followed the 6th Army, covering the flank against Verdun while maintaining contact with Metz. The 7th Army included three corps and a reserve corps. It was to fix the French in place in Lorraine. It had to be prepared to withdraw as far as Metz and the Nied River position (*Niedstellung*) if faced with stronger enemy forces. It was also to be prepared to reinforce the right wing. Once again, the plan notes that the arrival of Italian forces 'was dependent on the political situation'. Nevertheless, the deployment of five Italian corps to the upper Alsace was written into the plan.

The Schlieffen plan rests on the rosy assumption of a one-front war, which was obviously not entirely valid because in the 1906/07 plan there is an *Aufmarsch* II for a two-front war, and this plan bears no resemblance to the Schlieffen plan. In

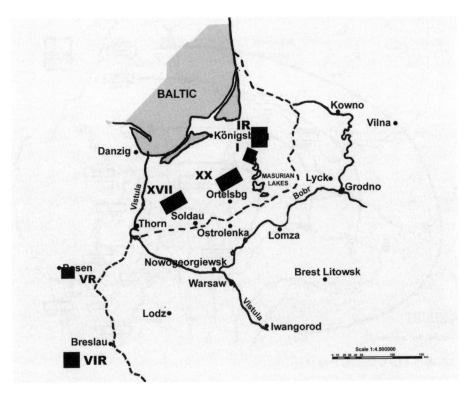

1906/07, 1907/08, 1908/09 East II, 1909/10 IIa

Aufmarsch II an army is deployed to East Prussia with three active corps, three reserve corps and a reserve division, probably thirteen divisions in total. These forces are mostly drawn from the right wing. The forces north of the Meuse were reduced from sixteen corps to ten. The crucial 2nd Army is dissolved entirely. The *Westheer* was now only about fifty-eight divisions strong; that is, thirty-eight divisions short of the force required by the Schlieffen plan, and in effect the French and Germans were numerically equal. Moreover, it is this *Aufmarsch* II that most closely resembles the two-front situation that the Germans faced in 1914.

The Schlieffen Plan Map: 'Little Maps, Big Arrows'

The most commonly used 'evidence' for the Schlieffen plan is the standard Schlieffen plan map, particularly Map 2 in the second volume of *The West Point Atlas of American Wars*,[41] which is found on Wikipedia and just about everywhere else.[42] The title of the *West Point Atlas* map is 'Western Front 1914. Schlieffen Plan of 1905. French Plan XVII', which obviously implies that in 1914 the

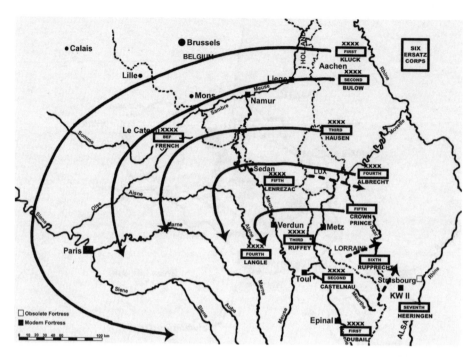

West Point Atlas Schlieffen Plan Map

Germans attempted to implement the Schlieffen plan. The *West Point Atlas* map is a mishmash of the actual Schlieffen plan map, the German 1914 plan and the 1914 campaign. This results in a map that does not accurately depict the Schlieffen plan or the German war plan in 1914 or the conduct of the Marne campaign. It is an attempt to substitute 'little map, big arrows' for the systematic study of all three.

On the actual Schlieffen plan map,[43] the centre armies stop on the Aisne and the Oise, which is where the Schlieffen plan *Denkschrift* said that the French might succeed at halting the German right wing. In the *West Point Atlas* map, the arrows depicting the German centre, the 2nd through to the 5th Armies, point south towards the Seine. The mapmaker apparently thought that if the Germans were going to push the French into Switzerland, then this was the way the Schlieffen plan map would look. He was wrong.

Neither is the *West Point Atlas* map an accurate depiction of the German 1914 war plan. It would have us believe that the German plan in 1914 ordered the 1st Army to march around Paris. In fact, the 1914 German plan did no such thing. The real, principal mission for the 1st Army was to act as flank guard. Due to a lack of troops in 1914, marching the 1st Army around Paris was a physical impossibility. In fact, the German plan in 1914 said nothing about the right-wing

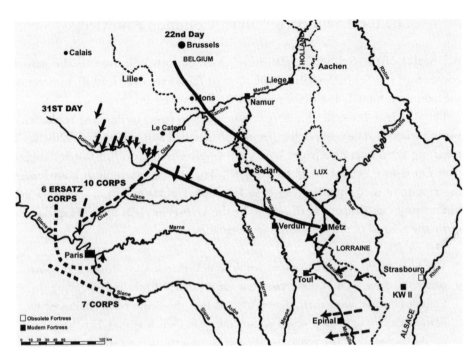

Actual Schlieffen Plan Map

advance after they reached the French border. Nor, as we shall see, do the *West Point Atlas* arrows accurately depict German orders and actions in 1914.

In the *West Point Atlas* map there are six ersatz corps (twelve ersatz divisions) behind the German right wing, as in the Schlieffen plan. In 1914 there were actually only six ersatz divisions, and these were sent to reinforce the German 6th and 7th Armies in Lorraine.

The French deployment in the *West Point Atlas* is misleading, making it look as though the Schlieffen plan had caught the French completely unprepared. As of 2 August, the first day of mobilisation, Joffre began to modify the peacetime deployment plan, so that by the time the French and German armies made contact, the French 5th Army was west of Namur, the 4th was south-east of Sedan and the 3rd north-west of Metz.

The Schlieffen plan map is the armchair strategist's dream. Based on this map the armchair strategist feels justified in making sweeping generalisations about German war planning, militarism, foreign policy and war guilt, which confirm his preconceived ideas, all without the need to actually read and understand the German plans, orders and actions.

The Real Schlieffen Plan *vs* 'Common Knowledge'

Advocates of the Schlieffen plan have a cavalier attitude towards the actual contents of the Schlieffen plan *Denkschrift* (if they have ever read it), preferring the 'common knowledge' description of Schlieffen's planning.

The Reichsarchiv official history required eleven pages to describe Schlieffen's planning and it is not especially specific.[44] A detailed appreciation of Schlieffen's planning takes over 100 pages.[45] A typed English translation of the Schlieffen plan *Denkschrift* occupies eighteen pages.[46] The standard 'common knowledge' description of the Schlieffen plan, as in Herwig's *The Marne 1914*, is accomplished in four pages, accompanied, of course, by the *West Point Atlas* map.[47] Herwig can recite the Schlieffen plan catechism in seven lines:

> The bulk of the German armies would quick-march west through the low countries, drive around the French left (or northern) flank; and, sweeping the English Channel with their 'sleeves', wheel into the Seine basin southwest of Fortress Paris, where they would destroy the main French armies. This 'hammer' would then pound any remaining enemy units against the German 'anvil' in Lorraine, or against the Swiss border.[48]

Herwig says that the Schlieffen plan was for a two-front war against France and Russia. The first line of the *Denkschrift* says '*Krieg gegen Frankreich*' – war against France; that is, a one-front war. There is no mention in the *Denkschrift*, as Herwig contends, that the Russian mobilisation (sic: deployment) would take forty days, because Russians were not expected to be belligerents. It is not as though this is a recent discovery: in 1925 the Reichsarchiv official history expressly said – twice – that the Schlieffen plan was based on *Aufmarsch* I for a one-front war against France.[49]

The *Denkschrift* said that the Germans would raise eight ersatz corps (sixteen ersatz divisions); six ersatz corps (twelve divisions) would, if possible, follow the right wing. Since there were only six ersatz divisions available in 1914, Herwig says that the Schlieffen plan provided for six divisions to follow the right wing.

Since the 1914 plan provided for six Italian divisions to deploy to the upper Alsace (none actually did), Herwig says that in the *Denkschrift* an Italian army with three corps would be deployed on the upper Rhine; however, there is no mention in the *Denkschrift* whatsoever of Italian forces, as the Reichsarchiv official history specifically points out.[50]

The Schlieffen plan is so well entrenched that its proponents feel no requirement to make their description of it internally consistent. Herwig says that the left wing made up 15 per cent 'of the German forces', the right wing 85 per cent,[51] making up 100 per cent 'of the German forces'. Herwig then says that the Schlieffen plan deployed another army in East Prussia. In the 1906/07 *Aufmarsch* II, a two-front war, Schlieffen deployed thirteen divisions in the east. Herwig never specifies how big his East Prussian army was, but if this is the size of the army that Herwig is talking about, then according to Herwig's own calculations, Schlieffen employed 120 per cent of the available German strength.

Herwig contends that 'Schlieffen meticulously crafted his grand design. The first twenty days of mobilization were laid out to the minute for 20,800 trains ...' On the next page he acknowledges 'that Germany was eight corps [sic: twelve] short of Schlieffen's actual prescription'. According to Herwig, Schlieffen's 'meticulously crafted grand design' depended on sixteen (actually twenty-four) 'ghost divisions'. Twenty-five per cent of the Schlieffen plan-sized German army, the equivalent of two strong armies, was imaginary.

What Herwig has done, just as the *West Point Atlas* did, is to improve on the Schlieffen plan, mixing the one-front 1906 *Denkschrift* with the two-front German war plan in 1914 so that they appear to agree with each other. While this may be a very satisfying procedure for armchair strategists, it is completely bereft of military, documentary and historical accuracy.

Notes

1 A. Marchand, *Plans de Concentration de 1871 à 1914* (Paris, 1926), pp. 129–43.
2 T. Zuber, *German War Planning 1891–1914: Sources and Interpretations* (Boydell & Brewer, 2002), pp. 7–22.
3 B. Gudmundson, *On Artillery* (Westport CT, 1993), pp. 6–7.
4 T. Zuber, *Inventing the Schlieffen Plan*, pp. 151–2, 163–4.
5 Ibid., pp. 167–8, 174–5.
6 Ibid., pp. 147–9, 181–3, 185–9, 273, 300.
7 Marchand, *Plans de Concentration*, pp. 140–3.
8 Zuber, *Inventing the Schlieffen Plan*, p. 203.
9 Letter from Dr Büttner, Bundesarchiv-Militärarchiv (BA-MA) dated 14 December 2004.
10 It was not available from 1996 to 2002 when I was conducting my research for *Inventing the Schlieffen Plan*.
11 The 1912/13 and 1914/15 *Aufmarschpläne* were transcribed from the stenographic notes into modern German by Herr Hans Gebhardt of the Forschungs- und Ausbildungstätte für Kurzschrift und Textverarbeitung, Bayreuth, Germany. The stenography used was the system devised by Franz Xavier Gabelsberger (*b.* 1789, *d.* 1849) in Munich in 1834, which was revised in 1857, 1895 and a last time in 1902. Gabelsberger's system was taught at higher-level educational institutions and stenographic associations, and widely used in academic circles. There were also other competing stenographic systems used until the introduction of a unified system in 1924.
12 Two 'Kriegskorps', which were to be established at the outbreak of war, were disestablished in 1904, reducing the German army by four divisions. C. Jany, *Geschichte der Preußischen Armee* (2nd edn, Osnabrück, 1967), IV, pp. 296–7.
13 Zuber, *Inventing the Schlieffen Plan*, pp. 191–202.
14 Ibid., p. 267.
15 Ibid., pp. 157, 185–9, 273, 300.

16 T. Zuber, *German War Planning*, pp. 22–3; Marchand, *Plans de Concentration*.

17 Greiner footnote: 'On the basis of evidence that is no longer available, it was assumed that there was a I and II Colonial Corps.'

18 Marchand, *Plans de Concentration*, pp. 148–9.

19 Ibid., pp. 147–56.

20 Bayerisches Kriegsarchiv München, Generalstab 207, Großer Generalstab, 1. Abteilung, *Zusammenstellung der wichtigsten Veranderungen im Heerewswesen Rußlands im Jahre 1905*.

21 Bayerisches Kriegsarchiv München, Nachlass Krafft von Dellmensingen 336, *Operationsstudie Januar 1905*.

22 Hauptstaatsarchiv Dresden, *Sächsischer Militärbevollmächtigter 1905 (1426)*, Blätter 45–6.

23 Zoellner, 'Schlieffen's Vermächtnis' in *Militärwissenschaftlicher Rundschau 1938. Sonderheft*.

24 Zuber, *Inventing the Schlieffen Plan*, pp. 203–6.

25 F. Boetticher, 'Der Lehrmeister des neuzeitlichen Krieges' in *Von Scharnhorst zu Schlieffen 1806–1906*, von Cochenhausen (ed.) (Berlin, 1933), pp. 249–316, especially pp. 309–12.

26 G. Gross, 'There was a Schlieffen Plan' (English version), p. 396.

27 T. Zuber, 'The Schlieffen Plan Reconsidered' in *War in History*, 1999 6 (3), pp. 291–3.

28 Zuber, *Inventing the Schlieffen Plan*, pp. 203–6.

29 G. Gross, 'There was a Schlieffen Plan' (German version) in *Der Schlieffenplan. Analysen und Dokumente*, H. Ehlert, M. Epkenhans and G. Gross (eds) (Paderborn, 2006), p. 140.

30 Bundesarchiv-Militärarchiv (BA-MA) Freiburg, *Nachlass* Boetticher N323/9.

31 Zuber, *German War Planning*, pp. 22–3. The total French force was forty-one active and fourteen reserve divisions, from which four active and two reserve divisions were assumed to be on the Italian border.

32 Gross, 'There was a Schlieffen Plan' (German version), pp. 144–6.

33 The sketches are accurate reproductions of the originals.

34 Gross, 'There was a Schlieffen Plan' (English version), p. 416.

35 *Chef des Generalstabes der Armee I Nr 13083 Z. Berlin, den 23. Dezember, 1905. Kriegsspiel November/Dezember 1905 Schlussbesprechung. Geheim!* BA-MA PH 3/646. Maps *Nachlass* Schlieffen BA-MA N 43/133. The Bayerisches Kriegsarchiv also has a complete copy, with maps, Generalstab 1237.

36 Gross, 'There was a Schlieffen plan' (German version), p. 137.

37 The possibility of a German invasion of Belgium and Holland in a British-German war caused by the growing strength of the German High Seas Fleet was expressly mentioned in the November 1911 German intelligence estimate. BA-MA PH 3/445 'Die militärpolitische Lage Deutschlands Ende November 1911'.

38 *Les Armées Françaises*, I, Annexes, p. 7.

39 Marchand, *Plans de Concentration*, pp. 164–7.

40 E. Ludendorff, *Mein militärischer Werdegang* (Munich, 1933), p. 100.

41 *The West Point Atlas of American Wars*, Vincent Esposito (ed.) (New York, 1959), Vol. II, Map 2.

42 Herwig, *Marne*, pp. 38–9.

43 BA-MA *Nachlass* (papers) Schlieffen N43, 141K Schlieffen plan maps.

44 *Weltkrieg* I, pp. 49–61.

45 Zuber, *Inventing the Schlieffen Plan*, pp. 1–51, 135–219.

46 Zuber, 'The Schlieffen Plan' in *German War Planning 1891–1914. Sources and Interpretations* (Boydell and Brewer, 2004), pp. 187–90, 192–200, 202–4.

47 Holger Herwig, *The Marne 1914* (New York, 2009), pp. 34–7, 40–1.

48 Ibid., pp. 35–6.

49 *Weltkrieg* I, pp. 55, 61.

50 Ibid., p. 61.

51 Herwig says that the transfer of two corps from the left wing to the right would result in the right wing constituting 91 per cent 'of his [Schlieffen's] forces': Herwig, *Marne*, p. 36.

THE WAR PLANNING OF THE YOUNGER MOLTKE, 1906–14

According to the advocates of the Schlieffen plan, Schlieffen bequeathed the 'perfect plan' to the younger Moltke, and being perfect, it was the only German war plan from 1906 to 1914. Moltke's baleful contribution to German war planning was his failure to understand the concept of the plan – to 'keep the right wing strong' – 'watering down' Schlieffen's brilliant plan by strengthening the left wing.[1]

Document RH 61/v.96 gives us, for the first time, a summary of the younger Moltke's deployment plans. It shows conclusively that the Schlieffen plan was never the German war plan. It should come as no surprise that there was not one 'perfect plan', but that Moltke modified German war planning to meet the changing political and military situation, including Russia's industrial growth and military build-up, the weakening position of the Triple Alliance and the worsening situation in the Balkans.

1906 *Generalstabsreise West*

If Moltke had adopted or even just inherited the Schlieffen plan as his war plan, it would be natural to assume that he would conduct an exercise to test it, particularly since such an exercise had not yet taken place. Since the Reichsarchiv never published any of Moltke's operational work or allowed access to it, it was not possible to verify this theory. Now, thanks to recent acquisitions at the Militärarchiv in Freiburg, we know the content of two of Moltke's earliest *Generalstabsreisen*, the staff rides in the west in 1906 and 1908.

For the *Generalstabsreise West* of 1906,[2] Moltke provided East Prussia with an unusually strong army: six corps and nine reserve divisions, twenty-one infantry divisions in all. This exercise was therefore testing the western component of *Aufmarsch* II: simultaneous French and Russian offensives. This would be incomprehensible if the Germans really considered that the Russian army was not combat-effective at the beginning of 1906, as the Schlieffen plan assumed. In the west, the right wing had fifteen corps (thirty divisions) deployed between Diedenhofen and Eupen, with a corps at Metz, seven corps (fourteen divisions) in Lorraine, two corps at Strasbourg and two corps in Alsace. This is clearly not the Schlieffen plan deployment.

Moltke stated that it was not in French interest to violate Belgian neutrality and therefore the French would attack in Lorraine. This attack was conducted en masse with fourteen corps. Moltke had to acknowledge that such a horde would be practically impossible to supply and have virtually no ability to manoeuvre. The French left flank army, to the north of Verdun, contained nine divisions and four divisions attacked in Alsace.

In the face of this mass French attack in Lorraine, the German commander decided immediately to launch his main attack through Belgium with the three right-wing armies. This was the solution that Schlieffen advocated, but never carried out, in the second 1904 *Generalstabsreise*. Moltke disagreed with this solution; he preferred to counter-attack with the right wing through Metz. Moltke said that one needed to be clear about the purpose of the right wing: it was to force the French to leave their fortress line and fight in the open. If the French launched their main attack in Lorraine, then the decisive battle would be fought in Lorraine and that was where the German right wing needed to march. This statement was practically the only part of Moltke's planning that was made public by the Reichsarchiv. It has been repeatedly cited to demonstrate that Moltke did not understand the concept of the Schlieffen plan.

In fact, having said that the 'school solution' was to counter-attack through Metz, Moltke allowed the German right wing advance through Belgium to proceed! On the fifteenth day the Germans also counter-attacked against the French invasion of upper Alsace, but this manoeuvre failed to trap the French forces. The Germans then abandoned Alsace altogether. On the eighteenth day the Germans were forced to send two corps from the right wing to reinforce the left. By the twentieth day the decisive battle was being fought by ten French and ten German corps on a 70km-long west–east line inside German territory from Metz to Bleikastel. A mass German frontal attack to the east of Metz failed in the face of the 'murderous fire of modern weapons', while the French slowly turned the open German left (!) flank. On the twenty-first day the last three corps of the German 3rd Army had to be sent from the right wing to Metz. The German right wing (1st and 2nd Armies) encountered no significant French forces and spent the exercise foot-marching through the Ardennes. Moltke ended

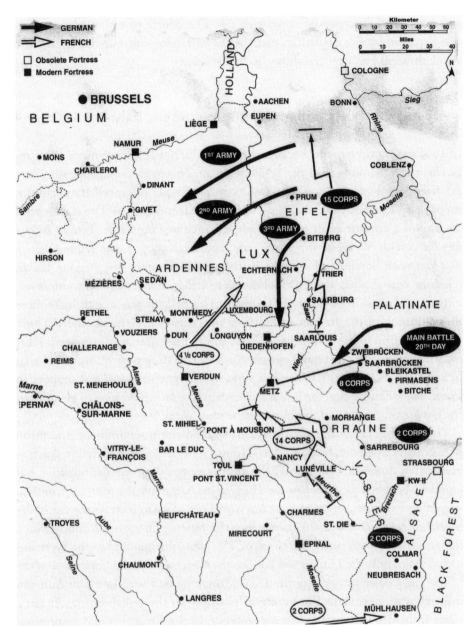

1906 *Generalstabsreise West*

the exercise without allowing it to come to a climactic battle of annihilation.
According to the results of this exercise, the German army would be forced to
meet a French attack in Lorraine with at least equal force. The decisive battle was
fought in Lorraine long before the right wing, marching through the Ardennes

and northern France, could make itself felt. The course of action advocated in this situation by the Schlieffen plan *Denkschrift* – to continue the right flank attack through France – was shown to be ineffective.

German 1906 Intelligence Summaries for Italy & Austria

In 1906 two developments became apparent which would have more effect on German war planning than the Schlieffen plan. The 1906 intelligence summary for Italy noted Italy's decreasing loyalty to the Triple Alliance.[3] Italy had not supported Germany diplomatically during the Morocco crisis. The Italian press advocated a continuation of the Triple Alliance but only if it allowed Italy a free hand with the western powers. Italy would not support the Triple Alliance in a war with Britain and an Italo-British rapprochement was evident. Italian relations with Austria were bad. There were Italian irredentist demonstrations in parts of Austria, particularly in Dalmatia. The Balkans was a continual source of friction, with the Italians supporting anti-Austrian elements there. There was speculation in the Italian press about an offensive war against Austria. Fleet manoeuvres seemed oriented against Austria. The only positive note was that in a war with Austria the Italian rail and fortress systems would not support an immediate offensive, and the initial Italian deployment would have to be far from the border, on the Po and Etsch, or even further west.

The intelligence summary for Austria noted the poor military condition of Germany's principal ally, Austria-Hungary.[4] The decisive factor in Austro-Hungarian domestic politics was the animosity between the nationalities, but especially between the Germans and Hungarians. As a result, the Austrian army was stagnating. In particular, the Hungarians would not agree to increase the size of the annual conscript class without gaining more Hungarian autonomy in return, which the government was unwilling to grant. The elements opposed to the Germans included not only the Hungarians but also the Czechs, Poles and South Slavs.

The only common enemy the Dual Monarchy had was Italy. The Austrian military was continually improving its position on the Italian border: shifting units from the east to the west, constructing fortifications and improving communications in the South Tyrol and the Adriatic. The Austro-Hungarian press fanned the war spirit against Italy.

The performance of the Austrian troops in the 1906 manoeuvres was poor; indeed, it had got worse, particularly at the higher command echelons. The exercise as a whole had been badly run. At the operational level units were deployed on too broad a front and employed piecemeal. Operations orders were unclear and marching routes conflicted.

Austrian relations with Russia were in some respects good. The Austrians had demonstrated their goodwill towards Russia and had not used the Russo-Japanese War to make trouble in the Balkans. Nevertheless, the Austrians wanted to expand towards Salonika and the Balkans remained the Achilles heel of Russo-Austrian relations.

French Plan XV Modified (1906)

In early 1906 the French Plan XV was changed significantly – the French left was strengthened – and Marchand said that this was de facto an entirely new plan.[5] A 5th Army was assembled out of the IV, X and Colonial Corps in the area north-east of St Dizier, behind the left flank 4th Army (VI, I, III and IX Corps), which was moved forward to the line Verdun–Challerange. The remaining three armies generally maintained the positions they had been assigned in Plan XV. The French now had six corps massed around Verdun. Marchand says the changes in question were due to the French two-year conscription law of 1905, which increased the total number of conscripts, and the fact that the French could count firmly on being able to commit the XIV and XV Corps not against the Italians but against the Germans.

German 1907 West Front Intelligence Estimate

In the summer of 1906 Agent 35 delivered what he said was the complete deployment of the active French corps, including their transportation routes to the 3rd Department of the German general staff. He named as his sources three officials in the French general staff and war ministry whom he had befriended for a considerable period. He explained that the march plans were compiled only by officers, but over the years the necessary changes were made by officials working under the supervision of officers. In this way his friends had become aware of the actual deployment plan and had conveyed this information in conversation to Agent 35, who they held to be a good patriot. According to Agent 35, the corps deployed as follows: four corps in the south at Toul–Besançon–Epinal, five corps near Toul, a corps at Verdun, three corps near Montmédy on the Belgian border and three corps at Châlons sur Marne. The three covering force corps were not mentioned. If compared to the modified Plan XV (1906), Agent 35's information placed the left-wing army at Montmédy too far forward and the reserve army at Châlons sur Marne too far to the north.

In a *Denkschrift* of January 1907 the 3rd Department thoroughly evaluated the probability of this information from the agent and compared it with its August

1904 estimate of the French deployment. After elaborate calculations, it developed a modified estimate of the French deployment that reflected a synthesis of the 1904 estimate and Agent 35's information. The 3rd Department estimate was also labouring under the misconception that the French had fourteen deployment rail lines available, when in fact they only planned to use nine.

If the German estimate compared to Plan XV (1906) the 3rd Department made the French too strong on the left, ten corps as opposed to the actual seven, and too far to the north, while the French had an entire four-corps army in the centre and the 3rd Department had none.[6] It is quite likely that the Germans were 'mirror-imagining' – writing the French plan from the perspective of German, not French, doctrine.

1907/08

French Plan XV*bis* (1907)

The French Plan XV was significantly changed again and became Plan XV*bis*, which went into effect on 22 May 1907. A mass of three armies (1st, 3rd and 4th) with fourteen corps between them were now to deploy on the border with German Lorraine. The main body was covered to the north by the 5th Army, consisting of two corps and two cavalry divisions, while only one army (2nd), consisting of four corps, was now deployed in the south on the Vosges front. The northern group of reserve divisions was widely dispersed from the Camp de Châlons to La Fère. The middle group was deployed behind the 3rd Army, the southern group south of Langres. Plan XV*bis* was in effect until the spring of 1909.[7]

The 3rd Army in the centre, five corps strong, formed the base of manoeuvre and was itself deployed in depth, also facilitating manoeuvre. The 1st Army, on its right, would act against the enemy left; the 4th Army, on its left, could act with the 3rd or 5th on the far left flank. The mission of the two flank armies, the 5th on the left and 2nd on the right, was essentially defensive, but could also act offensively. Aside from the IXX and XXI Corps, which would deploy late, there was no reserve army – it would have been necessary to subtract corps from the front-line armies to conduct a strategic manoeuvre.

Aufmarsch 1907/08: Moltke's First Plan

There were thirteen original documents available from the 1907/08 war plan: the mobilisation calendar; order of battle in the west, east and north; covering force maps in the west and east; some documents from the instructions for the covering force; deployment maps for the west (1:500,000, with enemy estimate, which reflect the 1907 changes; 1:300,000 and 1:200,000); and the *Aufmarschanweisungen*

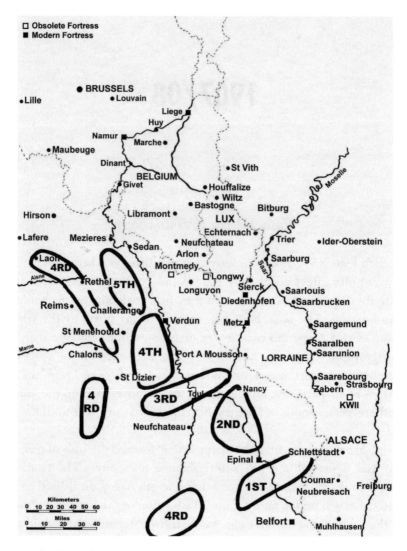

French Plan XV*bis* (1907)

West (including the Italian army) and *Ost* (neither included the annexes). The summary of the 1907/08 plan is twelve typed pages long (with handwritten annotations). There is also an *Aufmarsch* I deployment map (1:2,000,000) and a handwritten comparison of the strength of the German deployments from 1900/01 to 1905/06.

The 1907/08 plan included both an *Aufmarsch* I and II. Once again, only the concept of the operation for *Aufmarsch* I was discussed. The order of battle states there were twenty reserve divisions; that is, seven of the reserve corps still consisted of only one division.

The attitude of both Belgium and Holland was now characterised as 'doubtful'. The intervention of the British army was considered 'likely'. The British could move through Holland, land at Antwerp or at Calais and link up with the French. The German intelligence estimate said that the French left wing had been moved somewhat to the north and had been reinforced by one and a half corps to a total of six corps.

There is now only one German army north of the Roer River, the 1st, with four active and four reserve corps. This army was to march on Brussels while covering the right flank against Antwerp. The 2nd Army (five corps, two reserve

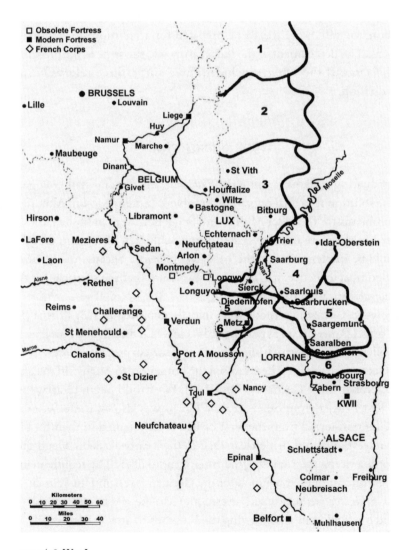

1907/08 *West* I

corps) had its zone of operations extended 25km to the south. It was to advance on both sides of Liège, begin the siege of the fortress, then concentrate north of the Meuse at Huy and advance through Wavre–Gembloux. The 3rd Army (six corps) was to advance on the Meuse at between Namur and Mézières; the 4th Army (six corps, one reserve corps) between Sedan and Longuyon in the Ardennes. The deployment of the 5th Army (two corps, three reserve corps) was echeloned far to the rear into the Palatinate. Its mission was to protect Metz and block a French attack originating out of Verdun. The 6th Army (three corps, two reserve corps) had the same complex mission as the 7th in the preceding plan: defend the south side of Metz, if necessary by withdrawing to the Nied, yet fixing the French forces on the Moselle and Meurthe, if necessary by attacking Nancy. After completing its mission, the 6th Army was to be prepared for a rail move to 'another area of operations'. The deployment of the Italian army was the same as the preceding year.

In *Aufmarsch* II the *Ostheer* included three corps, three reserve corps and a reserve division.

1907 *Schlussaufgabe*

Each graduating student at the *Kriegsakademie*, the general staff college, had to write the solution to a final operational problem (*Schlussaufgabe*). Although some of the problems for the elder Moltke and Schlieffen were published, those of the younger Moltke were not. Advocates of the Schlieffen plan claim that the great plan could be implemented in the 1906/07 *Aufmarsch* because the Russian army was not combat-effective. It is therefore surprising that the scenario for the 1907 *Schlussaufgabe* was for a two-front war.[8]

Only seven German divisions were initially deployed in East Prussia (I Corps, XVII Corps, I Reserve Corps plus the 3rd Reserve Division). The Russians attacked with a Niemen (northern) army of three to four corps and a Narew (southern) army of six to seven corps. These crossed the border on 30 August. In the afternoon of 1 September three German corps (II, III, IV) would begin to arrive in west-central East Prussia 'from other areas'. V Corps was also en route. Whether they were being transferred from the west or had been retained in their mobilisation areas as reserves was not made clear. Due to their early availability and the vague wording describing their transfer, the latter is more likely. The requirement was to develop a concept of the operation for the German forces in East Prussia.

In the *Schlussbesprechung* (exercise critique) Moltke said that this problem could be solved by digging in and allowing the Russians to attack. Fortunately, none of the officers had chosen this solution. If the Germans defeated the enemy attack, Moltke said, the enemy would retain his freedom of manoeuvre and would move to outflank them the next day. Eventually the defender would be forced out of his position. It was necessary not just to throw back the enemy attack, but defeat him, and this could only be accomplished by attacking. Since the German army was not strong enough to attack both Russian armies, it had to concentrate against one. The Niemen army would probably withdraw in the face of a German attack. Even if it stood and fought, the Germans would probably not be able to defeat it before the Narew army appeared in the German rear. A German attack on the Niemen army would be largely frontal and in modern combat frontal attacks are long, drawn-out and bloody affairs. Recent experience had shown that a decision could be won only by enveloping an enemy flank. In discussing the German intelligence concerning the Niemen army, Moltke said that officers must always keep in mind that they would never have a complete picture of the enemy forces and that if the location of the enemy flank were known a great deal had been accomplished. Determining the enemy situation was more a question of rational deduction than of waiting for reconnaissance reports to come in.

Moltke's solution was to attack the left flank of the Narew army with IV and V Corps, arriving by rail from the west, and drive the army into the Masurian Lakes. III, II and XVII Corps would block the Narew army's attack at Allenstein in the middle of East Prussia. I Reserve Corps would delay the Niemen army on a position along the Alle. Moltke said that this was safer than attacking the right flank of the Narew army, which had been Schlieffen's solution in 1894. Even if the Niemen army did break the German defensive line on the Alle line, it could not threaten the decisive right-wing attack of the German main body, whereas if the German *Schwerpunkt* were on the left, the Niemen army might pose a danger. Moltke also warned against taking the offensive under all circumstances. I Reserve Corps was simply not strong enough to attack the Niemen army but had to defend the relatively strong position on the Alle. Once engaged, the corps would not be able to withdraw until nightfall, but then a withdrawal would be absolutely necessary. I Reserve Corps should not withdraw to the south-west on the main body. It would be best to conduct an eccentric retreat to the west to draw the Russians after it. The enemy would be uncertain as to the I Reserve Corps' whereabouts and would have to divide his forces to pursue it.

Moltke warned against occupying a *Flankenstellung* with I Reserve Corps. The *Flankenstellung* was the elder Moltke's favourite 'school solution' to war game problems.[9] A defending force would occupy a strong position parallel to the advancing enemy. Theoretically, the advancing force would be placed on the horns of an insoluble dilemma, unable to attack the *Flankenstellung* while prevented from continuing the advance because the *Flankenstellung* threatened its rear. The *Flankenstellung* was a throwback to eighteenth-century positional warfare. Neither the elder Moltke nor his generals had ever used a *Flankenstellung* in actual combat. The younger Moltke said that the Russians would merely mask the *Flankenstellung* and continue their advance. Evidently the younger Moltke's pupils had been reading the elder Moltke's war games and theories, and were trying to apply them – a development that the younger Moltke had to suppress if they were to learn effective modern doctrine.

This was a classic Schlieffen-style problem: Germany's interior position and rail net allowed the transfer of four corps to the east, where the Germans would mass against one of the Russian armies and destroy it, while holding off the other enemy force with an economy of force operation.

Obviously, in 1907 the Germans were planning to fight a two-front war in which both the Russians and the French would be attacking. Just as obviously, Moltke had wholeheartedly adopted Schlieffen's counter-attack doctrine. There is no trace of the Schlieffen plan to be seen.

German 1907 Intelligence Summary for Russia

In 1907 the Germans thought that Russia had sixty infantry and twenty-eight cavalry divisions available for a war with Germany and Austria-Hungary.[10] Twenty-eight infantry divisions would deploy against Germany, twenty-four against Austria. Eight divisions would be retained in Moscow and St Petersburg for internal security duties. The Russians would still have to be concerned that the Japanese would take this opportunity to renew hostilities in Manchuria. Therefore, Russia would initially stand on the defensive in the west.

Most important, the Stolypin government was in complete control: its reforms had made the government popular and internal security had been fully restored. Russia was interested in peace to repair the problems caused by the war and revolution.

Russian military readiness was a decidedly mixed bag. The Russian army had grown by 111,000 men between 1904 and the end of 1907. New units had been created in the east and all the western units had returned from Asia to their home stations. There was an 11 per cent shortage of company-grade officers and a 17 per cent shortage of non-commissioned officers. Every line infantry regiment had two machine guns, and the artillery was equipped with telephones for fire control, but losses in equipment and expenditures on ammunition were such that the units had 25 per cent shortages. Improvements in the rail net and organisation of the mobilisation meant that the deployment had speeded up by three days. Nevertheless, the Russians would not complete the deployment on time. Training suffered from internal security duties but was getting better. The annual imperial manoeuvres and live-fire exercises demonstrated that the units had weaknesses which the Russian army was trying to overcome.

While the Russian army had serious deficiencies, the picture presented by the 1907 Russian intelligence estimate is a far cry from the insistence by advocates of the Schlieffen plan that the Russian army was completely helpless.

German 1907 Intelligence Summary for Austria

There was no improvement in pressing military questions (introducing a two-year conscript service, increasing the size of the conscript classes and raising the number of field artillery pieces) in 1907.[11] The government merely kicked the can of military reform down the road, postponing the question until 1908. The 9th Department, which was responsible for this estimate, thought that nothing was likely to change in 1908 either. The only positive point was the appointment of Conrad von Hötzendorf as chief of the Austrian general staff. Conrad was felt to have had a favourable effect on Austrian high-level manoeuvres and operational training.

Austrian relations with Russia were good, as they were with Romania.

Austria and Italy continued to compete in the Adriatic and the Balkans. Austria moved more troops from Galicia and the interior to the Italian border. The principal threat to peace was Serbia's inner political instability, combined with tension in Serbia's relations with Bulgaria and Montenegro.

The Austrian intelligence estimate complained of Britain's policy of 'encircling' Germany and of overwhelming British influence in the Balkans.

German 1907 Intelligence Summary for Italy

The 1907 Italian intelligence summary stated that Italy would not side with the Triple Alliance in a war against the western powers.[12] The Italians also thought that the Triple Alliance was militarily inferior to the western powers, which the 9th Department confirmed. Italy continued to seek closer relations with Britain. Italy was building four dreadnought battleships to challenge Austria for control of the Adriatic.

German 1907 Intelligence Summary for Bulgaria

Trouble was brewing in the Balkans.[13] Bulgaria was systematically preparing for war with Turkey, which the intelligence estimate said was 'unavoidable'. The Bulgarian army was growing. Bulgaria was coming to an understanding with Romania and would seek one with Russia. The Germans foresaw the First Balkan War, which would break out in October 1912, far in advance.

1908/09

Aufmarsch 1908/09

There were twelve original documents available from the 1908/09 *Aufmarsch*: 'instructions' (not further specified) for the west and east; a covering force map for the west and two for the east; an order of battle for the west, east and north, and separate orders of battle for the west and east; three deployment maps for the west (1:500,000, 1:300,000, 1:200,000); and the *Aufmarschanweisungen West und Ost* (without the annexes). These documents were boiled down to a summary seven typed pages long (with handwritten annotations) and a map of the deployment in the west (1:2,000,000).

In *Aufmarsch* I the 2nd Army now had the mission of taking Liège 'at once': 'The 2nd Army will open the roads blocked by Liège and Huy. It will begin operations even before the completion of deployment (on about the 10th or 11th day of mobilization).' Dutch neutrality was only to be violated if the 2nd Army did not succeed in taking Liège and a regular siege of Liège was necessary. The 1st Army was reduced by two reserve corps to four corps and two reserve corps, the 2nd Army by an active corps to four corps and two reserve corps, and the 3rd Army was reduced by a corps to four corps and two reserve corps, but also given a much narrower area of operations between Namur and Givet. The 4th Army lost two corps and now consisted of three corps and two reserve corps. Its objective was the middle of the Meuse. The 5th Army gained two active corps, lost a reserve corps, and was now four active corps and two reserve corps strong and directed at the Meuse north of Longuyon. The 6th Army, with four active and a reserve corps, took over the 5th Army's former mission and defended north of Verdun. A new 7th Army, with three corps and a reserve corps, was given the complex offensive-defensive mission in Lorraine.

The Italian army was not mentioned. On the other hand, XIV Corps was now to cover the upper Alsace against minor enemy operations but fall back to Strasbourg or the left bank of the Rhine in the face of a serious enemy offensive.

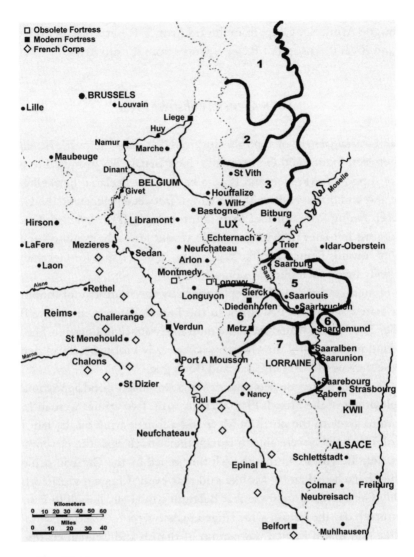

Legend:
□ Obsolete Fortress
■ Modern Fortress
◇ French Corps

1908/09 *West* I

This reflects a declining faith in the probability that the Italians would arrive and recognition that Alsace would require a degree of protection.

The intent of these changes was to create more uniform armies five or six corps strong which were smaller and easier to control. At the same time, however, the forces north of the Meuse were reduced by three corps and the forces in the Ardennes, between Namur and Metz, were increased by the same amount. There is no mention whatsoever of ersatz units.

The size of the *Ostheer* was unchanged. In order to form the *Ostheer*, I Corps and I Reserve Corps would be detached from the 1st Army, 3rd Reserve Division from the 2nd Army, XX Corps from the 3rd Army, V Reserve Corps from the 5th Army, and XVII Corps and VI Reserve Corps from the 6th Army.

1908 *Generalstabsreise West*

Moltke's *Generalstabsreise* of 1908 also survived.[14] It plays the pure *Westaufmarsch*: a war between France and Germany in which Britain has promised to provide effective support for France, and Russia has not yet declared her belligerency. Moltke also said that even though Russia was not yet a belligerent, the Germans must keep strong forces in East Prussia (probably 5 ID – *Infanteriedivision*) to guard against her later intervention. Italy would probably exercise benevolent neutrality towards France. Moltke was saying, in effect, that for Germany there would really be no such thing as a one-front war.

The French completed their deployment by the ninth day of mobilisation. Moltke stated again that it was not in the French interest to violate Belgian neutrality. The French would therefore most likely attack in Lorraine. The British would land in Antwerp if the Germans had already violated Belgian neutrality; otherwise they would land in Calais and Boulogne.

Moltke's French exercise deployment was a reasonably good approximation of the deployment in the French Plan XVII in 1914. Two armies were in Lorraine with a third army to the north of Metz and a fourth army on the left flank of the third. The French were able to launch their attack as of the eleventh day of mobilisation. Belgium said that she felt threatened by the German deployment and allied herself to France. Moltke said that even if France violated Belgian neutrality, Germany must assume that Belgium would ally herself to France. On the thirteenth day the British army landed in Antwerp.

Moltke said that if France was certain of British and Belgian co-operation, her best course of action would be to launch her main attack immediately with fifteen corps and nine reserve divisions from a line Verdun–Maubeuge to a line Diedenhofen–Liège, while remaining on the defensive between Belfort and Verdun with six corps and ten reserve divisions. After the eighth day of mobilisation, however, it was too late for the French to change their deployment from an attack in Lorraine to one in the Ardennes. Since, in 1914, both Britain and Belgium were at war with Germany by the fourth mobilisation day, Moltke was probably anticipating Plan XVII's offensive in the Ardennes, which was conducted by the French 3rd and 4th Armies.

The Germans deployed 66 ID in the west with four armies between Metz and Aachen, an army echeloned behind Metz, one in Lorraine and one in southern Lorraine and in Alsace. The Entente had the equivalent of ninety-two divisions,

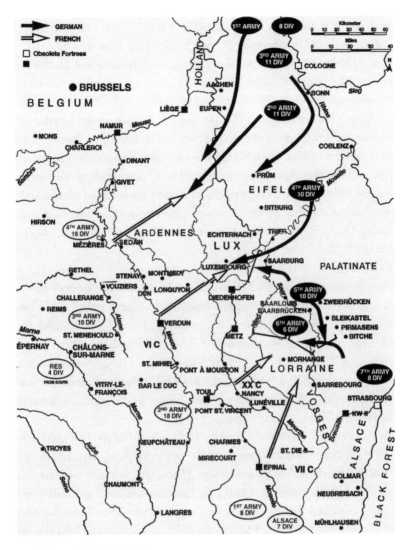

1908 General Staff Ride West

a numerical superiority of twenty-six divisions, but Moltke seemed to feel that this would be offset to a large part by German qualitative superiority. The German intent was to launch the main attack with the right wing into Belgium and Luxembourg, but the German army would fight a decisive battle wherever the French main force was to be found.

If the French launched their main attack between Metz and Strasbourg, the 3rd, 4th, 5th and 6th Armies would swing south to occupy a line Metz–Coblenz – that is, a 170km-long line entirely on German territory – and attack with a strong right wing to the south-west. The 1st and 2nd Armies would guard the right flank of the main body to the north of Metz and the 7th Army, on the left, would fall back to the north along the left bank of the Rhine.

The most likely French course of action was a main attack with the left wing between the Meuse and Verdun. This would be met by the German right wing, whose *Schwerpunkt* would be in an enveloping movement by the 1st and 2nd Armies on the right or a breakthrough by the 4th and 5th Armies on the left; the 6th Army would cover the left flank of the main body in Lorraine. The French might also attack to both sides of Metz. In this case, the 1st and 2nd Armies would march south.

Moltke said that the great difficulty would lie in determining what strategy the French were using. He then repeated a common concern of all soldiers before the Great War, saying that no one had any experience in conducting a war with a mass army. In the face of these questions, deciding on his own strategy was no higher than Moltke's third priority problem.

Moltke's analysis of the situation in the west in 1908 was founded directly on the results obtained by Schlieffen's last staff rides. This concept has nothing in common with the Schlieffen plan *Denkschrift*. There was also no provision for a pure French defence because every chief of staff from Moltke the elder to Moltke the younger maintained that it was very unlikely there would even be a war unless the French wanted one, and if the French wanted a war, then the French would attack. This was not a plan for invading France but a plan for meeting the French offensive head on. This is also, in concept, the same estimate of the situation Moltke used in 1914.

In this exercise, the French attacked on both sides of Metz. The most significant departure from Plan XVII was that elements of the 1st Army attacked directly over the crest of the northern Vosges into lower Alsace, which is also what the Germans expected the French to do in 1914. The German 1st, 2nd, 3rd and 4th Armies on the right marched directly south. The 5th held the Moselle to the north-east of Metz, the 6th held the Nied to the south-east, and the 7th held the line Han (south-east of Metz)–Saarburg in Lorraine. On the thirteenth and fourteenth days, nine French corps attacked eight and a half German corps defending a position on the German Nied. On the fifteenth day the German 2nd and French 4th Armies were manoeuvring against each other in the Ardennes, with the German 1st Army echeloned to the right rear of the 2nd, and the 3rd Army arriving to the left rear of the 2nd. The French 3rd Army was defending Luxembourg and the German 4th had crossed the Mosel to attack it. The German 6th, 7th and 5th Armies (west to east) were defending a position on a line Metz–Saargemünd–Pirmasens – a 110km-long line on German territory – against frontal attacks by the French 2nd and 1st Armies. The French frontal attacks failed, as Moltke said: frontal attacks would fail no matter how overwhelming the attacker's superiority in infantry. Nevertheless, the Germans were unable to prevent the defeated French forces from successfully withdrawing to their fortress line. The Germans, said Moltke, were now faced with a difficult second campaign. In his opinion, the first battle would come quickly and might well decide the final outcome of the war, but it would be followed by a long war in the enemy heartland.

1908 *Schlussaufgabe*

The situation for the 1908 *Schlussaufgabe* was for a defence against a landing of three corps (100,000 men) – pretty obviously the British army – in Denmark.[15] This was recognised to be a favourite scenario of the elder Moltke – the cover sheet for the problem called it a 'Moltke exercise' (*Moltkeaufgabe*). The Danes protested but otherwise remained neutral. Initially, the Germans could oppose this landing with only three Landwehr brigades, an ersatz brigade and assorted Landsturm battalions. On the fourth day, IX Corps and the 17th Reserve Division arrived by rail in Hamburg. On the eighth, the X Corps would begin to arrive. At the same time, the approach of another fleet of enemy transports was reported.

In the *Schlussbesprechung* Moltke said that the purpose of the landing was to divert German forces from the decisive front, strike at German morale and destroy the Kaiser Wilhelm Canal as well as the naval installations at Kiel and Hamburg. This meant that the landing force would try to achieve its objectives before the Germans could bring up reinforcements. Moltke said that neither a static defence forward of the Kaiser Wilhelm Canal nor a *Flankenstellung* at Kiel would prevent the enemy from taking the canal and destroying the installations. The Germans, although outnumbered, must attack. If they defeated the landing force they might prevent it from re-embarking and destroy it. Most of the officers decided to attack the enemy main body, which consisted of two corps on the east side of the Eider River. Moltke approved of this solution. He also agreed with those officers who decided to attack the enemy flank, but cautioned that the attack would succeed only if the Germans surprised their enemy. The Germans would be aided by the fact that the enemy could not conduct reconnaissance over the canal. By concentrating everything against the enemy left, part of the canal would fall into enemy hands. This had to be accepted in order to secure a decisive victory. Nevertheless, Moltke did not predict an easy time of it for the Germans. The enemy would move his units to the east to meet the German attack and success would come only after heavy fighting and at the price of severe losses. The enemy position was, however, unfavourable. He would withdraw during the night to occupy a stronger line. He could not be allowed to do this unhindered: the Germans needed to continue the attack during the night while at the same time moving to turn the enemy left flank.

German 1908 West Front Intelligence Estimate

There was considerable discussion in the French press and Parliament that in case of war, five armies would be deployed to the north-east border, including a 'covering force army'.[16] Furthermore, according to a private report that was considered very reliable, General Lacroix had inspected the three border corps (VI, VII and XX) as 'inspector of the army' and repeatedly toured the eastern border. Before being named the Generalissimo in 1907 he was supposed to have been selected to be the commander of an army composed of these three corps. On the basis of these reports, the 3rd Department now thought there would be five French armies, the 5th Army being a covering force army composed of the VI, VII and XX Corps. They considered the role of this commander at the beginning of the campaign to consist of bringing the movements of the widely dispersed covering force troops into harmony with each other, as well as with the intentions of the army command. It was left undecided how long after the commencement of operations this army would continue to exist. Agent 35 delivered a deployment plan that was very similar to the one he had delivered in 1906, and he too said that a covering force army had been formed.[17] The 3rd Department maintained its January 1907 estimate for the 1908/09 mobilisation year,[18] with the exception that it now thought the three border corps had been consolidated into a 5th, border security, Army. In fact, this army was a figment of the Germans' imagination. The covering force army issue is, however, indicative of the difficulties the 3rd Department was experiencing.

German 1908 Intelligence Summary for Austria

The Austrian army continued to stagnate.[19] The military budgets were little changed from 1907. Military reforms were postponed once again. Machine gun sections had been established in thirty-nine infantry and two cavalry regiments in March 1908. By February 1909 every active infantry regiment was to include a MG section. Since the size of the army was fixed, the machine gun sections could only be created by further decreasing the strength of the infantry battalions. About 3,500 additional personnel for the navy were obtained by raiding the infantry battalions.

Austria's international position was coming under increasing pressure. Relations with Russia were cooling after Austria announced the intention to build the Sanjak railway line to Salonika, while Russia was getting closer to Britain. Unstated was the fact that Britain and Japan were allies, and a British-Russian rapprochement would reduce significantly any Japanese threat to

Manchuria. The victory of the Young Turks stirred up conditions in the Balkans and made a Bulgarian-Turkish war more likely.

German 1908 Intelligence Summary for Italy

Italian foreign policy vacillated, trying to gain advantages from both power groups. The Italians wanted to fight Austria, but were aware that they were not strong enough to do so.[20] Such weakness was a topic of open political discussion. This reinforced Italian adherence to the Triple Alliance. On the other hand, Italy enjoyed cordial relations with France and Britain, and hoped to be able to co-operate in the Balkans against Austria.

French 1908 Intelligence Estimate

The French said: 'The tendencies which obtained in the German deployment in 1905 manifested themselves to an even greater degree with the subsequent rail construction, either completed or in progress, and reinforced the likelihood of the intelligence estimate.'[21] The 'tendency' the French intelligence estimate referred to was the expected German desire to conduct an offensive in the west as rapidly as possible. The French intelligence estimate noted that the Germans had begun constructing four new bridges across the Rhine, and when they were finished the Germans would have eighteen railway bridges across the Rhine between the Dutch and Swiss borders, two of which had four railway lines, fifteen had two lines and only one had one line. The Germans had also constructed additional rail installations at Aachen, in particular a line from Malmedy to Stavelot, which would give a German army operating on the south bank of the Meuse two lines of communication, which were not interdicted by Liège and Namur.

More important, however, was the large quantity of railway construction in 1907 around Metz and Saarbrücken, as well as at Trier and to the north, while there was little work around Strasbourg. This would reinforce the French estimate that the German centre of gravity would be placed behind Metz.

In 1908 there was little work behind Metz and more on the flanks, particularly in the north, where 'considerable improvements' had been made. The increase in the number of railway lines in the north, however, might not signify an increase in the deployment strength there, but merely increased the speed of the deployment in order to allow the right wing to cross Belgium and catch up with the centre more quickly. This, in turn, would allow the general advance to take place sooner.

1909/10

French Plan XVI (1909)

The adoption of the two-year law in France in 1905, which also involved conscripting everyone physically capable of serving, led to significant growth in the French order of battle, including an increase to twenty-two corps and the assignment of a reserve infantry brigade to most of the corps. There were also twelve reserve divisions available for the field army. These troop increases, plus the prospect of British participation in a war with Germany, led to the adoption of a much more confident Plan XVI in 1909. The plan provided for five armies to deploy on line from the east of Reims in the north to Belfort in the south, backed up by a reserve army of four corps behind Verdun.[22] As Greiner noted, this concentrated ten corps on the front line opposite Lorraine with an army of two corps on each flank. The French now also had ten deployment railway lines available instead of nine.

Crisis Over Austrian Annexation of Bosnia-Herzegovina

The Balkans was beginning to have a major negative effect on Austria's military position and, by extension, that of Germany as well.[23] The Austrian annexation of Bosnia-Herzegovina on 6 October 1908 ignited outrage in Serbia, Macedonia, Turkey and Russia. Serbia demanded territorial and economic compensation, and was supported by Russia. A special intelligence estimate was written for the crisis period for 1908/09, which made express reference to the fact that Serbia's internal instability was a destabilising factor in Balkan politics. In November 1908 the Austrians began a gradual partial mobilisation in Bosnia, bringing the force there to seventy-eight battalions (about three corps) with the two neighbouring corps also being reinforced. 'At the end of March [1909] the peace of Europe was seriously threatened', the annual report said. 'It was

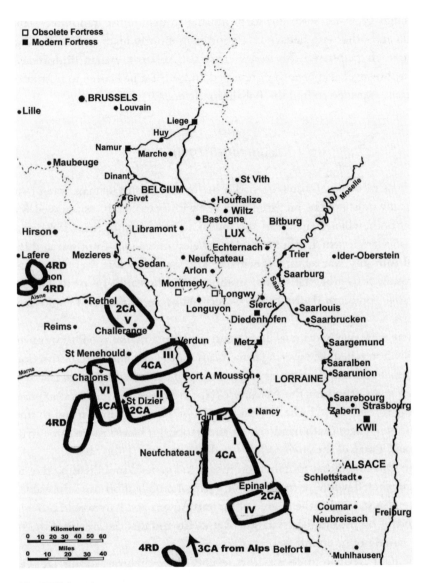

Plan XVI (1909)

doubtful that the expected war between Austria and Serbia could have been
localised, because Russia's relationship with Serbia encouraged it to continually
increase its demands.'

The intelligence estimates said the war was averted only because the Russians
were not ready to fight, and because the Russians also recognised that, in a
Russo-Austrian war, Germany would support Austria. The Russians told the
Serbs to drop their objections to the Austrian annexation of Bosnia, and on

30 March 1909 the Serbs did so, promising to demobilise, renounce claims to Bosnia and otherwise behave in a good neighbourly manner. The intelligence estimate characterised this as a victory for Austro-German diplomacy. The Italians, however, had been very reserved. Indeed, if it had come to hostilities, the Austrians expected to find the Italians in the enemy camp.

Aufmarsch 1909/10

The Balkan crisis of 1908/09 had a major effect on German war planning. 'Germany must now be prepared for a war with France or Russia as well as a war against both, which Britain can also join.' The war might begin in the Balkans as a one-front war, which would quickly develop into a two-front war and Britain could join any war against Germany. The war plan was therefore changed to provide for a war that started in the west – *Aufmarsch* I – or that started in the east – *Aufmarsch* II, also called *Grosser Ostaufmarsch*, the great deployment to the east.

There were twelve original documents available from the 1909/10 war plan: the mobilisation schedule; covering force maps for the east and west; instructions for the *Aufmarsch* I and II covering forces; orders of battle for *Aufmarsch* I *West*, I *Ost*, II *West und Ost* and for the *Nordarmee* (North Army); and *Aufmarschanweisungen* for *Aufmärsche* I *West*, I *Ost*, II *West* and II *Ost*. This was summarised in thirteen typewritten pages (with handwritten annotations), a handwritten force structure table and a map of the *Aufmarsch* II *Ost* deployment (1:4,500,000).

The plan noted that mobilisation meant full general mobilisation; due to the interconnected nature of mobilisation, a partial mobilisation was impossible.

The plan stated that the degree of support Austria and Italy would provide was dependent on the political situation. But it also said that the arrival of the Italian army could not be counted on.

The total German force was now seventy-three divisions strong. IX RK was still assigned to provide coastal defence in north Germany. In *Aufmarsch* I, a one-front war in the west, the strength and missions of the 1st and 2nd Armies are unchanged. The 2nd Army would receive general staff officers who had reconnoitred the routes and would serve as guides of the attack columns for the *coup de main* against Liège. The 3rd Army area of operations was extended south to the middle of Luxembourg. The 4th Army, with an additional corps and reserve corps, had its zone of operations extended south to cover the rest of Luxembourg. The 5th Army was now at Metz–Diedenhofen; the 6th Army, with three corps and a reserve corps, assumed the 7th Army's mission in Lorraine; and the 7th Army was pulled back to Strasbourg.

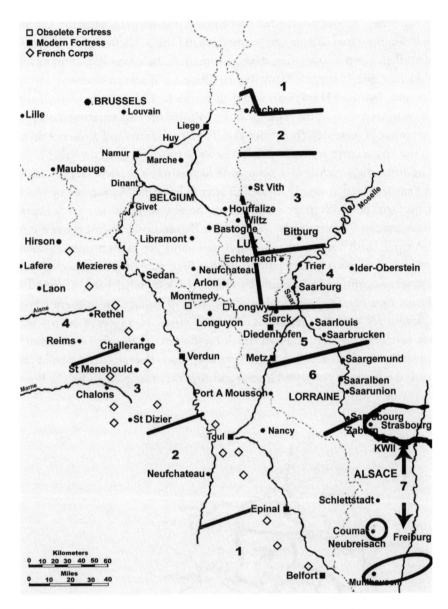

1909/10 *West* I

It is possible that the enemy will attack with strong forces from Belfort and across the Vosges into the upper Alsace, while at the same time advancing on Fortress Kaiser Wilhelm II. Initially, the 7th Army will be held back to cover the upper Alsace, to be committed on the left flank of the 6th Army, or to be transported by rail to another theatre of operations.

The Schlieffen School contended that Moltke was strengthening the left wing, which demonstrated that he did not understand the Schlieffen plan. In fact, it is evident that, given a worsening strategic situation, including Italian unreliability, Moltke had created the 7th Army to guard Alsace and act as a reserve.

The old *Aufmarsch* II was now called *Aufmarsch* Ia. Ten divisions were deployed in the east, sixty-one in the west. In order to form the eastern army, a corps and a reserve corps were detached from the 1st Army, a corps and a reserve division from the 2nd, a corps from the 3rd and two reserve corps from the 5th.

The new *Aufmarsch* II is a *Grosser Ostaufmarsch*, a massive deployment to East Prussia which is clearly modelled after Schlieffen's *Aufmärsche* of 1900/01 and 1901/02, but with more emphasis on the offensive and less on Schlieffen's counter-attack.[24] It was surely written for a Balkan crisis, a war between Russia and Austria, with Germany assisting Austria and the French initially neutral. Forty-two divisions would deploy to the east. The 1st Army, with two corps and two reserve corps, had to deploy by rail to the left (west) bank of the Vistula and then foot-march about 100km to the west of Soldau. From there it would attack towards Warsaw. The 2nd Army (four corps, two reserve corps) would attack towards Lomza, though an attack on the heavily fortified town itself was considered 'hopeless'. The 3rd Army (five corps, two reserve corps) would attack towards the Niemen between Grodno and Kowno, principally to fix the Russian

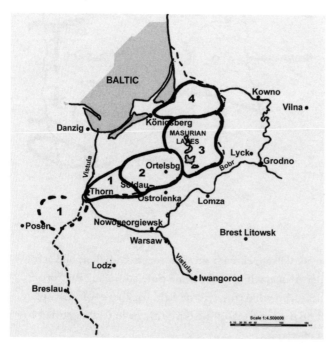

1909/10 *Ost* II

forces there in place; the 4th Army (four corps, two reserve corps) would outflank the Niemen line to the north of Vilna.

This would have been a slow-motion deployment using only two or three double-tracked railway lines (in 1914 the German west front deployment used thirteen double-tracked railway lines). Marching the 1st Army 100km would have taken five days. Deploying the 3rd and 4th Armies, with a total of thirteen corps, would have taken weeks. The (unstated) problem of the *Ostaufmarsch* was that, slow as the Russian deployment might be compared to the German deployment in the west, the Russian deployment was faster than the German *Ostaufmarsch* deployment.

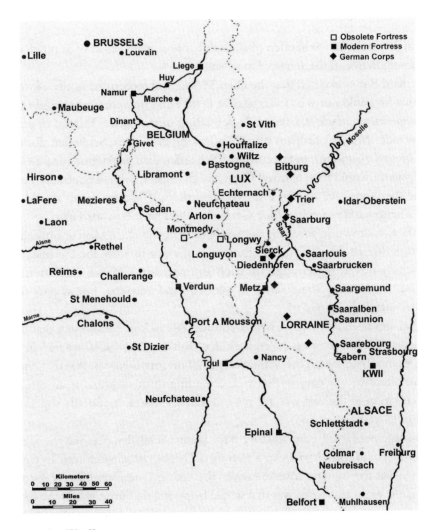

1909/10 *West* II

Twenty-nine divisions would remain in their garrisons. When the French mobilised, these units would move by rail-march and attack. Initially, the German forces which had already begun or completed their mobilisation would have a head start over the French, and if possible would use this advantage to attack. This operation was known as *Aufmarsch* IIa. The 5th Army, with four corps and three reserve corps, would deploy between Metz and Bitburg; the 6th Army, with the three Bavarian corps and reserve corps, would deploy behind the Saar north of Saargemünd; and the 7th Army, with four corps and a reserve corps, was spread out from Saarburg to the upper Rhine.

Grosser Ostaufmarsch, the Bugbear of the Schlieffen Plan

No single part of the Schlieffen plan myth has been the subject of as much error and contradiction as the *Grosser Ostaufmarsch*.

Gerhard Ritter claimed that the elder Moltke had recognised in the 1870s and '80s that he could not win a war against France and therefore developed *Grosser Ostaufmarsch* to attack Russia while defending in the west.[25] Instead of relying on the elder Moltke's brilliant plan for attacking in the east, Schlieffen discarded the *Grosser Ostaufmarsch* in favour of the Schlieffen plan. In August 1914 a *Grosser Ostaufmarsch* would have allowed Germany to respect Belgian neutrality. Britain would therefore have had no cause to enter the war, and the result would have been a negotiated peace in which Germany could have expanded east.

In fact, as shown in *Inventing the Schlieffen Plan*, the elder Moltke himself was forced to discard the plan for an offensive in the east in 1888: the German army was simply not strong enough for such an operation.[26] It was Schlieffen who revived the *Grosser Ostaufmarsch* in 1900/01 and 1901/02, but as part of his counter-attack doctrine.

It has also been contended, with a considerable lack of consistency, that it was the *younger* Moltke who cancelled the elder Moltke's *Grosser Ostaufmarsch* in 1913 in order to rely solely on the Schlieffen plan. This supposedly proves that Moltke had an offensive war plan in the west; according to this argument, an offensive concentration in the east was, for reasons that are not clear, morally superior to one in the west.

This argument is self-contradictory. If the perfect Schlieffen plan was the sole war plan, how could there have been a plan for a *Grosser Ostaufmarsch* too? In fact, we now see that the younger Moltke revived the *Grosser Ostaufmarsch* in 1909/10, this time in the expectation of a war that would begin as a one-front war in the east.

According to the myth, Schlieffen bequeathed the Schlieffen plan, the sole and 'perfect' plan, to the younger Moltke. The 1909/10 *Aufmarschanweisungen* show that this is utter nonsense. Moltke modified his planning to meet the changing military and political situation, in particular, Russian military recovery and political tension in the Balkans: 'keeping the right wing strong' was hardly the only issue the younger Moltke had to deal with. This meant that in the 1909/10 mobilisation year Moltke did not just have the 'perfect' Schlieffen plan, but four plans: *Aufmarsch* I was for a one-front war in the west; *Aufmarsch* Ia for the most likely circumstance, a simultaneous two-front war; *Aufmarsch* II (*Grosser Ostaufmarsch*) for a war that grew out of a Balkan crisis; and *Aufmarsch* IIa for French intervention in the east front war.

1909 *Schlussaufgabe*

The German deployment in the 1909 *Schlussaufgabe* was an *Ostaufmarsch*: the German army in the west contained only twenty-three divisions, so the French were 'massively superior'.[27] The 1st Army was in Lorraine with three corps; the 2nd Army was on the east bank of the Rhine defending southern Germany with three corps; the 3rd Army with five and a half corps was in reserve on the Saar. The French attacked with the mass of their forces (eight to eleven corps) in Lorraine, supported by an attack with an army to the north of Diedenhofen and another with about six corps in Alsace. Groener took part in this exercise.

Moltke said that in the next war the Germans were going to be severely outnumbered and they were not going to be given any easy problems to solve. The French also had their difficulties, as their armies were divided into three parts by Metz–Diedenhofen and the Vosges–Strasbourg. The Germans, therefore, had to attack and strike at the heart of the French army before the French had a chance to unite their force: partial success would not be adequate.

A German counter-attack into Alsace was out of the question. The Germans would not be able to mass a significant force there. In addition, it was completely immaterial to the Germans whether the French could cross the Rhine into Baden. Except for a few Landwehr brigades, the Germans could have pulled all their troops out of Alsace.

A counter-attack against the French army in Luxembourg had attractive advantages. However, in the current situation the Germans could not turn the French left in time. A German frontal attack in Luxembourg would accomplish nothing, because at the same time the French main body would drive the Germans out of Lorraine.

Only victory over the French main army in Lorraine would be decisive. The Germans had eight corps for the decisive battle in Lorraine, and would certainly not be numerically superior to the eight to eleven French corps there. There would be four ways to attack the French: frontally, on their eastern (right) flank, on the western (left) flank or both flanks.

Moltke said that a frontal attack would merely drive the French directly to the rear. The Japanese had pushed the Russians back in Manchuria with frontal attacks with little result. At the same time, the French army in Luxembourg would cross the Moselle in the German rear and the campaign would end in disaster for the Germans. The German deployment did not permit a strong attack on the French right. Neither, with only eight corps, could the Germans conduct a double envelopment. The only possible solution was an attack from Metz against the French left. The Germans had to be conscious of the fact that the French would recognise the threat to their left and would be very strong there. Tactically this would be a frontal attack. The Germans would be faced with successive French defensive positions and fresh French forces. The operation might drag on, a situation the Germans could not tolerate. The German army needed quick, decisive victories.

But this attack had the advantage that it would be directed against the strategic flank of the enemy army, and that was the most important thing. The area to the south-east of Metz was the most sensitive point in the entire French operation. A victory here must have decisive results. Moltke said that the majority of the officers had come to this conclusion, but that most had not been ruthless enough in its application. Many expected that if the Germans withdrew to the east, the French main body would follow and so present a flank to attack. Moltke said there was no reason why the French would make such an obvious mistake. It was better to stick with the principle that the enemy would act in the most effective manner possible.[28]

A surprise attack could only be launched through Fortress Metz. This attack should be conducted using the entire 3rd Army, supported by all of Metz's available guns and troops. The French could not fall back, but would have to stand and fight to defend their flank, and it would be likely that the Germans would push in the French flank. At the same time, the German 1st Army would occupy a defensive position behind the Nied with the left flank on the Saar, south of Saargemünd. Moltke noted that this operation was risky, but that it was impossible to defeat an enemy that was twice the German army's strength without taking risks. This operational problem is important in understanding Moltke's concept for the defence of Lorraine in 1914.

German 1909 Intelligence Summary for Russia

The Russian political class was judged to be solidly anti-German: Germany got no thanks for supporting Russia during the Manchurian War.

Finland was in a pre-revolutionary state, but in general, Russian political stability had advanced to the degree that, in case of mobilisation, only one division would remain in Moscow to maintain security, instead of the previous two divisions.

Russian troop strength was unchanged from 1908: 47,750 officers and 1,297,000 men (in 1908 the German army consisted of 613,333 officers and men). The annual army conscript class was 432,539 men; the German conscript class was around 250,000.[29] These numbers were enough to give any German war planner pause for thought. The Russian peacetime army was twice as large as the German. Each year, the Russians trained 180,000 more men than the Germans did, which meant that each year the Russians gained 180,000 more reservists – the equivalent of about five reserve corps.

The Russian army still had not recovered completely from the Manchurian War. It suffered from a shortage of infantry officers and of NCOs of all branches. At the beginning of the year, twenty-three battalions and sixty-six cavalry squadrons were on internal security duty. This was reduced by the end of the year to eight battalions and fifteen Cossack *sotnia* in the military district of Warsaw. Losses of clothing and equipment in the Manchurian War still had not been fully replaced. Practice mobilisations had been introduced, with good results. Marksmanship training was still poor, due in most part to a lack of garrison firing ranges.

In a war with Germany and Austria, Russia would employ fifty-six divisions, as opposed to sixty divisions in 1907. This is probably because the Germans thought that fifteen divisions (nine active, six reserve) would remain in Siberia, their peacetime stations. The intelligence estimate said that if Russia became involved in a war on her western border, then Japan would attack in Manchuria. This was the reason why the Russians were planning to redeploy units from Poland to the interior of Russia, and the basis of rumours that the Russians had adopted a defensive war plan on its western border. The new Russian deployment line would probably be Rowno–Kowel–Brest-Litovsk–Kowno. The conclusion drawn was that the Russians had little offensive power in a war against Germany and Austria. (The 1909/10 *Aufmarsch* plan said that according to the Austrian intelligence estimate, the Russian army would deploy fifty-two divisions against Austria and Germany, the same number as in 1902; that is to say, the Russians had reached the same high level of readiness that they had attained before the Japanese War.)

The Germans had drawn the wrong conclusions from the rumours of the pending Russian reorganisation. Japan had nothing to do with it. The Russians were planning to pull back units from Poland to the interior in order to co-locate them with their recruiting districts, where their reservists lived, which would speed up mobilisation. They also intended to reduce their fortress garrisons, as the Germans suspected, in order to create additional manoeuvre units. The Russian goal was not to adopt a defensive strategy, but to be able to assume the offensive faster and with greater force.

The Germans were not impressed by the new Russian tactical doctrine. The Russians seemed to have introduced a standard infantry attack procedure (*Normalangriff*) which did not give any consideration to the terrain and situation. It prescribed early deployment from column into a line and what the Germans felt was excessive dispersion, and displayed too much concern with utilising cover, with the advance by small groups and individuals being too slow and inadequately supported by fire. Cavalry battlefield reconnaissance was insufficient. Russian artillery took up covered positions at long ranges and stayed there for the course of the engagement. Because of the poor horse teams and heavy guns, the Russian artillery was not very mobile in any case. In each particular, the Russian stereotyped offensive tactical doctrine was the antithesis of flexible German doctrine, and the conclusion the Germans must have drawn was that a Russian attack would not be effective.

In 1909 the Russian army made several further improvements. Combined-arms live-fire exercises were reintroduced. Large-scale field training exercises now practised meeting engagements. Reservists were again being recalled to the colours for training. The state of discipline had improved. Russian artillery range firing was better than that of the infantry or cavalry. The field artillery, to include reserve and replacement units, had been completely re-equipped with fast-firing guns. In spite of revolutionary propaganda, especially in Polish regiments, there was no sign of serious indiscipline, much less mutinies. Rail construction still focused on the east; little was being done in the west.

German 1909 Intelligence Summary for Austria

Internally, the Austro-Hungarian conflict worsened. In the Hungarian parliament the Constitutional Party wanted expanded use of the Hungarian language in the joint army, while the Independence Party wanted an independent Hungarian army.[30] Forty-nine South Slavs were accused of high treason for agitating for a Great Serb state.

The infantry units were still being raided to provide manpower for new units and to raise the strength of units in Bosnia. The average infantry company now had a daily present-for-duty strength of fifty to sixty men (less than half the peacetime strength of a German company), which made realistic training impossible. On the positive side, the Austrians finally began providing their artillery with modern equipment: guns with recoil brakes and armoured shields, aiming circles and telephones for fire control.

German 1909 Intelligence Summary for Italy

All aspects of Italian political, military and naval activity pointed to a sharpening of Italian animosity towards Austria.[31] Characteristic was the continual improvement of Italian fortifications on the Austrian border, while nothing of the sort was being done on the French border.

German 1909 Intelligence Summary for Serbia

The Serbian state was arming itself to the teeth.[32] In the 1908/09 fiscal year the Serb state spent a sum equal to the receipts of the ordinary budget (80 million gold marks), then borrowed another 100 million gold marks, mostly from France (but some from Germany too), for armaments. The 1910 report said that they used the French money to acquire high-end equipment: modern artillery, artillery shells and machine guns.

1910/11

Aufmarsch 1910/11

There were twelve original documents pertaining to the 1910/11 war plan: the mobilisation schedule; orders of battle for *Aufmärsche* I *West und Ost* and II *West und Ost*, plus a special order of battle for the IX Corps military district; instructions for the covering forces in the west, east and north; maps of the covering force for the west and east; maps for *Aufmarsch* I *West*, II *West und Ost*; and *Aufmarschanweisungen* for I *West und Ost* and II *West und Ost*. The summary of these documents was twelve typed pages long, including a handwritten strength chart. There was also a map of *Aufmarsch* I (1:2,000,000).

The total German force had risen to seventy-nine divisions. All of the reserve corps now consisted of two divisions, though the reserve corps were still nineteen infantry battalions short of full strength. IX RK still conducted coast defence. In *Aufmarsch* I *West* (*Grosser Westaufmarsch*), seventy-seven divisions deployed against France. In *Aufmarsch* I *West und Ost* (the old *Aufmarsch* II), sixty-four divisions deployed to the west, thirteen to the east. In *Aufmarsch* II *Ost* (*Grosser Ostaufmarsch*), forty-three divisions deployed in the east and thirty-four remained at their mobilisation stations. In *Aufmarsch* II *West* these thirty-four divisions deployed against France. The ersatz troops from nine corps areas were to be organised into manoeuvre units as quickly as possible so as to be deployed for coast defence in the north. The caveat was included that Italian and Austrian support was once again dependent on the political situation: 'Given the current political constellation, the arrival of Italian forces cannot be counted on.'

Aufmarsch I was similar to that of the preceding year, excepting only that the 3rd Army gave up a corps to the 4th Army. The 7th Army received the same offensive-defensive mission in Lorraine as had the 6th Army, and now it was the 6th Army that might be transferred to another theatre.

In order to create the eastern army for *Aufmarsch* I *Ost*, a corps, a reserve corps and a reserve division were detached from the 1st Army and a corps from the

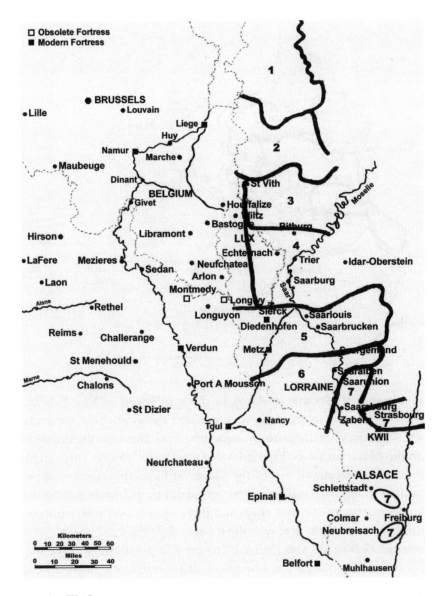

Obsolete Fortress
Modern Fortress

1910/11 *West* I

2nd. The forces north of the Meuse were reduced by more than 25 per cent, from twelve corps and a reserve division in *Aufmarsch* I to nine corps under *Aufmarsch* I *Ost*. A corps was also detached from the 3rd Army and two reserve corps from the 5th Army.

In *Aufmarsch* I *Ost* the enemy estimate stated that the Russian offensive would probably be directed against Prussia east of the Vistula, and that the Germans might have to abandon the province.

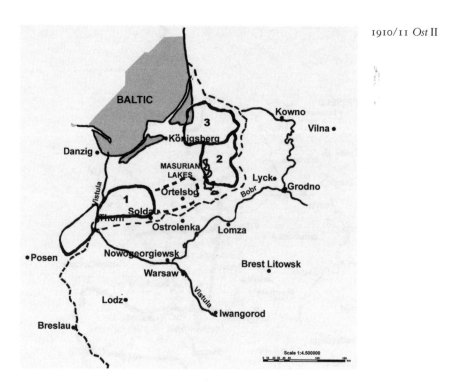

In *Aufmarsch* II *Ost* the 1st Army, in the south-west of East Prussia, was massively reinforced to comprise six corps and a reserve corps, with a sector initially along the Vistula, eventually expanding from Thorn on the Vistula all the way to the Masurian Lakes. The 2nd Army now included four corps and three reserve corps. It deployed east of the Masurian Lakes. The army mission was presumably to fix the Russians on the Niemen. The 3rd Army was on the left around Königsberg with four corps and three reserve corps. No mission was given, but it was most likely to turn the Russian right flank.

Aufmarsch II *West* was also changed. The 4th Army, with three corps and two reserve corps, would deploy in a bow west of Trier, with the northern flank at St Vith. The 5th Army (three corps, one reserve corps) deployed behind Metz–Diedenhofen; the 6th Army (three corps, one reserve corps) behind the Saar from Saarlouis to Zweibrücken; and the 7th Army (three corps, one reserve corps) from Sarrebourg to Strasbourg.

German 1910 Intelligence Summary for Russia

The German 1910 intelligence summary said that the combat power of the Russian army had increased significantly.[33] The Russians had conducted a massive

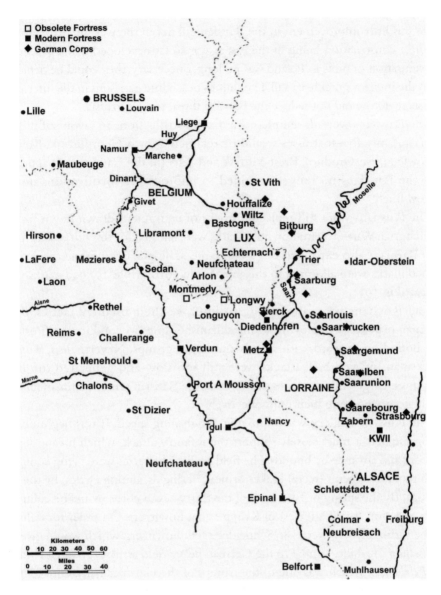

□ Obsolete Fortress
■ Modern Fortress
◆ German Corps

1910/11 *West* II

reorganisation: reserve cadres and fortress garrisons had been transformed into manoeuvre units. Together with some existing active army formations, this allowed the creation of four new corps in European Russia (XXIII–XXV and III Caucasus), as well as two new corps in Siberia (IV and V Siberian), producing a significant gain in combat power with no increase in peacetime strength. The peacetime garrisons of a number of units were moved out of Poland to the east to co-locate with their recruiting districts, allowing a faster mobilisation. Although there was little improvement in the Russian rail net in the west in 1910, most of the new construction being in the east, it was so far developed that a peacetime concentration of units in Poland was no longer necessary: they could be deployed from the interior quickly by rail. The shift to peacetime garrisons in the interior of Russia therefore did not reduce the Russian threat to East Prussia.

The Russians were de-emphasising fixed fortifications in favour of mobile warfare. Only five fortresses would be retained: Nowo Georgievesk, Kowno, Ossowiec (near Grodno), Brest-Litovsk and Kars (in the Caucasus). It appeared that the Russians no longer intended to improve the fortifications on the Narew line.

The Russians were still replacing stocks of equipment drawn down for the Manchurian War – 100 million gold marks were allotted for this purpose in 1911. The Russians also expanded the use of large-scale practice mobilisations; only 86,000 marks were allocated to this purpose in 1910, while 259,000 marks were allocated in 1911.

The Russians were attempting to improve their infantry tactics along German principles, deploying strong skirmisher lines to conduct the fire-fight and bounding forward with squads and larger groups. Nevertheless, Russian marksmanship was bad; attacks were still too slow and generated too little firepower. Large-scale exercises showed that the Russian senior commanders still could not manoeuvre their units effectively.

The Russian artillery was improving at lightning speed. It was beginning to recognise that it must closely support the infantry attack, which meant deploy forward and advance by bounds. The field artillery batteries were being equipped with modern systems (recoil brakes, armoured shields, aiming circles) by the end of 1911. By the spring of 1911 each of the thirty-seven corps would be equipped with a section (two batteries) of Krupp 12cm howitzers. On order for delivery in the spring of 1912 were 180 Schneider 15cm howitzers, which would give the Russians a capability similar to the German heavy field artillery (*Schwere Artillerie des Feldheeres*), which was one of the trumps of the German army. On order for the Russian siege artillery were 180 Schneider 10.7cm cannon.

Internal security in Russia was good. Discipline in the army continued to improve, although there were still incidents of revolutionary agitation. The harvests in 1909 and 1910 had been good, and for the first time in many years the Russian government enjoyed a budget surplus. Overall budgetary spending in 1911 was to increase by 230 million marks.

Further increases in Russian combat power were to be expected in 1911. The nationalistic majority in the Duma had approved increasing defence expenditures without demur, and an exceptionally large extra-budgetary request – perhaps 2.9 million marks – was expected in 1911.

German 1910 Intelligence Summary for Austria

The aftermath of the Bosnian crisis kept tension high in the Balkans, though Russo-Austrian relations seemed to have improved, particularly after the replacement of the Russian foreign minister, Isvolsky. Both Austria and Russia wanted to preserve the status quo in the Balkans.[34]

Significant reform of the Austro-Hungarian army continued to be blocked by Hungarian opposition. The condition of the infantry companies remained deplorable due to low present-for-duty strength and the consequent inadequate training. Four officers had received their pilot's licences and the Austrians hoped to buy their first aircraft in 1911.

Austrian military preparations continued to focus on Italy. In February 1910 a plan was drawn up for improving the fortifications on the Italian border. The Austrians succeeded in dragging a 24cm siege mortar over snow on sleds to the 1,842m-high Panacrotta pass – training for attacking Italian border fortifications. The Austrian general staff ride took place in the South Tyrol and played combat on the Isonzo River. Most tactical exercises were held on the Italian border. Two dreadnought battleships were laid down without budgetary approval as an emergency measure to counter Italian battleship construction, and Hungary (!) demanded the building of a third.

1911/12

Second Moroccan Crisis

French intervention in Fez, Morocco, in 1911 presented the Germans with an opportunity to assert the right to be heard as a world power. The German challenge to French and British overseas influence gave rise to a war scare in the last half of 1911, which in 1912 led to a European arms race of unprecedented dimensions.

Franco-Russian Offensive War Plan

In 1911 the French and Russians agreed to conduct simultaneous offensives against Germany by the sixteenth day of mobilisation.[35] In 1913 this was reduced to the fifteenth day. All of Schlieffen's two-front exercises had assumed that the French and Russians would conduct near-simultaneous offensives. But German intelligence could never be sure that this would occur, and always accepted the possibility that the French or Russians would initially remain on the defensive.

French 1911/12 Intelligence Estimate

Marchand said that German operational security was good and that the French had no knowledge of the German war plan.[36] German 'open sources' conveyed German tendencies well enough, but the French knew nothing of the German distribution of forces. Once again the French sought indicators of German intent for rail construction in 1910 and 1911. The sort of errors that this could lead to becomes quickly apparent. The French thought they had observed enough rail construction in the upper Alsace to support the deployment of an army, which would have the mission of turning the French flank south of Belfort. In fact, the

Germans never entertained such an operation. A total of six independent double-tracked lines terminated in what the French thought were the principal German deployment areas 'for the major part of the German forces', at Saarburg–Metz, Saargemünd–Diedenhofen and Saarbrücken–Trier. Further rail construction here was unnecessary.

The principal German emphasis on rail construction was in the Eifel, a thinly populated, infertile and economically unimportant area. In 1896 this area possessed two double-tracked lines with four military platforms. In 1911 it could boast four double-tracked lines (and one partially so) with fifteen platforms. A fifth line was in construction since 1910. The rail net in the area between Trier and Aachen could support the movement of seven corps and several reserve divisions. In 1914 the Germans deployed eight corps to this immediate area, plus two closer to Cologne and Bonn.

The French felt that an army deployed to the Eifel could transit the Belgian Ardennes and attack the French left flank. The violation of Belgian neutrality, which had been under discussion until 1910, now seemed to be more and more likely. However, it was felt that the centre of mass of the German rail net in the Eifel was near Prüm, and that there were no military platforms north of Aachen. The Germans would therefore operate south of the Meuse, and out of range of the guns of Liège and Namur.

The Germans were too convinced of the need to operate in mass and seek a quick decision to attack north of the Meuse. Even if the Belgians retreated immediately to Antwerp and offered the Germans no resistance, the length of time that it would require for these forces to join the fight would delay the general engagement for a dangerously long period. This was precisely the argument Schlieffen had made against the right-wing attack, and in all the war games from 1904 to 1908 the far right-wing armies achieved little or nothing.

Against Russia, the Germans would deploy five active corps, a 'doubled' corps (how this was accomplished was not stated) and ten reserve divisions, twenty-two divisions in the field army with three reserve divisions as fortress garrisons. Including Landwehr, the French estimated the German force to be the equivalent of twenty-four divisions.

Against France, the Germans would deploy eighteen corps, two 'doubled' corps and ten reserve corps, sixty divisions in the field army, plus three reserve divisions as fortress garrisons and the equivalent of four divisions of reserves and Landwehr for coast defence.

The Germans had seventy-nine divisions, not the eighty-four or so the French estimated. Minus the twenty-four divisions that the French thought the Germans would deploy in East Prussia, the French thought they were going to face sixty German divisions; in *Aufmarsch I West* the Germans would have deployed sixty-four. The French were obviously very sanguine concerning the power of the Russian army, estimating that the Germans would have to deploy twenty-two divisions in the east, while in *Aufmarsch I Ost* the Germans only deployed thirteen.

The French thought the Germans had fourteen rail deployment lines (which was correct). The largest part of the combat elements of the active corps could debark on the tenth or eleventh day of mobilisation; the deployment would be complete, supply units included, during the fifteenth mobilisation day. The French had to be prepared to meet the German attack as of the thirteenth mobilisation day. (This was five days too soon.) The Rhine railway lines would be used to shift forces behind the front.

The French were very impressed by the capabilities that the German rail net provided and developed four possible German deployments. In Deployment I the Germans massed the greatest forces possible: thirteen corps in Lorraine, behind Metz, with a group of five corps at Strasbourg–Zabern, four corps in Alsace, six corps between Trier and Malmédy (just north of St Vith) and two corps near Cologne. This option failed to utilise fully the rail net recently established in the north and was so unlikely that it could be disregarded. Deployment II was similar to I, but differed in that it created a two-corps 'army of observation' near Aachen, linked to the main body in Lorraine by an army of six corps in the Eifel. In this case, the Germans would advance to the south of the Meuse. Deployment III nudged Deployment II a bit to the north, but not much. Nevertheless, in this case the Germans would advance on both banks of the Meuse.

Deployment IV reduced the forces in Lorraine to two armies and deployed the maximum forces possible north of the line Aachen–Cologne. This deployment, which was in fact the actual German deployment, was considered unlikely because of the difficulty in executing the transport and the fact that it under-utilised the new rail installations in the Eifel.

Deployment II was considered the most likely German deployment: the Germans would not be able to resist the opportunity of concentrating the mass of their forces behind Metz, in close striking distance of the French border, which would allow them to immediately fight a decisive battle.

In 1911/12 it appeared that the Germans would attack in two masses: the central mass at Metz and to the south in the direction of Nancy–Toul; the second from the Eifel in the direction of Givet–Sedan, linked by an army originating from Trier. To the north the 'army of observation' had the mission of screening the Belgians. To the south an active corps and two or three reserve corps would defend the Alsace. The central (Metz) mass would stand on the defensive until the northern (Eifel) mass had reached the French frontier. This was a critical period

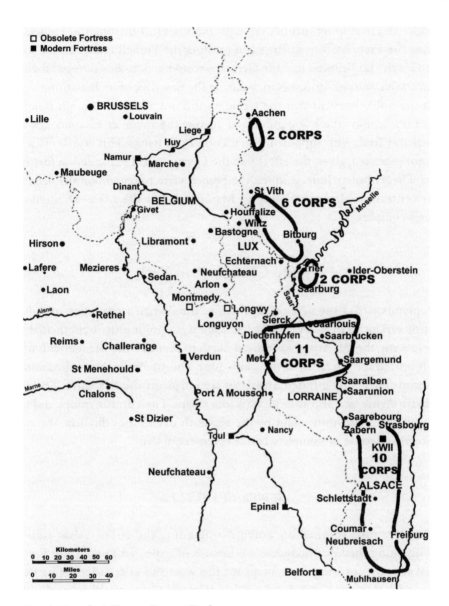

French Hypothesis II 1912 German Deployment

for the German forces: the French might attack the forces deployed behind Metz before the German right wing in the Eifel could arrive. As Marchand said, this was what disposed the French to think that the Germans would advance south of the Meuse.

The German right wing advancing from the Eifel had to be strong enough to advance to the Meuse and then, after a frontal engagement with the French left, conduct an enveloping manoeuvre with the intent of turning the French left, cutting the French off from Paris and pushing the French armies to the south. The French also believed that the Germans would seek to free (*dégager*) their left by an *attaque brusquée* against Nancy during the first days of mobilisation.

In the unlikely event that the Germans did not advance through Belgium, then they would attack straight ahead against the *trouée de Charmes* between Epinal and Toul, with supporting attacks on both flanks. This course of action was not expected, given the effort that the Germans had expended in fortifying Metz–Diedenhofen. Indeed, unless the French were to remain on the defensive, their central problem, according to Marchand, was the Metz–Diedenhofen fortress complex.

Joffre Changes Plan XVI

In September 1911 the new chief of staff of the French army, Joffre, introduced the first variant to Plan XVI.[37] The left wing was significantly strengthened. The reserve army, the 6th Army, was moved north to Reims – Ste Menehould, where it was behind the 5th Army to the south-west. The 5th Army was pushed forward to Sedan. This concentrated a mass of six corps on the left flank. The right flank 4th Army was also increased to four corps. The combat troops and their trains would finish movement by the eleventh day of mobilisation; the entire deployment would be complete by the seventeenth day.

Aufmarsch 1911/12

There were nine original documents concerning the 1911/12 war plan: the mobilisation schedule; intelligence estimates of expected French and Russian initial actions; covering force maps for the west and east; orders of battle for *Aufmarsch* I *West und Ost* and *Aufmarsch* II *West und Ost*; maps of *Aufmarsch* I *West* and II *Ost*; and the *Aufmarschanweisungen* I and II *West und Ost*, without annexes. The summary of these documents was eleven typed pages long with handwritten corrections and a table with the forces in each *Aufmarsch*. There was a map for *Aufmarsch* I and II *West* and one for I and II *Ost*.

The German army was now facing a critical shortage of manoeuvre units. The *Aufmarschanweisungen* stated: 'In every *Aufmarsch* the utmost measures are to be taken to create new maneuver units … In an emergency, the fortification of Berlin must be considered.' There is no specific mention of numbers or employment of ersatz units, other than the warning that ersatz formations lacked

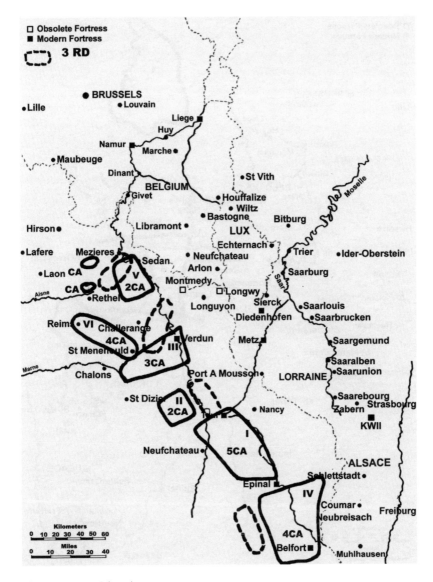

Plan XV Variant I (1911)

the unit cohesion necessary in combat and that they needed to be retained in the deployment assembly areas until this had been attained.

In *Aufmarsch* I, seventy-seven divisions deployed against France. There was no change in the order of battle or deployment. The Germans now had a plan to take Liège by *coup de main*. If it failed, the decision had to be taken as to whether the German forces needed to transit Dutch territory. The French might conduct a division-sized cavalry raid into Lorraine on the fourth mobilisation day, as

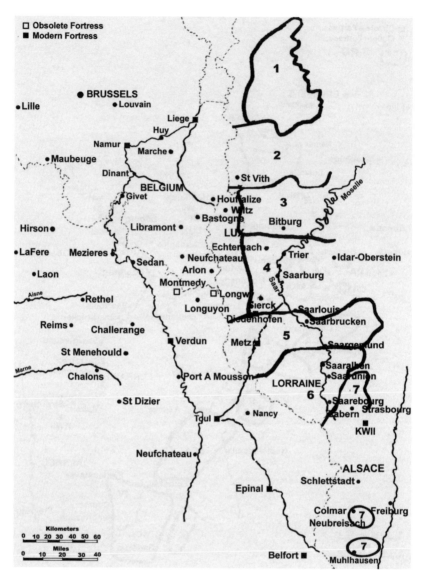

□ Obsolete Fortress
■ Modern Fortress

1911/12 *West* I

well as an early offensive into the upper Alsace, perhaps on the eleventh day of
mobilisation.

It was now considered possible that the British would send only elements of
their field army to the continent, and that these would conduct a demonstration
but not engage in serious combat. (Why the British would take this unlikely
course of action is not stated.) The British could also land at Calais–Antwerp on
the fourteenth day of mobilisation, or in Jutland on the sixteenth day.

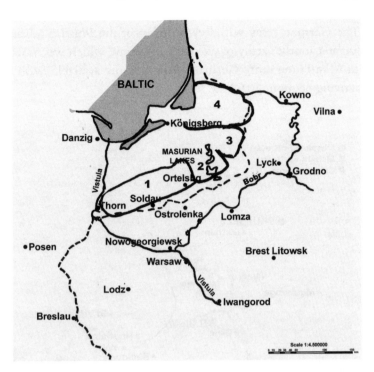

In the east, the German situation was rapidly becoming alarming. The *Aufmarschanweisung* now warned that the Russians might conduct a secret partial mobilisation during periods of political tension. To disrupt the German mobilisation and deployment, the Russians might also conduct cavalry raids into East and perhaps West Prussia even before the declaration of war, but upon declaration of war at the latest. The warning of the previous year was also repeated: in the case of *Aufmarsch* I *Ost* the Russians might overrun the Prussian lands to the east of the Vistula before reinforcements could arrive from the west. In 1914 the Germans were using *Aufmarsch* I *Ost*, and for the German leadership such a catastrophe was a very real possibility.

Aufmarsch II *Ost* was essentially unchanged, except that the forces in the 2nd and 3rd Armies were divided between the 2nd, 3rd and 4th Armies. In *Aufmarsch* II *West* the forces in Lorraine were strengthened by two corps drawn from Alsace.

1911 *Schlussaufgabe*

The initial situation for the 1911 *Schlussaufgabe* was similar to that of 1907.[38] The Germans conducted a *Westaufmarsch*. Only six divisions were initially deployed in East Prussia. The Russians attacked from the Niemen with seven to eight corps.

The German army withdrew in front of the Russian advance. The Russians formed another army of six corps at Warsaw, which was moving north-west on 14 May. Three more German corps 'became available' with the lead elements arriving beginning 16 May.

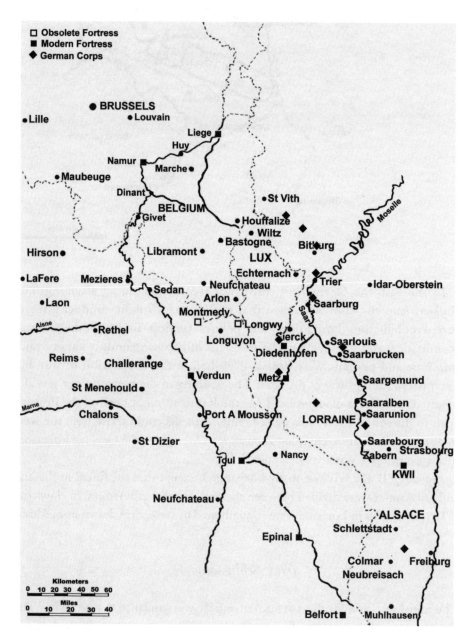

1911/12 *West* II

Moltke said that the Russians knew their Niemen army was nearly three times stronger than the German army in East Prussia and thought the Germans would withdraw and defend the Vistula. Here the Germans would be able to hold up the Russian advance for a considerable time. The Russians had therefore sent a second army from Warsaw down the Vistula to turn this defensive line. The Russians would know that the Germans had sent reinforcements to the east, but would not know where they would be employed. Once they had detrained, however, the Russians would become aware of their presence.

The German mission was to defeat the two Russian armies in detail. Most of the officers chose to attack the Warsaw army. Moltke agreed. He did not believe that the Germans could gain numerical superiority over the Russians in East Prussia, while the Warsaw army would be forced to advance between Thorn and Posen. In the second requirement the Germans decided to attack the Warsaw army as it advanced up the south bank of the Vistula. The three arriving corps were directed to Posen. The three German corps in East Prussia crossed to the west bank of the Vistula at Thorn. The German force opposite the Russian Warsaw army, therefore, included all available active and reserve units, plus the equivalent of more than three Landwehr divisions. The troops were assembled by 19 May and the German attack began on the 20th.

Moltke said that the evaluation of the Russian situation was relatively easy. Only one corps from the Niemen army was across the Vistula and it was a day's march to the east. Six Landwehr brigades could defend the Vistula against attempts by the rest of the Niemen army to force a crossing. The Warsaw army was tangled up in the lake district south of Thorn, where withdrawal was difficult and it was possible that the Russians would dig in and attempt to defend in place. All available German forces must be concentrated against the Warsaw army to achieve its destruction. It was essential to close the sack behind the Warsaw army with the Guard and XVII Corps. The troops would be tired but it was necessary to push them on.

This exercise was based on a likely real-world situation. It was also a classic 'Schlieffen problem'. The German force defending East Prussia was small, massively outnumbered by the Russians and had been forced to retreat to the Vistula. It had, however, gained enough time for forces to be shifted by rail from the west. The Germans could now concentrate against the divided Russian forces.

German 1911 Intelligence Summary for Russia

The Russians had overcome the effects of the Manchurian War and the resulting revolution to such a degree that Russia had resumed expansionistic policies in the

Far East and Middle East (Persia).[39] The stocks used during the Manchurian War had been replaced and no funds were allocated in 1912 for this purpose, but there was still a shortage of officers for troop units. Revolutionary propaganda had not been eliminated entirely, either in the army or civil society. Bank robberies for revolutionary purposes increased, particularly in Poland and the Caucasus. Some provinces were still under a state of emergency.

The Russian army was making great efforts to speed up mobilisation and deployment, adopting procedures similar to those of the French army. The combat elements of the border units could be ready on the sixth day of mobilisation. It was estimated that the Russians would mobilise thirty-four reserve divisions in European Russia and three in East Asia (in 1914 the Russians mobilised thirty-five reserve divisions in the west). In 1911 320,000 reservists of the 1904 and 1906 year groups were called up for practice mobilisations, as well as 136,000 men from the Russian equivalent of the German Landwehr. These exercises were thought to have produced good results.

Tactical training was stereotyped and still showed serious deficiencies, particularly in preparation for mobile warfare. Meeting engagements were seldom practised. Neither troops nor units were able to react to new or unforeseen situations. Local security failed frequently, as did liaison between units. Nevertheless, the Russians seemed to have mastered the technique for the infantry attack. Cavalry reconnaissance had got worse. The artillery was becoming more mobile and displaying an increased willingness to adopt open positions, deploy closer to the infantry and to bound forward in order to provide better fire support. Nevertheless, the employment of artillery masses posed problems. The field guns still did not have armoured shields or aiming circles, and the heavy field artillery was made up of obsolete guns.

Field training exercises appeared to provide useful training, except in St Petersburg (the Guard Corps), where they were military spectacles. The Russians now had 100 trained pilots. Aircraft appeared in a field training exercise in 1911 for the first time, as did heavy field artillery. The Russians sent an experimental column of trucks from St Petersburg to Moscow, which showed that the poor condition of Russian roads and bridges severely restricted the usefulness of motor vehicles.

Indicative of the Russian military build-up was the decision to build a new battle fleet, which by 1930 would include twenty-four battleships. Four dreadnoughts, which had been laid down in 1909, were launched in 1911.

Rail construction was still concentrated in the east and the Caucasus. The 1911 state budget was 284 million marks higher than the previous year; nevertheless, the budget was balanced.

German 1911 Intelligence Summary for Austria

This document was quite short (twelve pages) and one-third of the size of the 1910 report.[40] No army reform had taken place in 1911. Any improvements were intended for a war with Italy. Six batteries of vehicle-drawn 24cm mortars had been established and the assembly of one battery of 30.5cm mortars was proceeding; all were intended to break the Italian border fortifications. The corps at Graz added a brigade, the corps in Innsbruck three brigades, which, particularly in the case of the Innsbruck corps, were directed against Italy. In 1911 the Austrian fleet programme was approved, which was also directed against Italy. One dreadnought had been launched; another would be launched in 1912. By 1916 the Austrian navy would have four modern battleships. Landing operations were also practised on the Dalmatian coast.

German 1911 General Intelligence Estimate

Due to a lack of new information, the 3rd Department retained the 1907 west front estimate until 1911.[41] In 1909 it was acknowledged that the estimate was based on a wide range of indicators of uncertain value, and the estimate could be partially or totally wrong. Greiner said that up until 1909 the Germans thought that the French expected them to launch a frontal attack from Lorraine and the Vosges, with an attack through Luxembourg and south Belgium being considered a strong possibility, but not a certainty. The French military literature seems to indicate that after 1909 the French expected the German main attack through Belgium and Luxembourg. The French no longer felt that the Germans would launch a serious attack in Lorraine. The Germans would only deploy weak forces in Lorraine, which would demonstrate against the French fortress line or stand on the defensive. Indeed, they suspected that the Germans might advance to the north of the Meuse and even march through Holland.

In November 1911 the 3rd Department wrote a political-military appreciation of the German situation, which the Militärarchiv in Freiburg obtained from the East German military archive.[42] The *Denkschrift* began by saying that any consideration of Germany's military-political situation must be based on the possibility of war with France. It did not appear, in November 1911, that France was seeking war with Germany. The factors in France which served to maintain the peace were universal conscription, colonialism and the government's own interest in self-preservation. The elements which could lead to war were the propaganda of the French nationalists, the support that France would receive from her allies, the recent reawakening of French self-confidence and the excitability of the French national character. A successful war promised France revenge, national power, glory and the return of Alsace-Lorraine. In any war, France would therefore be the political aggressor. Germany, which had no other continental goal than the preservation of the status quo, was politically on the defensive. However, in terms of *Weltpolitik*, Germany had offensive political goals – colonial and naval expansion – which must come up against British interests.

The *Denkschrift* said that French confidence had increased significantly recently, particularly in the army. This was due in good part to the assurance that the Triple Entente would stand together in a war against Germany. The Russians had recovered from the effects of the Japanese War and the 1905 revolution. Above all, the French were encouraged by the certainty that Britain would support France in a war against Germany. At the same time, pro-war propaganda was stirring up the easily excited French population. German military prowess was being called into question, particularly by the British military expert Colonel Repington, who said that the latest *Kaisermanöver* showed that the French army was in many areas superior to the German, while the German army had in many areas sunk to the status of a second-rank power. Numerous books, including those written by senior French officers, proclaimed French military superiority. Success in aviation (the cutting-edge technology of the early twentieth century) further built French confidence. As a consequence France, borne on a wave of popular enthusiasm, could go to war at any time.

Given the current political constellation, an isolated Franco-German war was impossible. The corollary to this was that the outcome of the war would largely depend on the degree of support given to Germany and France by their allies. Italian adherence to the Triple Alliance was purely formal: there was no possibility that Italy would fight if opposed by British sea-power. The best that could be expected of Italy was that she did not attack Austria. If Italy declared war on Austria, Austria would be crippled in the east. For their part, the Austrians would rather attack Italy and defend in the east. On the other hand, if Russia was neutral, Austria would remain neutral also, and Germany had nothing to fear (on the land) from a war with France and Great Britain.

In any possible war, the general staff maintained that the German *Schwerpunkt* must be directed against France. If Russia was a belligerent in a Franco-German war, Germany could deploy to the east only the minimum forces necessary to defend the eastern provinces. The war would be decided in the west. France was the most dangerous opponent and the Germans had the prospect of reaching a quick decision in the west. If France were defeated in great battles, the French lacked the manpower reserves necessary to conduct a long war. If the Russians lost the initial battles, they could always withdraw into their vast interior and drag the war out for an unforeseeably long period. Germany's entire effort must be directed at winning the war on one front before turning to the other.

(After the *attaque brusqueé* on Liège, this may be considered Moltke's second break with Schlieffen's doctrine. Schlieffen foresaw a rapid shift of forces from one front to the other. Moltke was hoping to first gain a decisive victory on one front before shifting to the other, which would have required more time than Schlieffen would have allowed.)

The Italian-Turkish war had further complicated Italy's relationship with the Triple Alliance. Germany now ran the risk of losing a friend (Turkey) or an ally (Italy). The general staff decided that the Turkish alliance was more useful in a European war. Military reforms had increased the offensive capability of the Turkish army. Turkey alone could threaten England on land. A Turkish campaign against the Suez Canal and Aden would divert significant British forces from the continent. The Turks could also assist against the Russians. In conjunction with the Bulgarians, the Turks could keep the Romanians in check.

The numerical balance was shifting in favour of the Entente. The Russians had raised six new corps by reorganising fortress and reserve troops. They had spent vast sums on new field guns and heavy artillery. In the last five years, due to rail improvements and a more effective distribution of peacetime garrisons, the Russian army had halved the time needed to complete its deployment (probably from forty to twenty days). The most important improvements in the Russian army had already been completed. The German general staff concluded that it was no longer correct to say that Russia was not capable of conducting a European war.

The British had also done all they could to increase their military strength. By drawing in their colonial garrisons, the British would be able to put an army of 150,000 men on to the continent. Great Britain would not be unhappy to see a war between Germany and France. The British recognised that a German defeat would present an opportunity to eliminate the German fleet. To achieve this objective, the British were willing to commit their entire strength to the war.

In an isolated Anglo-German war, the British would rely on a naval blockade to destroy German trade and industry. The British would also seize the German colonies. There was no military solution for an Anglo-German war. Germany could injure Britain only by seizing the Low Countries. The British would never land troops on the mainland and a German invasion of Britain was impossible, even if the Germans won a naval battle. A German naval victory could never bring the war to a favourable conclusion. Even if the British lost a naval battle, given their vast fleet it would still retain naval superiority.

(This was an explicit rejection of Tirpitz's 'Risk Theory', which maintained that although the British could destroy the German High Seas Fleet, they would lose too many ships, and their naval supremacy, while doing so. 'Risk Theory' notwithstanding, German naval policy was not to immolate itself, and in the Great War the German fleet consistently avoided a decisive naval battle. It is now clear that this was German naval strategy in 1911, if not earlier.)

Occupying the Low Countries meant war with France. The French could never tolerate a combat-ready German army in Belgium. If Great Britain declared war on Germany, the only possible German response could be the mobilisation of the entire army for a war with France, before France mobilised and attacked an unprepared Germany. Germany's strength, now as in the past, rested on her military power.

The general staff traced the cause of the current tension in European politics back to the Morocco crisis of 1905. Prior to that time a reduction in the military spirit and interest in defence was discernable in France. The Morocco crisis caused a complete reversal in French defence policy, as well as revived and strengthened French chauvinism. The second Morocco crisis of 1911 only reinforced these tendencies. Franco-German tensions then led to a European arms race. All the powers in Europe were now preparing for a great war, which they believed to be inevitable sooner or later.

Only Germany and her Austrian ally had not taken part in the European military build-up. Austria had done nothing for years to strengthen her army. The build-up of the German army had been blocked by financial considerations. In particular, there was a glaring failure to completely utilise Germany's manpower. The general staff did not say so outright, but the implication was clear – Germany had devoted all of her resources to the fleet and that was dangerous.

The course of European politics in the near future would be decided by war, the general staff maintained. This war would judge whether the individual states had demonstrated the inner strength that alone justified their future existence. The general staff concluded that German defence policy needed to move in two directions: towards a further build-up of the fleet, as well as the reinforcement of the army through genuine universal conscription.

The general staff was pessimistic: since 1905 tensions had been increasing and would probably lead to war. The general staff saw the attack coming most likely from France, but perhaps from Great Britain with the Entente acting in concert. The Italians, on the other hand, would probably desert the Triple Alliance. The Entente was ready for war and the Austro-Germans were not. Neither the Austrian nor the German armies had kept pace with the Entente build-up and they were losing the arms race. For Germany this would be a three-front war. Britain was impregnable and had absolute control of the seas: the German colonies were lost and her overseas trade would be destroyed. An invasion of Russia was pointless. The Germans could hope only to defeat the French and then rescue the Austrians. German victory might be possible, but the difficulties were very great.

The German Army in Crisis

The German military situation was becoming critical. In the west, the Germans were increasingly faced with the possibility of an early French offensive into Lorraine. As of 1909 the Russian army had fully recovered from the effects of the Japanese War and was once again a formidable opponent. *Aufmarsch* I, a Schlieffen plan one-front war, was now an academic exercise, a fond hope. In 1911/12 it was feared that the Russians would stage massive 'bolt from the blue' cavalry raids even before the declaration of war. The Russians could conduct a partial secret mobilisation in peacetime which would reduce the time lag between the French and Russian offensives. In 1910 there is even a warning that, in the case of *Aufmarsch* I *Ost*, the Russians might overrun German territory up to the Vistula.

If war came, the French might well initiate it, and the Germans were going to be massively outnumbered on one front at least. Germany should attempt to defeat the French first. 'Defeat' meant just that: it did not necessarily mean 'annihilate', and by no means meant 'attack'. The French might well be the ones who were doing the attacking.

This intelligence estimate, which was approved by Moltke and which was still in force in 1914, makes it clear that the German army did not advocate war 'now rather than later', as historians of the German 'war guilt school' contend. At no point does it state that a German attack in the west would have any certain prospect of quickly winning a decisive victory. In the east the condition of the Austrian army made the situation positively grim.

The solution that the intelligence estimate recommended to the military impasse in which Germany found herself was pure Schlieffen: Germany must institute genuine universal conscription.

1912/13

First Balkan War Crisis

On 18 October 1912 the First Balkan War broke out between Bulgaria, Serbia and Greece on one side and Turkey on the other. The Bulgarians pushed to the gates of Constantinople, while the Serbs overran northern Albania and reached the Adriatic. The Austrians were opposed to the Serbs gaining a base on the Adriatic. Austria began to mobilise in November and December to stop the Serbs; the Russians began to mobilise to support the Serbs. The German army issued sixteen intelligence estimates during the big-power crisis, five of which (21 November and 10 December 1912 and 2 January, 28 January and 18 February 1913) were preserved at the Kriegsarchiv in Munich.[43]

It was clear to the Germans on 21 November that the Russians were conducting a gradual undeclared mobilisation. The Russians did not discharge the oldest group of draftees, as they normally would have done. This meant that the peacetime strength of the Russian army increased by 400,000 men. The active army regiments in the military districts of Vilna and Warsaw, opposite East Prussia, rose to a present-for-duty strength of 3,400 men, higher than the wartime strength. Especially in October, practice mobilisations and reserve training became unusually frequent. The Germans reached the conclusion that under these conditions, on mobilisation, and before the declaration of war, the Russians would launch raids on the German border. The Russians had begun mobilisation of their rail assets: empty trains were assembled and coal reserves topped off, sometimes by confiscation. Railway personnel were being augmented. The railway lines in western Russia were under military guard. Austrian sources reported of reservists being recalled and of the movement of mobilised units from the interior of Russia to the Austrian border. On the other hand, there were no indications that the French were taking any mobilisation measures, and the French border population and press were unruffled, in contrast to the anti-German attitude during the second Moroccan crisis in the summer of 1911.

The intelligence estimate of 10 December said that German suspicions had been confirmed: the Russians had initiated an extensive series of pre-mobilisation measures. The only measures that pointed to deployment were the preparation of the railway lines for long-term high-intensity service. Large-scale troop movements had not yet taken place. The training of the newest recruit class was to be completed in six weeks instead of the usual four months. Equipment such as vehicles, searchlights, telegraphs and telephones were being purchased overseas in conspicuous quantities and with short delivery times. This was in contrast to France, where the mood was calm. Politically informed sources said that the French did not approve of the Russian actions. (This was wrong. In fact, the French had let it be known to the Russians that if Russia went to war, so would France.)[44]

The 2 January 1913 intelligence estimate showed a continuation of the previous Russian measures to increase readiness. Individual reservists had probably been called up. Mobilisation plans had been reviewed at all levels. The rail system repeatedly conducted practice mobilisations. Overseas, the Russians were buying small-arms ammunition, field railway equipment, gasoline-driven personnel and cargo vehicles in 'extraordinary numbers'. Recently a news blackout concerning military matters was promulgated, closing off 'open source' intelligence to the Germans. Although there were no movements of troops from the interior, war-strength units on the border were continually conducting field training exercises. This reinforced the German belief that, simultaneous with their mobilisation, the Russians would conduct raids to disrupt German mobilisation.

The French had taken no obvious military measures, but since the beginning of November the British fleet had been at the highest state of readiness possible short of mobilising.

By 28 January 1913 the accelerated training of the 1912 recruit class should have been completed, while the class that was to have been discharged in 1912 was still with the colours. Russian infantry companies on the western border, therefore, had a present-for-duty strength of 215, little short of the war strength of 250. According to French newspapers, the Russian war minister said that the Russian army was ready, more so than ever before, a statement that the German intelligence section agreed with.

On 18 February the Germans estimated that when the Russian army announced mobilisation, it would in fact already have mobilised (this was underlined in pencil in the original document), and Russian mobilisation meant the beginning of Russian hostilities.

After 18 February the crisis began to wind down. The fact that it would have been impossible to conduct major offensive operations in the middle of winter, and that the political pot would not continue to boil until the summer campaigning season arrived, was certainly a major factor in preserving the peace. Europe now set out on an even more massive arms race.

Such extensive Russian use of pre-mobilisation measures came as an unpleasant surprise to the Germans and immensely complicated war planning. Pre-mobilisation measures offered the Russians a means to significantly speed up their actual mobilisation and deployment, reducing the disparity between the completion of French and Russian deployments. The Germans were faced not only with the prospect of a war on two fronts, but of near-simultaneous attacks on both fronts.

Aufmarsch 1912/13

The only information in document RH 61/v.96 consists of three pages of shorthand notes concerning *Aufmarsch* II. This would indicate that, faced with a Balkan crisis that appeared to be the catalyst for a European war, the Germans were relying solely on the *Grosser Ostaufmarsch*.

Four armies were to deploy in the east. The German rail net was not equal to the task and the deployment would have been slow. In particular, the 2nd Army, with 10 ID, would offload from its rail transport near the Vistula and then foot-march 100km to its assembly area at Ortelsburg – a week-long process.

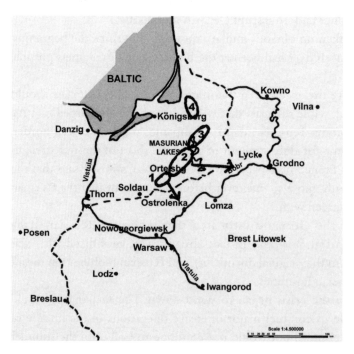

1912/13 *Ost* II

The 1st Army, with 14 ID, would advance on the right towards Novogeorgiewsk
– Ostrolenka. The 2nd Army, on the 1st Army's left, would advance on Lomza
and take the fortified position there. The 3rd Army, with 10 ID, would deploy
to the left of the 2nd, but would not initially advance across the border. The 4th
Army, with 8 ID, would deploy to eastern East Prussia, but be so delayed by the
overloaded rail net that its initial mission would be to defend in place. It would
later follow echeloned left of the 3rd Army.

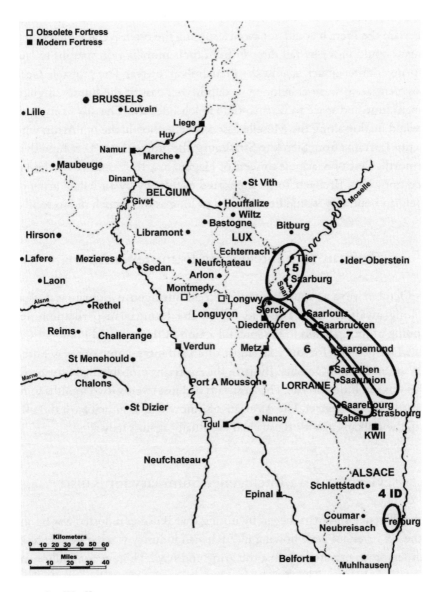

In this plan, France was initially neutral. All possible measures were to be taken to avoid threatening France. The corps designated for western deployment would be retained in their mobilisation stations. If war with France did come, the commander-in-chief west (*Oberkommando des Westheeres*) with the 5th, 6th and 7th Armies would be given complete freedom of action. In spite of the enemy numerical superiority, if the *Westheer* had a head start over the French in deployment, it should attack. The plan noted that this represented a significant departure from the 1901/02 concept, which surrendered the initiative to the French. Nevertheless, as in Schlieffen's planning, the 1912/13 plan stated that it was certain the French could not avoid assuming the offensive, at which point the Germans could move by rail directly from their mobilisation stations to launch a surprise counter-attack against the French flank or rear. The probable German deployment areas were echeloned in depth well east of the border, giving the Germans time and space to react to the French offensive. The 5th Army, with 10 ID, would deploy along the Moselle east of Diedenhofen; the 6th Army, with 10 ID, across Lorraine from Sierck to Strasbourg; the 7th, with 10 ID, behind the 6th, from north-west of Saarlouis to west of Hagenau; 4 ID would cover the upper Alsace from Neu Breisach, to be supported eventually by an Italian army of 10 ID. Belgian neutrality would be respected so long as the French did so too.

German 1912 Intelligence Estimate for Austria

On 5 October 1912 a supplementary Austrian intelligence estimate was issued.[45] The long-awaited Army Bill had passed the Hungarian parliament at the beginning of June, 'thanks to the forceful action of [Hungarian] President Count Tisza'. The present-for-duty strength of an infantry company was raised to ninety-seven men in October. By 1912 the Austrians probably had fifty aircraft.

This was too little, too late. The Austrians had just twenty-two months to make up for decades of neglect. The Austrians also now had to anticipate a three-front war: in the Balkans, against Russia and eventually against Italy also.

German 1912 Intelligence Summary for Russia

The intelligence summary began by noting that Russian industry was booming and the tax revenues were flowing in.[46] Russian industry was hardly able to meet the orders from private industry, the army and navy. There was a million-mark positive trade balance. The state budget had grown by 285 million marks but yet was in balance; 110 million marks in state debt were redeemed ahead of schedule.

The budget recommendations for 1913 provided for an increase of 19.3 per cent, or 768 million marks, without increasing indebtedness.

Nevertheless, the country had not been entirely pacified. The number of strikes had increased and these had a connection to revolutionary propaganda. Emergency decrees had been extended by a further year. The Russians continued their attempts at expanding in the Far East and Middle East. Northern Persia was under Russian military occupation and Russia had established a military protectorate over Outer Mongolia. In spite of nationalistic and pan-Slav agitation for war with Austria, the Russians had exercised restraint during the Balkan crisis.

The Russians had increased the speed of their mobilisation in 1911 by one day. Active army units in the more heavily populated areas would be ready to deploy on the evening of the fifth mobilisation day, reserve units on the evening of the eighth day. The Russians were continually improving and testing their mobilisation and deployment procedures. Practice mobilisations included calling up both reservists and horses, and testing the mobilisation procedures and staffs. Commissions at the war ministry, military district and corps commander levels inspected mobilisation planning and then practised it using troops from other units.

The estimate said that Russian readiness for war in 1912 was significantly improved over that of 1911: Russia had never attained such a high state of readiness.

Infantry training had improved, but both infantry fire control and artillery fire support were still inadequate. The Russian military traced the continuing deficiencies in combat proficiency to the lack of individual field training. Marksmanship training still suffered from the insufficiency of local garrison rifle ranges. Cavalry reconnaissance was still ineffective. The low educational level of the soldiers had a strong negative effect on training.

The priority for the expansion of the state rail net was still in the east, although economic expansion led to private-capital rail construction in the west.

French Offensive Tactics

In October 1912 the German general staff issued an intelligence estimate which noted the increasing emphasis on the offensive in the French army.[47] In effect, the French now had two tactical doctrines. The old doctrine (Bonnal's doctrine, though he is not named) emphasised security: the ability to meet all tactical possibilities. Bonnal used deep formations in the approach march. At the army level, the advance was conducted in a tight formation, with a corps- or division-sized advance guard and a strong reserve. The enemy would concentrate against the advance guard, allowing the mass of the army to conduct a carefully controlled manoeuvre. Envelopments were avoided in favour of concentration of force at a chosen point for a breakthrough. Artillery was to be committed sparingly, with reserves held back to feed the battle, although a group of young officers advocated concentration of artillery for mass fire.

The new doctrine (Grandmaison's doctrine, although he is also not named) was the antithesis of the old. The advance guard and the detachments could be defeated in detail, so they were kept relatively weak. The new doctrine emphasised 'in the strongest terms' the offensive on a broad front.

The old French doctrine focused on defence in depth and the counter-attack. The new French school did not change defensive doctrine, in fact, it hardly addressed it.

German 1912 West Front Intelligence Estimate

In May 1912 the 3rd Department issued a *Denkschrift* titled '*Aufmarsch und operative Absichten der Franzosen in einem zukunftigen deutsch-französischen Krieg*' (French deployment and operational intentions in a future Franco-German war).[48] This represented a fundamental reassessment and revision of the German intelligence estimate. It was updated on 9 November 1912, updated again for the 1913/1914 plan and finally reviewed a last time in April 1914. This is therefore the final German west front intelligence estimate. This is an unusually thorough document, some seventy pages in total, and is worth a detailed summary.

The 3rd Department acknowledged that it had no hard intelligence data concerning the French deployment or intentions. Apparently the only important agent material it possessed concerned the transfer of the North African units to France. It believed, however, that it could develop an accurate estimate using published works by French military authors.

So long as the French thought that the German main effort would be made in Lorraine, the *Denkschrift* began, the French massed their forces at Toul–Epinal. Now that the French thought the Germans would make a major effort in the Ardennes, they had moved their deployment to the north. In particular, in the October 1911 issue of the *Revue Militaire Général*, General Langlois said that a German *Westaufmarsch* was a practical certainty and that it was virtually impossible for the Germans to stay on the defensive in the west. The Germans would leave a minimum of forces in the east and seek an early decision against France. General Bonnal said that the Germans would not leave more than two to three corps in the east. The Russians could not tie down more than a maximum of four German corps. In 1911 Bonnal suggested the Germans would send

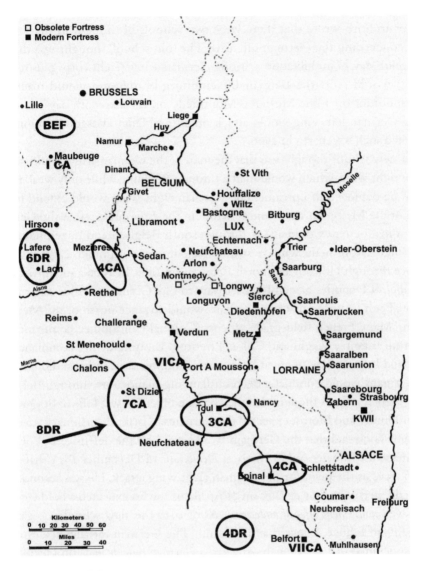

German West Estimate 1912–14

twenty to twenty-two corps against France. The German intelligence estimate noted that everyone in France, Belgium and England expected the Germans to attack through Belgium (*anderslautende Meinungen kommen überhaupt nicht mehr auf* – there are absolutely no dissenting opinions). The *Petit Parisien* and *Est Republican* said as much in 1909. The *Armée et Democratie* wrote in April 1911 that the Germans had no other choice. Senator de Lamarzelle said in the Senate on 6 April 1911 that the need to find room to deploy the army by itself forced the Germans to march through Belgium.

Captain Sorb wrote that there were two schools of thought in the French army concerning the German offensive. The 'old school' thought was that on the twelfth day of mobilisation a 'strong German army' (eight corps plus reserve troops) would cross the Belgian-Luxembourg border and would reach the French border on a line Mézières–Montmédy on the sixteenth day, when the strong German left wing would attack on a line Nancy–Vosges. Langlois had presented such a scenario in 1906.

The 'new school' thought was that the mass of the German army would deploy on the right wing, which would march through Belgium, while only weak forces would be deployed in Lorraine. The German right wing would extend to the north of the Meuse. In 1910 'Junius' wrote in the *Echo de Paris* that the German mass of manoeuvre would attack through south Belgium and Luxembourg on Maubeuge–Montmédy, while a 'strong detachment' with much cavalry would advance through Holland and north Belgium on Lille. In 1906 a member of the Chamber of Deputies named Rousset warned of a German advance as far north as Lille. Foch (!) wrote that the Germans would advance north of the Meuse at Namur. Many French field-grade officers (Colonel Cordonnier, commander of the 119th Infantry Regiment; Colonel (retired) Biottot, former commander of the 162nd Infantry Regiment at Verdun and Commandant Imhaus) thought that the Germans would conduct a deep outflanking manoeuvre through Belgium. Many French officers thought that the German objective was Lille or St Quentin.

Cordonnier and Biottot expected the Germans to make diversionary attacks in Lorraine. Foch said that the Germans would stand on the defensive in Lorraine. Commandant Imhaus said in *Armée et Démocratie* in December 1911 that Metz would serve as the pivot for the German right wing attack. He was seconded by General Cherfils in *Echo de Paris* on 21 April 1912, who expected a bold German offensive (*mouvement offensif audacieux*). As of 1910 the 'new school' was gaining adherents in France, England and Belgium. The German intelligence estimate even concluded that the French expected a German *coup de main* on Liège.

The German intelligence estimate stated that the French expected the Germans to make the main attack through Belgium and Luxembourg. The Germans felt that the French were certain that the German right would attack through Belgium, but uncertain concerning what the German left would do in Lorraine. The real question for the French stood between the 'old school', which expected a German attack on the front Verdun–Toul, and the 'new school', which expected the Germans to stay on the defensive in Lorraine. French apologists would attempt to justify French defeats in the Battle of the Frontiers and the retreat to the Marne by claiming that the German right wing had been much stronger than anticipated. This was an *ex post facto* explanation. The real cause for French confusion was the German intentions in Lorraine.

The French, according to the German intelligence estimate, expected the German mobilisation and deployment to be completed in ten to twelve days. This was a correct appreciation of the French estimate: in 1914 the French thought that the German forward movement could begin on the thirteenth day.[49] The German deployment in fact took seventeen days. When in 1914 the Germans failed to appear as expected, the French were puzzled.

The Germans thought the French would estimate the German approach march through south Belgium and Luxembourg to take five to seven days, that is, to the fifteenth to nineteenth day of mobilisation. The German forces moving to the north of the Meuse would take twenty-one to twenty-two days to reach the French border. Once again, this was a correct appreciation of the French estimate. In August 1914 the Germans began their march on the seventeenth day (18 August) and the 3rd, 4th and 5th Armies in the centre were one day's march from the Meuse by the twenty-first day of mobilisation and the 2nd Army on the right wing on the twenty-first day of mobilisation. On the one hand, the Germans started their forward movement five days later than the French expected. On the other hand, the German approach march was five to seven days faster than the French had estimated, and the French would be caught seriously off-balance.

Until 1911 the German intelligence estimate concluded that the French intended to conduct a strategic defensive operation. This was clear from Bonnal's 1906 book *La Prochaine Guerre* (The Next War). However, as of 1911 there were signs of increasing military confidence in France and therefore a turn to the doctrine of the strategic offensive. The 3rd Department said that French confidence had grown because of the prospect of English support in a war with Germany and of Italian neutrality. The French thought the German army was less capable than their own (*systematisch wurde das deutsche Heer herabgesetzt* – the German army is being systematically denigrated). They believed that their troops were better trained than the Germans. In the 1911 Balkan war the German-trained Turkish army was badly beaten; this was taken to be an indicator of the poor training of the German army itself. The French thought that they had achieved numerical parity with the German army, while enjoying technical superiority, especially in the most modern equipment such as aviation. The French expected the Belgians to withdraw to Antwerp and the Italians to join the winning side.

The 3rd Department said that the offensive spirit was strong in the French press, military literature and in parliament. The war minister and other representatives of the government were using the word 'offensive'. An important indicator of the new French offensive doctrine were the writings of Colonel Boucher, *La France victorieuse* (France victorious) and *L'offensive Contre l'Allemagne* (The Offensive

Against Germany), in which Boucher, with all the authority of a former chief of the operations section of the French general staff, strove to show that the French army was superior to the German regardless of whether the Germans were attacking or defending.

Nevertheless, the French were not yet really serious about launching a strategic offensive. They would initially still be on the strategic defensive, but were more and more emphasising the counter-attack. This estimate was repeated in 1913, when the 3rd Department noted that there were even more calls for a strategic offensive, but it felt that the French still had not adopted an outright offensive war plan. (This was perfectly accurate: Plan XVII, the purely offensive war plan, was not implemented until April 1914.) As proof of this estimate, Major Mordacq's views on the German offensive were cited. Mordacq wrote that the Germans would launch an offensive on a very broad front (*sur un front énorme*) with the *Schwerpunkt* directed on Dun-Stenay (that is, south of the Meuse in the Ardennes) against the French left flank. The Germans would try to divert French attention with supporting attacks between Belfort and Verdun. Mordacq said that the German plan left them no means to manoeuvre: it was merely a 'brutal push straight ahead which took not the least notice of the movement of the enemy'. The French would win by using their railways to manoeuvre. Therefore, the French would deploy in depth.

The German intelligence estimate said that the French High Command had replaced General Michel with Joffre in the spring of 1911 in order to institute a more aggressive war plan. Joffre had moved the French leftmost army nearer to Hirson–Maubeuge. This army would march 'under all circumstances' into Belgium. It could be supported by a second army of three corps located between Stenay and Montmédy. French military literature mentioned sending forces towards Namur to secure the French left flank and assist the Belgians and English, who would operate against the German right. The French were still uncertain as to whether the German attack would come to the north or south of the Meuse. The 3rd Department thought that Joffre estimated that the German right wing would need two days to reach Liège and a further five days to reach the French border; in other words, Joffre would think that he would have seven days in which he could concentrate forces on Hirson–Maubeuge and deploy them either to cover the Sambre–Meuse, or move north to meet the Germans on French soil.

However, the French mass of manoeuvre would still assemble on a line Epinal–Toul–Verdun, and the main French counter-attack would come either from Verdun to the north of Metz or into Lorraine. The French were conscious of the fact that an attack into Lorraine was a difficult undertaking. Bonnal had said that it was impossible. General Maitrot agreed, adding that the French should also not attack into the upper Alsace. Captain Sorb said the terrain was difficult and the Germans would probably reinforce their defence with field fortifications. Metz and Strasbourg threatened the flanks of the French attack, while the entire French army was in danger of encirclement by a German attack over Sedan. Sorb felt that the French should extend their deployment more to the north.

The French would not deploy all the way to the Channel (as Michel had proposed), for in that case they would expose the right flank of their main body to an attack from Lorraine (Metz) and they ran the danger of being thrown into the sea (shades of Dunkirk). Therefore, if the Germans did launch their main attack through Belgium, the French would not be able to outflank the German right but would only be able to meet the German attack in a frontal battle.

The 3rd Department estimated that the French army included twenty-two active corps with forty-five infantry divisions (plus twenty attached reserve infantry brigades), perhaps eighteen reserve divisions, sixty-three active and reserve divisions in total (plus twelve third-rate Territorial divisions). In 1914 the French field army initially deployed forty-six active divisions and twenty-one reserve divisions, sixty-seven divisions in total (with four more reserve divisions as fortress garrisons). Eight Territorial divisions were available for field operations, four served as fortress garrisons.[50]

The 3rd Department estimated that the French active army would deploy by the tenth day of mobilisation, the reserve divisions by the thirteenth, and the Territorial divisions by the eighteenth. In 1914 the combat elements of the French active units were deployed by the tenth day. The reserve units, as well as the combat and field trains (supply units), deployed by the seventeenth day. The African units would arrive on the sixteenth or seventeenth day.[51]

In 1914 the French began their offensive in Lorraine on the fourteenth day of French mobilisation (the fifteenth day of Russian mobilisation), but largely without the reserve divisions, some of which were still deploying on the seventeenth day and then needed to move forward to catch up with the advancing French armies.

Both the Germans and the French thought that their opponents could deploy faster than was actually the case. In the July crisis this would have reinforced the pressure on both general staffs to begin their own mobilisation as soon as possible.

The 3rd Department's map of the French deployment carried the caveat that the estimate was based on 'uncertain sources'. In the front line there was, from north to south: I Corps at Maubeuge; a left-flank army of four corps at Vouziers–Rethel–Mézières; a centre army of four corps (including VI CA – *corps d'armée* – army corps) at Toul; a southern army of five corps (including VII CA at Belfort) at Epinal, and an enormous mass of manoeuvre, two armies with seven corps concentrated west of Verdun–Nancy. Six reserve divisions were deployed behind the left flank at Laon–La Fère, four behind the right flank at Lure–Vesoul and no less than eight reserve divisions would be added to the mass of manoeuvre.

Compared to the French Plan XVI or XVII the German general staff estimate of the French deployment was once more far from the mark. The 3rd Department still thought that the French would deploy in depth when in fact they intended to deploy almost on line and much closer to the border. It estimated that the French left consisted of an army at Maubeuge. This extended the French left too far to the north and made it too strong. In fact, the French left was much weaker and went only as far north as Mézières.

The only offensive action that the French would take at the outset would be an immediate attack by the VII Corps from Belfort into the upper Alsace. This was seen as a means for the French to get a cheap propaganda victory and occupy time until the main battle took place on the fifteenth to the seventeenth day of mobilisation in Lorraine, or on the twentieth to twenty-second day in Belgium or northern France. Once the French had begun their rail deployment, changes in the deployment were no longer possible.

In 1914 the French VII Corps attacked into upper Alsace on 7 August, into Lorraine on 15 August – the fourteenth day of French mobilisation – and across the Meuse into the Belgian Ardennes on 21 August – the twentieth day of mobilisation. The battle in Lorraine took place on 20 August, the nineteenth day of mobilisation, and in the Belgian Ardennes on 22 August, the twenty-first day of mobilisation.

The 3rd Department thought that the French could not count on the British army. Captain Sorb wrote in *Doctrine* that the value of the Entente should not be overestimated. The British would use the opportunity supplied by the war to destroy the German fleet and would provide full diplomatic support to France, but would not send the British army to France out of fear of a German invasion. From agent reports, the 3rd Department was aware of the secret 1911 British-French military staff discussions. It said that the French wanted the British Expeditionary Force to land at Dunkirk, Calais and Boulogne. The British would probably base their army at Lille. The French I Corps was deployed at Maubeuge to link up with the BEF. The British would probably advance from Lille on Namur–Liège.

This written estimate does not agree with the enemy estimate map, which puts the British army near Mons, where it actually assembled. Nevertheless, it appears that Moltke, Bülow and Kuhl had developed a preconceived notion that the British would be at Lille, which was to have serious consequences.

The primary concern of French intelligence would be to determine if the Germans would enter Belgium and Luxembourg and in what strength. Attacks by French agents against German bridges and rail installations were considered possible. The French would employ masses of cavalry in Belgium and send them deep into the country. It was also possible that the French would use airships to attack the Rhine bridges as well as German Zeppelins and Zeppelin bases.

There were only two possible French courses of action. In the first, the Germans attacked both in Belgium and in Lorraine. The French, according to Bonnal, Foch and Sorb, would then manoeuvre to concentrate superior forces against one half of the German army while conducting an economy of force operation against the other. It would be unlikely that the French would make their main effort between Metz and Strasbourg. The French would probably choose to meet the German right wing. They could either move forward to the Meuse between Givet and Namur, while the British and Belgians advanced between Namur and Liège, or they could hold a line in northern France. According to an article in the *Journal des Sciences Militaires* of April 1912, the mission of the French left-wing army was to defend in place and not yield a step in order to give the manoeuvre army time to conduct the counter-attack. The 3rd Department felt that the most likely French counter-attack would be from Verdun to the north-east to unhinge the German right wing. Colonel Biottot suggested an attack from Verdun towards Luxembourg and said that the French had played a war game concerning such an operation in March 1912. In this case, the French left would either join in the attack or defend on the Meuse, Argonne and Aisne.

In the second course of action the Germans attacked with the mass of their army through Holland-Belgium-Luxembourg. Only weak German forces deployed in Lorraine. These would defend or conduct diversionary attacks. In 1912 the 3rd Department did not think the French would respond with a major attack in Lorraine. By 1914 a major attack in Lorraine seemed more likely. The 3rd Department said that in 1913 many articles in the French military journals had been advocating a French counter-offensive in Lorraine: Captain Felix in the 15 May 1913 issue of the *Journal des Sciences Militaires*, General Lacroix and so on. In the 8 September 1913 issue of *France Militaire*, General X (presumably General Ferron) said that 'the stronger the Germans are in Belgium, the more favourable the conditions for an attack in Lorraine'. The German right wing would be delayed by the fortifications of Maubeuge and the northern army while the French mass of manoeuvre attacked the weak German forces in Lorraine with overwhelming numerical superiority.

If the Germans attempted a very wide envelopment the French would defend on the lines Maubeuge–Lille or Sambre–Oise. The German forces in Lorraine would be fixed in place by the French army attacking from Epinal. The French could also withdraw deep into the Champagne, to the line Reims–Laon–La Fère. The army at Toul could counter-attack to the north from the line Verdun–La

Fère against the German right wing's lines of communication. Mordacq had discussed this possibility in his book *Politique et Stratégie*.

The direction of the withdrawal of the French left wing had been widely discussed in the French press. The 3rd Department said that it was certain the French would not fall back on Paris. If necessary, the mass of the French army would pull back to the middle Loire. The *Monde Illustrée* had said in February 1906 that the main body of the French army could withdraw, if necessary, to Orleans on the Loire, with the right flank on Lyon and the left on Paris. The *Petit Journal* had presented a similar opinion in May 1906. The 3rd Department agreed. It also said that the Morvan – the plateau of Langres – was still an important refuge in case of a French withdrawal.

In case of a serious defeat, the 3rd Department was of the opinion that the French did not have the manpower to raise new armies on the scale of 1870/71. On the other hand, the initial German victories would not be on the order of Metz and Sedan in 1870. Even if the Germans won significant victories at the beginning of the next war, strong elements of the 2 million-man French field army would be able to withdraw to the middle Loire and the subsequent German operations would not be easy. Significant forces would have to be detailed to watch the French border fortifications. The German advance on the middle Loire would be flanked by Paris and Lyon. Fortress Paris was enormous and would be difficult to deal with.

An initial French offensive was considered extremely difficult – much more so than the German offensive – and therefore was very unlikely, unless the Germans committed significant forces in the east. The 3rd Department was implicitly saying that an *Ostaufmarsch* would assist and encourage a French offensive. If the French did attack, the most likely French course of action would be to attack on both sides of Metz (which was in fact Joffre's intent in Plan XVII). The attack by the French right between Metz and Strasbourg was extremely difficult and the left-wing French armies would be separated from those on the right by Metz. The further advance by the French left would be in eccentric directions towards the Moselle and the Rhine, and would be blocked by these rivers. A French advance across the upper Rhine into south Germany would be cut off.

In December 1912 the 3rd Department issued an intelligence estimate titled *Vermutete Erste Massnahmen der Franzosen 1913/14* (Anticipated Initial French Actions 1913/14).[52] The 3rd Department thought it likely that the French would take immediate action on the flanks at the start of the war. On the left, I Corps, and perhaps also II Corps, would probably assemble at Maubeuge and then enter Belgium to secure the line of the Meuse from Namur to Givet (in August 1914 the French eventually sent an entire army north to the Sambre–Meuse). At the same time, a large cavalry corps of up to four divisions was expected to move into the Belgian Ardennes and Luxembourg. On the French right flank an early attack by the French VII Corps and 8th Cavalry Division against Mühlhausen was anticipated (which occurred). The French were also likely to send light infantry detachments to seize the Vosges passes. It is clear from these documents that the general staff expected the French to immediately begin hostilities at the start of the war.

German uncertainty was evident throughout these intelligence estimates, which consist of analysing a widely varied list of possible French and British courses of action. Most important, the French expected a German attack through Belgium and were prepared to enter Belgium too. But the Germans literally had no idea what the French were going to do. While they expected that a French defensive-offensive was likely, an immediate French offensive in Lorraine, or on both sides of Metz, was not out of the question.

The Germans did not expect a quick, decisive victory. If the Germans won the first battles, the French were prepared to conduct a strategic withdrawal as far as the middle Loire, buying time for Russian pressure to make itself felt.

These analyses show conclusively that both the French and the Germans had weighed all the possible permutations of their own and their opponents' courses of action. There were no brilliant secret war plans. The trick, as Moltke had said in 1906, was in discerning which plan the enemy had actually adopted. In any case, war is not about planning but fighting. War plans notwithstanding, the army that fought best was likely to win the initial battles.

This estimate was probably decisive in motivating the general staff to simplify the German war plan. The strategic situation was plain and it was serious. The next war would be on two fronts. There was no need for two deployment plans, *Aufmarsch* I and II. By 1913 they were amalgamated into one plan for a general European war.

1913/14

Aufmarsch 1913/14

There were only seven original documents concerning the 1913/1914 war plan: the mobilisation schedule; instructions for the covering forces in the west, east and north; maps of the covering forces in the west and east; maps of *Aufmarsch* I *West und Ost* and of *Aufmarschstudien* (deployment plans studies) II *West und Ost*; *Aufmarschanweisungen* I *West und Ost*; and special orders for the first and second *coup de main* against Liège. The summary was fourteen typewritten pages long, with handwritten additions and a handwritten summary of the forces in each *Aufmarsch*. There was a map of *Aufmarsch* I *West* and for the *Aufmarsch* II *West* study.

German war planning now reaches a crucial stage. The preamble to the 1913/14 plan states:

> Germany's war planning must principally be directed against France ... It is probable that Russia and Britain will join a French war against Germany ... Due to French public opinion, a war between Germany and Russia or Britain alone is unlikely. Nevertheless, if Russia or England alone do declare war on Germany, German diplomacy must force France to definitively declare her position.

Austrian and Italian support was dependent on the circumstances, but in the best case, Italy would engage the French only on their common Alpine border. No Italian army would be sent to Alsace.

Only one *Aufmarschplan* was prepared, in effect *Aufmarsch* I *West und Ost*, which was Schlieffen's old *Aufmarsch* II: sixty-eight divisions in the west, two on the North Sea coast, and nine in the east. The order of battle is the same as in the 1911/12 *Aufmarsch* and remains the same in August 1914. (*Aufmarsch* II, the *Ostaufmarsch*, was prepared as a 'study', an abbreviated plan.) For the first time, ersatz units would be formed into an 'Ersatz Army', six divisions strong.

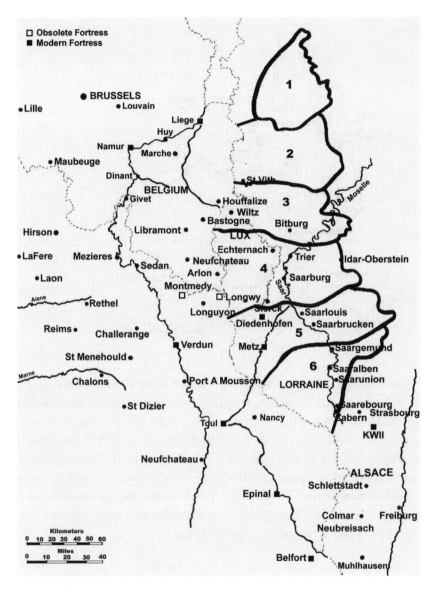

1913/14 *West* I

Germany could support Austria only by drawing off as many Russian forces as possible. A strong Russian offensive against Germany was favourable for the common cause. The German route of withdrawal over the Vistula had to be secure. If the Russians did not attack, then the German 8th Army in East Prussia would conduct its own offensive.

On the first day of mobilisation Belgium would be presented with an ultimatum requiring a prompt reply, to determine whether Belgium was

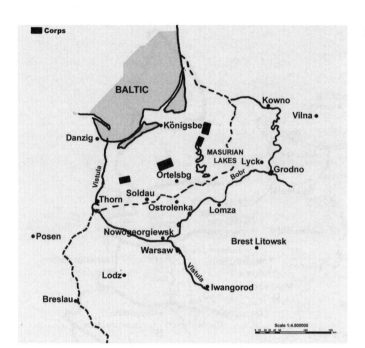

1913/14 *Ost* I

Germany's ally or enemy. A favourable reply would allow German troops to transit Belgium, open the fortresses of Liège and Namur, protect the railway lines and prevent a British landing. In case of a negative answer, a *coup de main* would be attempted against Liège on the night of the fourth to fifth mobilisation days. If this failed, a second attack would be conducted on the tenth mobilisation day. If Liège had not fallen by the twelfth day of mobilisation, it would be necessary to transit Dutch territory at Maastricht. A diplomatic attempt would be made to gain Dutch assent. The *Westaufmarsch* was little changed from 1912/13 and was essentially the same as that used in August 1914.

German 1913 Intelligence Summary for Russia

The annual intelligence summary emphasised the excellent state of the Russian economy.[53] The harvest in 1913 was good. Industrial expansion continued at full speed. The state budget grew for yet another year. Almost all sources of tax revenue increased. There was a budget surplus that allowed unforeseen expenditures to the tune of 800 million marks to be covered. The additional costs occasioned by the Balkan crisis were paid for without resorting to loans or increasing taxes. The budget estimate for 1914 was 660 million marks greater than 1913, including 230 million more marks for defence.

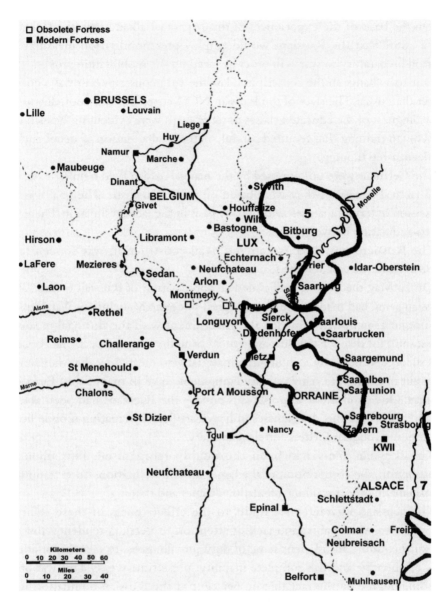

☐ Obsolete Fortress
■ Modern Fortress

1913/14 *West* II

On the other hand, there was considerable internal unrest. The 1912 wave of strikes continued into 1913. Revolutionary propaganda made gains. Dissatisfaction was evident in all social classes. The Duma was divided by conflicts between the reactionary, constitutional and left parties and was unable to produce a majority. The sole subject of unanimity was the willingness to sacrifice in the interest of national defence.

On the basis of the experiences of the 1912/13 Balkan crisis, the Germans were aware that the Russians would employ pre-mobilisation measures – a 'period preparatory to war' – in order to speed up the mobilisation proper.

Due to a change in the conscription law, the 1913 conscript class was a quarter larger than usual. The state of the Russian NCO corps was still poor, due to the unwillingness of the educated classes to serve. Gaps were evident in the elements of Russian training that required careful, methodical attention to detail, such as marksmanship training.

The Germans were unimpressed by the major Russian field training exercises. The tactical situations they were based on were unrealistic. The goal was the possession of terrain features, without any basis in the tactical situation. There was no co-ordination between units.

The Russians now had 250 aircraft. Rail construction was concentrated exclusively in the east and the Caucasus.

On 22 May the general staff issued an appreciation of Russian tactics.[54] The Russian army had made significant progress since the Manchurian War. Russian economic growth had provided the government with the financial means to invest sums for defence that surpassed those of all the other powers. The Russians had succeeded not only in filling the material gaps created by the Manchurian War, but in giving the army military equipment equal to that of west European powers. One prominent example was cited – the Russians had been able to correct their previous deficiencies in heavy artillery by creating mobile heavy artillery and modern fortress and siege artillery.

The Russian army had been thoroughly reorganised. This included conscription, the composition of the larger units, mobilisation, troop stationing, management, officer training, regulations, tactics and training.

The Russian character set limits to the effectiveness of these reforms: disorganised work habits and lack of attention to detail, a tendency towards personal comfort, insufficient sense of duty, unwillingness to take responsibility, lack of initiative and the complete inability to use time wisely. This was offset to some degree by the fact that 90 per cent of the Russian population were peasants, who made good soldiers. They were strong, needed little, and were brave. They were also mentally slow and lacked initiative. The Russian soldier would, however, recover quickly from defeat and be capable of conducting a tenacious defence. He was loyal, eager and reliable. Nevertheless, revolutionary propaganda had made some progress, especially among technical troops. A war against Germany and Austria 'would not be unpopular'. The Poles were completely unreliable.

Russian officers at all levels were poor trainers, and they had the Russian character faults in spades. They did not lack boldness, but their sense of duty and willingness to accept responsibility were lacking. Each level required close and continuous supervision by the superior level. They were cold-blooded and possessed good nerves, but also had a great tendency towards personal comfort and were physically and mentally lazy; they were not resourceful and failed during unforeseen circumstances. Russian bureaucrats were corrupt.

Russian tactical doctrine had been modernised, but there was no evidence in the manoeuvres of the last years that this had any effect on troop practice. Troop movements were executed with 'extreme slowness'. Russian leaders were not able to quickly exploit a favourable tactical situation. Troop-leading procedures – giving, transmitting and executing orders – broke down. Larger Russian units could not quickly transition from the defence to the offence or change the direction of march. Russian leadership in combat would be dominated by methodical slowness, waiting for orders and for neighbouring units, and attempting to operate according to standard, cookie-cutter procedures.

For these reasons, the Russian was a stranger to meeting engagements, and it would be easy for an energetic and mobile enemy to seize the initiative and throw the Russians on the defensive. In consequence, in combat with the Russians, German leaders may risk manoeuvres that would not be permissible against a fully capable enemy.

Recent Russian manoeuvres showed a preference for the defence and attack of field fortifications, in which the Russians had gained a certain degree of experience in Manchuria. In the defence the Russians made excessive use of detached forward positions which could not be supported by the main position. Due to their experience in the Manchurian War, the Russians had come to the conclusion that an attack on a well dug-in position would not succeed. The doctrinal procedure for an attack on field fortifications was to conduct a night approach march and a dawn attack. Pursuit was almost never practised: when the position was taken, the exercise was usually terminated.

In the offensive the Russians advanced on a broad front, aiming at envelopment. The most effective counter against Russian envelopments was a counter-attack, which would always catch the Russians unprepared, first because the Russians conducted neither cavalry nor infantry reconnaissance, and second because Russian leaders, when surprised, were helpless. If the Russians made unexpected contact they would stop and deploy, in spite of the doctrinal requirement to act aggressively to develop the situation. The Russian infantry remained maladroit in combat due to its lumbering movements and the incapacity of the officers.

In the attack, the Russians sought to reduce the effect of enemy fire by deployment in thin lines and use of the terrain. On the other hand, the Russians had no idea how to conduct the fire fight. There was no recognition that forward movement required fire support, much less of fire superiority. Counter-attacks against even a carefully deployed Russian infantry attack would always enjoy great success due to the clumsiness of the Russian officers.

Infantry training was mass training; individual training, such as marksmanship training, was not conducted due to the lack of energy and insufficient knowledge of the trainers. The Russian artillery was the best-trained arm, but nevertheless not the equal of German artillery.

Only the major Russian roads were hard-surfaced, and even these were so poorly maintained that automobiles and heavy wagons would run into great difficulties. The other roads were dirt, infrequently reinforced with gravel. Their usefulness was determined by the weather and soil conditions. Except for Poland, Russia was thinly inhabited. Great tracts of swamp and forest were practically unpopulated. Troop movement in Russia was therefore slow and laborious. In order to move, artillery would often need the assistance of infantry, and wagons would need additional teams. Off the main roads heavy artillery and supply columns might be significantly and unexpectedly delayed, or stopped completely by inadequate bridges. Older maps were not accurate. The most important factor in a German offensive against Russia was the vast and difficult Russian terrain.

This estimate demonstrated itself in combat to be completely correct. Russian units that tried to engage in manoeuvre battles with German units were destroyed. In 1915 and 1916 Russian units were never able to hold field fortifications against German combined-arms attacks. The only hope for the Russians was to massively outnumber their German opponents, and the best way to arrive at that situation was to defeat the Austrians.

1914/15

German 1914 Evaluation of Russian Training

The German army published a final evaluation of Russian training on 25 March 1914.[55] European armies strove to conduct their summer training at Major Training Areas (MTA). The German MTAs were the best of any army: each corps had its own MTA, generally about 8 x 8km in size (64 square km), which allowed live-fire with minimum safety restrictions and manoeuvre for large (brigade- and division-sized) units. Russian MTAs were of widely varying size, but often considerably smaller than the German. Finding suitable areas in Russia's vast swamps and forests was not easy. So while the Russian artillery MTA at Rembertow, near Warsaw, was 57 square km, where seventy batteries exercised at once (still pretty crowded), the X Corps MTA was only 12 square km, in which two infantry divisions and two artillery brigades tried to manoeuvre simultaneously – a virtual impossibility. The Wilna MTA was only 3 square km. The Russian war ministry had been trying to increase the size of the MTA since 1911, to no effect.

Russian infantry training was centralised at the regimental level; the regimental commander specified the training schedules for the battalions and companies. Every company conducted the same training at the same time. The company commander had very little influence on training, and therefore had little enthusiasm for it. This did not trouble him, for professional satisfaction and pride in personal accomplishments were unknown to Russian officers. Such stereotyped training and over-centralisation were ill-suited to developing a sense of personal responsibility, independence and initiative. The consequences were plain in larger exercises and later in combat.

The time available for field training at the MTA was poorly used. The duty day began late and training lasted only about two hours. Training was always conducted in the same spot directly behind the tents, with no attempt being made to find different terrain or to gradually increase the difficulty of the marches.

Artillery batteries were to live-fire fifteen times at the MTA. Due to the shortage of firing positions and inadequate training facilities they were rarely able to do so. In one case, during eight weeks at the MTA a battery fired seven times. Since each battery of eight guns was only allocated 600 shells, the fire mission was always terminated when the battery had adjusted on to the target: the battery had only one opportunity each year to fire for effect.

Kaiser Wilhelm is always criticised for conducting cavalry charges during the *Kaisermanöver*. He was not alone. In the 1913 manoeuvre of the Guard Corps, a cavalry brigade conducted a charge against the fully deployed enemy advanced guard and, 'aided by the favourable terrain', overran the infantry and penetrated as far as the 'surprised' artillery. On the other hand, the intelligence report noted that the charge against such strong unbroken infantry could just as well have ended in failure.

In any case, the 1913 Guard Corps exercise was 'canned': the tactical course of the exercise was established in advance and the leaders were not required to arrive at independent decisions. Reconnaissance was poor. The senior leadership was unequal to the requirements of their positions, was unable to co-ordinate unit operations and movement, to correctly evaluate the situation or to write effective orders. It also showed a serious lack of initiative.

The infantry attack at this exercise showed serious deficiencies in conducting the fire fight, moving reinforcements forward, gaining fire superiority and making the assault. Use of the terrain was good, but reconnaissance often failed completely.

The Guard Cavalry Division exercise was a pure parade manoeuvre. The intelligence report guessed that its purpose was to allow Grand Duke Nicholas, the presumptive commander-in-chief, the opportunity to show himself to his French guests at the head of a mass of cavalry.

The field training exercise at Krasnoje Selo, the imperial headquarters, constituted the highest level of training in the Russian army. It had been well known for decades that the point of the exercise was always to attack or defend the high ground in the manoeuvre area. Leaders at all levels displayed an indifference towards the conduct of the manoeuvre, as well as complete passivity and lack of initiative. Movements were executed slowly, probably because of late receipt of orders. Meeting engagements were seldom practised, and when they were, the leadership showed itself to be incapable of acting decisively in uncertain situations, but continually waited for further reports and information and finally slid into a passive defence.

The Russian defence was built around the counter-attack, with half the forces holding a thin front while the other half held in reserve. Preference for the defence was natural for the Russians – the product of their national character and years of practice.

Units also deployed on too broad a front. While the doctrinal divisional frontage in the attack was 3km, one division in the attack deployed on a 9–10km front. At another point, a regiment in the attack spread out on a 2.5km front. This was also true in the defence: in one over-extended position, 1.5km of front was held by twelve guns and an infantry company.

The German intelligence report clearly believed that, unit for unit, the German army was massively superior to the Russian. This was the sole consolation that the Germans would have in the east. The war there would not be fought under conditions of numerical parity: the Russians would begin with at least a 2:1 superiority and would bring up wave after wave of reinforcements.

But the real Achilles heel of the Central Powers was the Austrian army. Bad as the Russians were, the Austrians were probably worse. Whatever masterpieces the Germans could contrive from their superior manoeuvrability and combat power, they would at best balance out Austrian defeats. The Austrians would be outnumbered by the Russians, had inferior equipment (and less of it) and many of the minorities were unreliable. Unit for unit, they were probably inferior to the Russians.

German 1914 Evaluation of Russia's Readiness for War

In February 1914 the 1st (Russian) Department issued a special intelligence estimate, *Die Kriegsbereitschaft Russlands* (Russian Military Readiness). This was a warning to the German army that, whatever the Russian deficiencies, the Russians were not to be taken lightly. Quantity had a quality of its own. The estimate listed seven pages of improvements in the Russian army since the Russo-Japanese War. All the material deficiencies caused by the war had been made up by 1911. The military budget had increased from 351 million roubles in 1903 to 518 million in 1908, to 635 million in 1913. The transportation budget had increased from 542 million roubles in 1908 to 649 million in 1913. The size of the army had been increased by six corps. The units deployed on the border had been strengthened (infantry companies up from 116 men to 158), permitting quicker combat-readiness. The number of officers had increased, and their pay and training improved.

Cadres had been created in the interior to facilitate the mobilisation of reserve units. Refresher training for reservists had increased from 320,000 men in 1911 to 368,000 in 1912, 422,349 in 1913 and 490,000 scheduled for 1914. The refresher training period had been increased from four to six weeks.

The rail net had been developed through incremental upgrades and not through new railway construction. Existing track and installations had been improved. The quantity of rolling stock had been increased, as had the quantity of fuel. More personnel had been added. District rail committees provided for better use of the rail net.

The speed of mobilisation had increased greatly. The 1910 reform, which provided for territorial mobilisation, improved radio, telegraph and telephone nets and practice mobilisations, contributed to the fact that the line troops were now ready to move on the fifth day of mobilisation, the reserve troops by the eighth day, which was as fast as the Germans and the French; only the greater distances that the Russians had to move those troops made the deployment slower.

The speed of the mobilisation was further accelerated by the official introduction of a 'period preparatory to war' (*Kriegsvorbereitungsperiode*) in 1913.[56] This was in fact a secret mobilisation. These alert measures included the disguised call-up of reservists, horse purchases and the uploading of ammunition, rations and animal fodder.[57] German intelligence was especially sensitive to the Russian use of secret mobilisation because it had detected unmistakable signs that the Russians had conducted one such during the Balkan crisis in the winter of 1912/13. At that time the Russians had retained conscripts in the army who ought to have been discharged, while simultaneously calling up the next conscript class, which increased the peacetime strength of the Russian army by 400,000 men. The

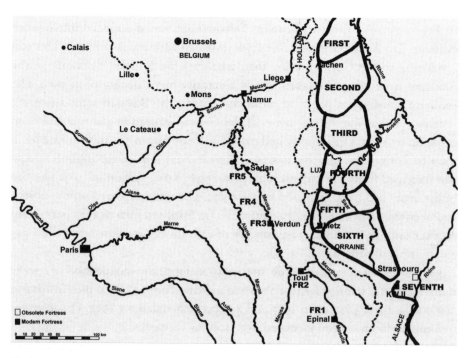

Deployment 1914

Russians had also conducted an unusual number of practice mobilisations and reserve exercises, prepared the railway system for troop movements and massed troops on the Austrian border.[58] Both in 1912/13 and in 1914 the German general staff would exercise great restraint in the face of the secret Russian mobilisation. Nevertheless, the Russian army was obviously trying to steal a march on the Germans – an enormously destabilising factor in times of international tension.

In summary, the estimate said that Russian readiness had made 'immense progress' and had reached hitherto unattained levels. In some areas Russian readiness exceeded that of the other Great Powers, including Germany; in particular the higher state of readiness in the winter, the frequent practice mobilisations and 'the extraordinary increase in the speed of mobilization provided by the "period preparatory to war"'.

There is no evidence, as has often been contended, that the Germans expected that the Russians would not be ready to attack until the thirtieth or even the forty-fifth day of mobilisation, and that this would have given them time to implement the Schlieffen plan. From 1909 onwards, the German intelligence estimates warned in ever more emphatic terms that the Russians were getting stronger and their mobilisation and deployment were getting faster. From all the evidence, it appears that the Germans thought the Russians would attack by the twentieth day of mobilisation at the latest.

Aufmarsch 1914/15

This *Aufmarsch* went into effect on 1 April 1914 and was implemented as the actual war plan on 2 August 1914. Only fragments of this *Aufmarsch* were presented in the German official history, and then they were heavily distorted in order to facilitate the Reichsarchiv's desire to propagate the Schlieffen plan.

In addition to the few pieces of the *Aufmarschanweisung* published in the official history, the *Aufmarschanweisungen* for three armies survived the destruction of the Reichsarchiv. The American army captured the German 5th Army's records at the end of the Great War. Some time after the Second World War the Americans returned a typewritten English translation of the 5th Army's *Aufmarschanweisung* to the Militärarchiv in Freiburg.[59] The US Army War College also retained a copy. Even more crucial was the survival of the Bavarian 6th Army's *Aufmarschanweisung* at the Kriegsarchiv in Munich.[60] Since the 6th Army had operational control over the 7th Army in Alsace, the 7th Army's *Aufmarschanweisung* also survived.[61] Just as important, the Bavarian chief of staff, Krafft von Dellmensingen, wrote an estimate of the situation (*Lagebeurteilung*) for the left wing of the German army, which is to be found in his *Nachlass* (papers).[62]

The German concept of the operation was contained in the fourth section of the *Aufmarschanweisung, Besondere Weisungen* (special instructions). These began with a general appreciation of the political situation. Holland was not expected to declare war on Germany. Belgium's position was uncertain. The intervention of the British army was considered 'not unlikely'. The British could move through Holland, occupy Antwerp or land at Calais–Dunkirk and move to link up with the French left wing.

The Germans had no idea what the French and Russians would do, and kept a completely open mind, refusing to prejudge entente intentions. A more-or-less simultaneous Franco-Russian offensive was the most dangerous entente course of action.

The Germans thought they would be opposed by a field force of sixty-three French, six British and six Belgian divisions – seventy-five in all. The French and Belgians could also count on the support of their elaborate systems of fortification.

The Germans deployed seven armies (sixty-eight divisions) in the west. IX RK (*Reservekorps* – reserve corps) with two divisions would watch the North Sea against a British landing. The Germans could calculate that the higher tactical quality of their troops would make up for their numerical inferiority. Nevertheless, the Germans could not count on an overall superiority in combat power.

In the east, the Germans would have nine divisions, the Austrians forty-nine – fifty-eight divisions in total. The Germans estimated that the Russians had fifty-nine active divisions, twelve light infantry brigades (the equivalent of six divisions) and thirty-five reserve divisions (not counting fifteen divisions in Siberia and Turkistan) – 100 divisions in total.[63] The Austrians estimated that the Serbs had twelve divisions, for 112 divisions in total. The Russians would probably deploy two armies against East Prussia, each numerically stronger than the German army there. While the German troops in East Prussia might well be able to hold their own against twice as many Russian divisions, this would still leave forty-nine low-quality Austrian divisions opposed to some ninety-four Russian and Serb divisions.

Germany's forces in East Prussia, as well as those of its Austro-Hungarian ally, would be massively outnumbered by the Russians. The Austrians would be constantly looking over their shoulders in anticipation of an Italian attack. A crisis in the east was likely, and soon. It was therefore necessary for the Germans to inflict a defeat on the French serious enough to force them on to the defensive and allow the transfer of forces to the east as soon as possible. Forcing the French completely out of the war would be a long process; there is no evidence that the Germans thought they could annihilate the French army in forty days, as proponents of the Schlieffen plan contend.

The concept of the German operation was for the main body to advance through Belgium and Luxembourg to France. The 5th Army would act as a pivot for the German movement by maintaining contact with Metz–Diedenhofen. The speed of the movement of the main body would be determined by the movement of the right flank. Rolling stock had been assembled behind the left, centre and right to permit the immediate rail movement of seven corps. This was the entire concept as stated in the *Aufmarschanweisungen*. In addition, each army received its own mission statement.

There was no attempt in the deployment instructions to prescribe the complete operation; neither did they say that the objective was the annihilation of the French army. The German war plan in August 1914 was not the Schlieffen plan.

The 7th Army, with 2 AK (*Armeekorps* – active corps) and 2 RK (*Reservekorps* – reserve corps), and the 6th Army (4 AK, 1 RK) in Alsace and Lorraine under the 6th Army commander Crown Prince Rupprecht of Bavaria, had a complex set of missions. The first was to hold Lorraine (and, if possible, Alsace too) to protect the German left flank. Metz was to be expanded into a fortified zone: seven Landwehr brigades reinforced with artillery would dig in along the Nied River (*Niedstellung*). If it appeared that the French were withdrawing forces from their right to reinforce their left, Rupprecht was to attack to fix them in place. How Rupprecht was to divine French strength and intentions with the necessary degree of accuracy was an interesting question.

There was also a third mission for the 6th Army – probably a follow-on from the other two – to attack west from Metz to break through the French fortress line. There was only one reason for such an operation: Moltke was trying to implement General von Beseler's 1900 plan for the German right wing to drive deep into France behind the French fortress line, which would be attacked front and rear and broken, linking up the German left and right wings and surrounding Verdun. Moltke had first broached the idea of an advance deep into France in the 1911 intelligence estimate, which had nothing to do with the Schlieffen plan.

The 5th Army (3 AK, 2 RK) was deployed on a narrow front and in depth behind Metz for a specific purpose: if the French attacked early and in strength into Lorraine, this formation would allow the 5th Army to swing through Metz to the south-east to counter-attack against the French left flank. Such a French attack was the theme of most of Schlieffen's west-front war games, as well as Moltke's two surviving war games. This would have changed the entire character of the campaign. The 4th Army (3 AK, 2 RK) would have had to cover the 5th Army rear and the operation would have looked exactly like one of the *Generalstabsreisen West*. Moltke clearly felt that there was a strong possibility that the French could launch their main attack into Lorraine.

If the French main attack did not come in Lorraine, then the 5th and 4th Armies would first move north-west, then west towards the Meuse. The 3rd Army (3 AK, 1 RK) would advance straight west towards the Meuse.

Liège would be taken by a *coup de main* on the night of the fourth day of mobilisation. The 1st Army (4 AK, 2 RK) would then cross the Meuse north of Liège, the 2nd Army to the south of it. If Liège was not silenced, the 1st Army (4 AK, 2 RK) would have to transit Dutch territory, an eventuality the Germans wanted to avoid. It was important for the 1st and 2nd Armies to reach the bottleneck at Brussels before the French.

The mission of the 1st Army on the right flank, commanded by Kluck, with Kuhl as his chief of staff, was not, as the Schlieffen plan would have it, to deliver the decisive attack but to march on Brussels, 'to protect the right flank of the army (*die rechte Flanke des Heeres zu decken*)'.[64] The 1st Army's mission throughout the campaign, from the initial *Aufmarschanweisung* to the end of the battle of the Marne, was always principally to act as flank guard.

Moltke clearly intended the 2nd Army to conduct the main attack. The army was led by Germany's senior active general officer, Karl von Bülow. Moltke would give Bülow operational control over the 1st Army on his right and the 3rd Army on his left.

Rail assets were to be assembled behind the left, centre and right in order to be able to simultaneously transport seven corps.

As the elder Moltke had said, 'no plan survives contact with the enemy'. The *Aufmarschanweisungen* did not prescribe actions beyond the deployment and initial movements. The one exception was the instructions for the German 6th and 7th Armies in Lorraine. After the initial advance, German actions would have to consider French movements.

Document RH 61/v.96 (German War Plans) 1914/15

As unlikely as it would seem, the only information concerning this vitally important *Aufmarsch* in the RH 61/v.96 file consists of five pages of shorthand notes. RH 61/v.96 adds only supplemental information to what we already know. There is no map of the west front deployment. There is no list of the documents that were available. There is no after-action report concerning the implementation of mobilisation and deployment – a strange oversight, particularly for the German army, where after-action reports were routine at all levels. There should have been estimates of the situation (*Lagebeurteilung*) written by each of the army chiefs of staff, indeed an estimate written by Moltke himself. There should have been mountains of original mobilisation and deployment documents.

RH 61/v.96 confirms that there was only one *Aufmarschplan*: 'German war planning is principally oriented against France. Russia will probably join France in a war against Germany: British hostility must also be anticipated.' Nevertheless, all possibilities had been considered. In case of war with Russia, an agreement had been concluded with the Austro-Hungarian general staff for a joint offensive. On the other hand, if it appeared that Russia might not be hostile, the German 8th Army could deploy immediately to East Prussia, or it could remain in its mobilisation stations. If Russia did declare neutrality, the 8th Army would be sent west. A 'garrison army' of six and a half ersatz divisions had been created, which could be deployed in the east, in the west, or for coast defence.

RH 61/v.96 makes the surprising assertion that the Germans thought Italy would probably participate with Germany in a war against France, sending three corps (not five, as previously planned) to south Germany and attacking across the Alps with the main body of her army. Previous estimates stated that Italian participation would be unlikely; anticipating Italian aid at this point must be considered wishful thinking, indeed desperation.

During periods of serious political tension, the chief of the general staff, the imperial chancellor, the foreign office, war minister, chief of the military cabinet and chief of the naval staff were to meet in order to co-ordinate measures to determine the position that friends, enemies and neutrals would take. The minutes of these meetings would be fascinating. Alas, RH 61/v.96 does not include them. The description of the concept of the operation and the orders to the army commanders in RH 61/v.96 is short and serves only to confirm what we already know.

The Concept of the German War Plan

The German war plan in 1914 was relatively simple. It followed Schlieffen's counter-attack doctrine. In the west, the German army would deploy on a broad front to make maximum utilisation of the rail net and the available space for manoeuvre. It would then find the French main body, move against it, and defeat it as quickly as possible. The French army would withdraw to the next defensive position. The Germans would probably use this pause in the west to transfer up to seven corps to the east for a counter-attack there.

In the east, the Germans would be outnumbered 2:1, but would use their interior position to mass against one of the two attacking Russian armies. If necessary, the Germans would fall back to the Vistula fortifications. The Central Powers' Achilles heel was the Austrian army, which was weak and outnumbered 2:1.

The German advantage lay in its interior position and rail mobility – the ability to mass on one front, win, and then mass on the other. This would make optimal use of German tactical and operational superiority over all of its opponents. This mobility is known today as a 'force multiplier' and was the sole means the Germans had of offsetting their numerical inferiority. Such a strategy would not produce strategic victory, but successive defeats of French and Russian armies would destroy their capacity for offensive action.

A German strategic offensive deep into the interior of either enemy territory negated the German advantages of interior position and rail mobility; indeed, the rail mobility advantage would pass over to Germany's opponent. A German strategic offensive, such as the one Moltke launched into France on 24 August, after he had won the Battle of the Frontiers, was a gamble that Germany had the means of winning an immediate victory on one front.

Document RH 61/v.96 *vs* the Schlieffen Plan

Most advocates of the Schlieffen plan contend that Schlieffen implemented it in the 1906/07 *Aufmarsch*.[65] The description of the 1906/07 *Aufmarsch* in Document RH 61/v.96 shows that this was untrue. RH 61/v.96, which gives the real force structure in the German army, eliminates the possibility that a 'Schlieffen plan' force was ever available.

All the plans from 1905/06 to 1909/10 included seventy-two divisions (fifty-two infantry divisions and twenty reserve divisions), not the ninety-six divisions required by the Schlieffen plan. The 1907/08 plan says in one passage that thirteen reserve corps and one reserve division equalled twenty reserve divisions; that is, seven reserve corps had only one division, not two as required in the Schlieffen plan. It says in another passage, on the same page, that twelve reserve corps and one reserve division would be deployed in the west, and that these made up nineteen reserve divisions, while IX RK, which had one division, would defend the North Sea coast: so, once again, the German army had twenty reserve divisions. Not until 1910/11 did all the reserve corps have two divisions; that is, only then were there the required twenty-seven reserve divisions.

The Schlieffen plan needed sixteen ersatz divisions. In 1905/06 the ersatz troops from five corps and one divisional area were to 'be prepared' to deploy to Holstein in northern Germany for coast defence. In the 1906/07 plan, IX Ersatz Corps (composition not specified) was to deploy to the North Sea coast. The Guard Ersatz Corps and a Landwehr corps were to deploy 'on order' after an enemy landing. If no landing occurred (and none ever did), then these corps were moot. The German army still had only seventy-two divisions available, plus two static coast defence divisions in Germany. In the 1907/08 plan, the ersatz troops of the IX AK area alone were to 'be prepared' to defend the North Sea coast. The only specific mention of ersatz troops was that thirteen squadrons of ersatz cavalry were to be prepared to move 'on order'. Ersatz troops were not mentioned in the 1908/09 plan. In the 1909/10 plan there was no specific mention of ersatz units, but elements of the 'Home Army' were to 'be prepared' to reinforce the IX RK in the coast defence mission. There is no further mention of ersatz units until 1913/14, when it was first planned to raise six (not sixteen) ersatz divisions.

By 1913/14 Germany faced the certainty of a two-front war, and could deploy only sixty-eight active and reserve divisions and six ersatz divisions in the west; that is twelve active and reserve, and ten ersatz divisions too few – in total twenty-two divisions, the equivalent of two armies.

The concept of the Schlieffen plan is not mentioned in any of the German war plans. There is no indication that the war would be concluded with the total annihilation of the French army in forty days, as advocates of the Schlieffen plan generally maintain.

Notes

1   T. Zuber, *German War Planning*, pp. 23–9.
2   *Geheim! Grosse Generalstabsreise 1906* BA-MA PH 3/663: twenty-three pages, typewritten, with maps.
3   Kriegsarchiv Munich, Generalstab 204, *Jahresbericht Italien 1906*.
4   Kriegsarchiv Munich, Generalstab 204, *Jahresbericht Österreich-Hungarn 1906*; Generalstab 203, *Österreich-Ungarn, Mitteilungen 1906*.
5   Greiner footnote: '*Les Armées Françaises*, p. 10; Marchand, *op. cit.*, p. (illegible) and map for Plan XV.' Marchand, *Plans de Concentration*, p. 155.
6   Greiner, 'German Intelligence Estimate' in Zuber, *German War Planning*, pp. 24–31.
7   Marchand, *Plans de Concentration*, pp. 162–4; Greiner, 'German Intelligence Estimate' in Zuber, *German War Planning*, p. 24.
8   Sächsisches Hauptstaatsarchiv Dresden KA(P) 9195 (XII Corps) contains both the *Aufgaben* and the *Schlissbesprechung*, with pages 2 and 3 of the latter missing. Groener's *Nachlass* (papers) (BA-MA N/46/111) contains the *Schlussbesprechung*. The Hauptstaatsarchiv Stuttgart has a copy of the *Aufgabe* M33/1 (XIII Corps) Bündel 35.
9   T. Zuber, *The Moltke Myth: Prussian War Planning 1857–1871* (UPA, 2008), pp. 47–51.
10   Kriegsarchiv Munich, Generalstab 207, *Jahresbericht Russland 1907*.
11   Kriegsarchiv Munich, Generalstab 204, *Jahresbericht Österreich-Ungarn 1907*.
12   Kriegsarchiv Munich, Generalstab 204, *Jahresbericht Italien 1907*.
13   Kriegsarchiv Munich, Generalstab 204, *Jahresbericht Bulgarien 1907*.
14   *Grosse Generalstabsreise 1908*, BA-MA PH 3/664: thirty-six pages, typewritten, with eight maps.
15   Hauptstaatsarchiv Stuttgart M33/1 (XIII Corps), Bündel 35.
16   Greiner, 'Nachrichten' in Zuber, *German War Planning*, pp. 29–31.
17   Greiner footnote: 'p. 100'.
18   Greiner footnote: '3rd Department *Denkschrift* of 31 March 1908 concerning the French deployment 1908/09.'

19 Kriegsarchiv Munich, Generalstab 204, *Jahresbericht Österreich-Ungarn 1908*.

20 Kriegsarchiv Munich, Generalstab 204, *Jahresbericht Italien 1908*.

21 Marchand, *Plans de Concentration*, pp. 105–6.

22 Ibid., pp. 169–89. Zuber, *German War Planning*, pp. 28–32.

23 Kriegsarchiv Munich, Generalstab 204, *Jahresbericht Österreich-Ungarn 1908–09; Jahresbericht Österreich-Ungarn 1909*; Generalstab 203, *Veränderungen Österreich-Ungarn 1909*.

24 Zuber, *Inventing the Schlieffen Plan*, pp. 174–7.

25 Ibid., pp. 47–9.

26 Ibid., pp. 121–3.

27 Hauptstaatsarchiv Stuttgart M33/1 *Schlußaufgabe 1909*.

28 Moltke noted that captive balloons had the ability to detect enemy troop movements far into the enemy rear. Future campaigns would begin with attempts to destroy enemy balloons. That was why in this exercise the assumption had been made that the French balloons had all been destroyed. (!) For the moment, Moltke said, the Zeppelin provided the Germans with the superior air reconnaissance vehicle.

29 Kriegsarchiv Munich, Generalstab 208, *Zusammenstellung der wichtigsten Veränderungen im Heerwesen Rußlands 1909; Jahresbericht Rußland 1909*; Jany, *Preußische Armee* IV, p. 326.

30 Kriegsarchiv Munich, Generalstab 204, *Jahresbericht Österreich-Ungarn 1909*; Generalstab 203, *Veränderungen Österreich-Ungarn 1909*.

31 Kriegsarchiv Munich, Generalstab 204, *Jahresbericht Italien 1909*; Generalstab 203, *Veränderungen Italien 1909*.

32 Kriegsarchiv Munich, Generalstab 208, *Jahresbericht Serbien 1909*.

33 Kriegsarchiv Munich, Generalstab 208, *Veränderungen Rußlands 1910; Jahresbericht Rußlands 1910*.

34 Kriegsarchiv Munich, Generalstab 204, *Jahresbericht 1910 Österreich-Ungarn 1910*; Generalstab 203, *Veränderungen Österreich-Ungarn 1910*.

35 Zuber, *Inventing the Schlieffen Plan*, pp. 255–7.

36 Marchand, *Plans de Concentration*, pp. 189–97.

37 Ibid., pp. 181–9.

38 Hauptstaatsarchiv Stuttgart M 33/1, *Schlußaufgabe 1911*.

39 Kriegsarchiv Munich, Generalstab 208, *Veränderungen Rußland 1911*.

40 Kriegsarchiv Munich, Generalstab 203, *Veränderungen Österreich-Ungarn 1911*.

41 Greiner, 'Nachrichten' in Zuber, *German War Planning*, p. 34.

42 BA-MA PH 3/529 *Die military-politische Lage Deutschlands Ende November 1911*.

43 Kriegsarchiv Munich, Generalstab 925, *Nachrichten über die militärische Lage in Rußland 21 November 1912; Nachrichten über die militärische Lage in Frankreich 10 Dezember 1912; Nachrichten über die militärische Lage in Rußland V, 2. Januar 1913; Nachrichten über die militärische Lage in Frankreich 5, 2. Januar 1913. Nachrichten über die militärische Lage in England 3, 2. Januar 1913; Nachrichten über die militärische Lage in Rußland VI, 28 Januar 1913; Nachrichten über die militärische Lage in Frankreich 6, 18. Februar 1913*.

44 M.B. Hayne, *The French Foreign Office and the Origins of the First World War* (Oxford, 1993) p. 245.

45 Kriegsarchiv Munich, Generalstab 203, *Veränderungen Österreich-Ungarn 1912*.

46 Kriegsarchiv Munich, Generalstab 203, *Veränderungen Rußland 1912*.

47 US National Archives, Papers of Wilhelm Groener M137/20, *Die Taktik der französischen Armee*.

48 Greiner, 'Nachrichten' in Zuber, *German War Planning*, pp. 34–7; Grosser Generalstab 3. Abteilung, Mai 1912, *Aufmarsch und operative Absichten der Franzosen in einem zukünftigen deutsch-französischen Krieg*, BA-MA PH 3/628. This copy was obtained from the Militärarchiv der DDR. The BA-MA also has a typed transcript of the *Denkschrift* which had been made by the Americans who had captured it after the First World War. The

original had belonged to the German IV Corps. The Americans had apparently returned the transcript to the BA-MA. The maps were missing, which probably goes a long way in accounting for the fact that this *Denkschrift* has never received the attention it deserved.

49 *Les Armées Françaises*, I, I, I, p. 40.

50 Ibid., pp. 21–2.

51 Ibid., pp. 26, 36.

52 Greiner, 'Nachrichten' in Zuber, *German War Planning*, pp. 37–8.

53 Hauptstaatsarchiv Dresden, KA (P) 9195 Generalstab XII Armeekorps, *Veränderung Rußland 1913*.

54 Hauptstaatsarchiv Dresden, Sässisches Kriegsministerium KA (P) 623, *Mitteilungüber die russische Taktik*.

55 Kriegsarchiv Munich, Generalstab 209, *Sommerausbildung russischer Truppen*.

56 Hauptstaatsarchiv Stuttgart M33/1 (XIII Corps) Bündel 1; Kriegsarchiv Munich, AOK 6 Bündel 925. In the copy issued to the Bavarian 6th Army the sections referring to the Russian *Kriegsvorbereitungsperiode* are highlighted in red.

57 G. Frantz, *Russlands Eintritt in den Weltkrieg* (Berlin, 1924), pp. 193–200. Frantz provides German translations of captured Russian mobilisation regulations.

58 Kriegsarchiv Munich, Generalstab 925, *Nachrichten über die militärische Lage in Rußland: politische Spannung 1912/13*.

59 BA-MA PH 3/284, *Aufmarschanweisung 5. Armee*.

60 Kriegsarchiv Munich, AOK 6 Bündel 369 Nr 45, *Aufmarschanweisung für Oberkommando 6. Armee*. This was handwritten in the German standard style. There is also a typed copy in the Kriegsarchiv Munich, Nachlass 145 Krafft von Dellmensingen.

61 Kriegsarchiv Munich, Nachlass 145 Krafft von Dellmensingen, *Aufmarschanweisungen für Oberkommando der 7. Armee*.

62 Kriegsarchiv Munich, Nachlass 145 Krafft von Dellmensingen.

63 Reichsarchiv, *Der Weltkrieg. Band II. Die Befreiung Ostpreussens* (Berlin, 1925), pp. 15–23.

64 *Weltkrieg* I, p. 73.

65 For example, Gerhard Gross, 'There was a Schlieffen Plan' in Hans Ehlert, Michael Epkenhans & Gerhard P. Gross (eds) *Der Schlieffenplan. Analysen und Dokumente* (Paderborn, 2006), p. 150.

THE MARNE CAMPAIGN

The French & Russian War Plans

Since the conclusion of the Franco-Russian military alliance in 1894 the two general staffs had held frequent, if not always annual, conversations. At the 1910 conference the French promised that, in case of war, they would launch an immediate offensive against Germany, and asked the Russians to do the same between the fifteenth and thirtieth day of mobilisation.[1] The year 1910 was also the first in which the Russian general staff's operations officer, Danilov, said that he could observe real improvement in the Russian army after the debacle of 1904/05.[2]

The Franco-Russian military conference of 1911 was of decisive importance in the lead-up to war: the Entente was co-ordinating a detailed offensive war plan. As Joffre reports, the French delegate, General Dubail, obtained the Russian commitment to attack Germany on the sixteenth day of mobilisation, when the Russian initial deployment was completed, without waiting until the reserve divisions or units from the east arrived. It was agreed that only a determined joint offensive against Germany would ensure success.[3]

Such an agreement had always been the French objective. It was a commitment that the Russians had always avoided making in anything other than the vaguest terms, due to their slow mobilisation and deployment, their preference for fighting the Austrians and their disinterest in fighting the Germans. In one of their last meetings before the Russo-Japanese War, in 1901, the Russian chief of staff, Kuropatkin, promised the French that he would mobilise and deploy by the fortieth day. He did not allow himself to be pinned down to a promise to attack the Germans at a specific time.[4] Presumably he was giving himself plenty of time to bring up his reserve divisions and forces from the east. Kuropatkin's timetable had an additional advantage for the Russians: by the fortieth day of mobilisation, the first battle would probably have been fought in the west.

The French and Russians were fully aware of the advantages that the German interior position and rail mobility afforded. By seizing the initiative, attacking simultaneously and as soon as possible, they intended to make it impossible for the Germans to utilise either advantage.

Joffre visited the Russians in 1913 to ensure that the joint attack plan was properly co-ordinated. Joffre explained to the Russians on several occasions that the most probable German course of action would be to commit their main body against the French, and that it was therefore urgently necessary for the Russians to attack as soon as possible, even if it meant doing so with only a portion of their forces. Joffre said that the Grand Duke Nicholas, the Russian commander-in-chief designate, expressed to him several times that he understood the need for an early Russian offensive. Tsar Nicholas said that he would attack on the fifteenth day with eleven corps in the Niemen army and nine corps in the Narew army. Joffre recommended that the Narew army be directed down the Vistula on Thorn.[5] The Convention went on to say that the Allied plan must be to attack Germany simultaneously from both sides with the maximum forces.[6]

Time was particularly crucial for the Russians; they, alone of all the Great Powers, were attacking at less than full strength. They, therefore, had every incentive to begin their mobilisation before the other powers. The need to mobilise early and strike quickly was an integral part of the Franco-Russian offensive war plan and not, as Ritter and others would have it, the unique characteristic of the German war plan.

The 1911 agreement was the foundation of all further French and Russian war planning, which thereafter would undergo a fundamental change in both countries. On the basis of this agreement the French would replace the defensive-offensive doctrine of Bonnal with Plan XVII, which was the strategic expression of the *offensive à outrance*. The Russians would replace their normal defensive war plan against Germany with Schedule 19, which provided for simultaneous offensives against Germany and Austria-Hungary.

In 1911, therefore, the military stage was set for the outbreak of the war. The Russian general mobilisation on 30 July 1914 set the clock ticking for the Franco-Russian offensive, which would start on the fifteenth day of mobilisation at the very latest – in the event, 14 August 1914. Schlieffen had predicted that this would be the case at least since 1902; indeed, he had built his entire counter-attack doctrine around it.

Russian Schedule 18 (modified)

Though the Russians never implemented Schedule 19, Schedule 18 was considerably modified and closely approximated Schedule 19. Probably in order to utilise the Russian rail net, the Russian armies were uniformly distributed along their western front. This meant that two armies would deploy against Germany, four against Austria, with a further army assembling at Warsaw, which could be used against either.

The Russians would attack Germany on the fifteenth day of mobilisation with two armies, the 1st (four active corps) from Lithuania, and the 2nd (five active corps) from the north-west of Warsaw. The two armies were about 100km apart and separated by the Masurian Lake district. The Russians' intent was either to attack the Germans on both flanks or to force the Germans to abandon East Prussia.

French Plan XVII (1914)

The French war plan assumed a Russo-French two-front war against Germany and Austria. There was never a provision in the French plan for an isolated Franco-German war. The French said that recent developments in the Balkans were going to divert Austria and prevent her from assisting Germany to the same degree that she could have in the past. The Russians would be able to commit twenty-four active army corps (forty-eight divisions) by the twentieth to the twenty-third days of mobilisation. The French wanted the Russians to put their main point of effort against Germany.

The French thought the Germans would employ at least ten active divisions in East Prussia (the Russian intelligence estimate is unknown). The Germans actually deployed six active divisions. They estimated that the Germans would deploy forty active and twenty-eight reserve divisions in the west. While the total of sixty-eight divisions was correct, the Germans actually deployed forty-six active divisions in the west.

The French field army included forty-six active and twenty-one reserve divisions – sixty-seven divisions in total – plus eight Territorial divisions of limited value. Four more reserve and four Territorial divisions garrisoned fortresses.[7] The French also anticipated the arrival of the BEF with six divisions.

The French believed that the Germans could begin forward movement on the thirteenth day of mobilisation, which was far too soon. They also estimated that the rail net would not allow the Germans to deploy more than eleven corps north of Trier, which was perhaps half right: the Germans actually deployed eleven active and five reserve corps north of Trier. The French felt that the well-developed rail net behind Metz would lead the Germans to mass there.[8]

It has generally been assumed that the Plan XVII deployment is well known. The *West Point Atlas* map shows that the 1st Army was deployed near Epinal, the 2nd at Toul, the 3rd behind Verdun, the 4th initially in reserve to the south-west of Verdun, and the 5th on the left at Ste Menehould.[9] The Cavalry Corps was on the far left at Mézières and Sedan. This represents the initial locations in Plan XVII when it was first issued on 7 February 1914. The Germans were expected to mass their armies 'on the common frontier with France'.[10]

Joffre claimed that he did not have a preconceived scheme of manoeuvre.[11] Nevertheless, the concept of the operation was purely offensive: 'in all cases, the intent of the commanding general is, once the armies are deployed, to attack the German army'. No preconceived scheme of manoeuvre notwithstanding, the expressly stated general concept of the operation was for the French right wing to attack between the Vosges and Toul, while the left attacked north of the line Verdun–Metz. Though not expressly stated, this movement would surround Metz and almost surely bring on a decisive battle with the mass of the German army assembled behind Metz. As has been noted, the French were sure of their operational and tactical superiority and were confident they would win a pitched battle in the open field.

According to the French 1911/12 intelligence estimate, an attack on the German forces deployed behind Metz would engage a part of the German army before the German forces in the Eifel (i.e. the German 'right wing') could march through Belgium and enter the fight: Joffre intended to defeat the German army in detail. In the German war games from 1904 to 1908 this was the correct French solution to the German right wing attack.

Each army was given a specific mission. The 1st Army, with five corps, was to be ready as of the twelfth day of mobilisation to attack towards Sarrebourg and Saargemünd. VII CA, on the 1st Army right, had the special mission of attacking from Belfort towards Mühlhausen on the fourth day of mobilisation. The 2nd Army, with five corps, was to attack towards Saarbrücken, directly east of Metz. As the 2nd Group of Reserve Divisions arrived, it would cover the army left flank against Metz. The 3rd Army, with three corps, was to link the two wings of the French army, with a 'be prepared' mission of beginning the investment of Metz on the west and north-west sides. The 4th Army, three corps, was the French reserve. It was to 'be prepared' to attack either to the left of the 2nd Army, south of Metz (three French armies would be attacking in Lorraine), or to the left of the 3rd Army, north of Metz. The 5th Army, with five corps, had the mission of operating against the enemy right flank, either by attacking east towards Diedenhofen or north-east towards Neufchâteau.

Plan XVII is normally described as having a 'variant' which would be implemented if the Germans invaded Belgium. In this variant, the 4th Army would move from its reserve position to the north of the 3rd Army, and the 5th Army would move north towards the Belgian border (see map on p. 142 – Deployment). All five French armies would be on line. At 1400 on 2 August

1914 the French government gave Joffre 'complete freedom of movement' and Joffre implemented the 'variant' at 1930 the same day, which was the first day of mobilisation for both the French and German armies.[12] The justification for doing so was that the Germans had entered Luxembourg and German violation of Belgium seemed 'more and more likely'.[13] The Germans did not enter Belgium until the late afternoon of 3 August. On 2 August the Germans had just begun to mobilise, and aside from security forces no German troops would move towards the border until around 6 August. The French could therefore have had no indicators whatsoever of the German deployment. Neither would the French begin their deployment for several days. Therefore, the 'Plan XVII' deployment as depicted in the *West Point Atlas* map is wrong. The real French deployment provided for five armies on line, with three of those armies, the French mass of manoeuvre, to the north of Verdun.

Given a deployment that placed three of the five French armies on the Belgian border, a war plan which called for an *immediate* French attack and an alliance that specified an offensive against Germany by the fifteenth day of mobilisation, the French were going to enter Belgium, irrespective of whether the Germans did or not. It will surely be argued that the French political leadership would never have allowed Joffre to invade Belgium. In fact, the French government approved of the war plan and was fully aware of its significance.

German intelligence had practically no idea of the scope of the changes in the Russo-French war plans since 1911.[14] Nevertheless, there is at least one strong indication that Joffre was going to launch an immediate attack which had not gone unnoticed by the general staff.[15] A long article in the last issue before the war of the general staff's professional publication, *Vierteljahresheft für Truppenführung und Heereskunde* (Quarterly Journal for Leadership and Military Studies) accurately and perceptively traced the rise of Grandmaison's *offensive à outrance* in some detail. It would have been difficult to have ignored such a development, because Grandmaison had published a book explaining his doctrine. The new French doctrinal manuals were also made public: the 28 October 1913 *Instruction sur la Conduite des Grands Unités* (the French doctrinal operations manual at army group, army and corps levels), as well as the 2 December 1913 *Service en Campagne* (division level and smaller units) and the 20 April 1914 manual for the individual soldier. All these documents emphasised the offensive, including Grandmaison's famous statement that 'the French army, returning to its traditions, recognises no other law in the conduct of operations but that of the offensive'. The objective was to destroy the enemy in a battle of annihilation. The new regulations were reflected almost verbatim in Joffre's concept of the operation in his 8 August 1914 General Instruction #1: 'The offensive will begin as soon as the army has assembled.' German intelligence estimates were justifiably sceptical that a complete change in French doctrine could have permeated the entire French army in so short a period of time, but regardless, the French had clearly stated their intent.

Mobilisation & Deployment

The Russians would implement the 'period preparatory to war' at 0326 hours on 26 July 1914. German intelligence got wind of this almost immediately. The general staff intelligence summary issued on 28 July 1914 said that the Russians were apparently conducting at least a partial mobilisation and that the *Kriegsvorbereitungsperiode* had 'probably' been declared in all of Russia.[16] It said it was certain that Russia was taking military measures in areas bordering Germany which could only be considered as preparations for war.

The German intelligence estimate of 29 July 1914 reported troop concentrations near the border of all arms in up to multi-regimental strength, the recall of reservists and the preparation of rail rolling stock. The Russians had obviously begun a secret mobilisation and in addition were preparing to begin deployment. The 30 July intelligence summary said that the Russian implementation of the 'period preparatory to war' was 'far advanced'. On 1 August the Russian mobilisation was so far along that German intelligence was able to identify specific Russian units.[17] The fact that the German army thought the Russian army had been mobilising since 27 July, if not earlier, must be considered in any evaluation of German actions during the July crisis.

The 29 July intelligence estimate also reported that the Belgians had mobilised, begun 'arming' the fortresses (digging field fortifications in the intervals between the permanent fortifications) and preparing bridges and railway lines for demolition. On 30 July it reported that the Meuse bridges were prepared for demolition, and on 31 July that Liège had been armed and the eastern viaducts and tunnels were ready to be destroyed.[18]

It should have been evident to Moltke by 31 July, even before Germany took any military measures whatsoever, that the *attaque brusquée* on Liège – and a night attack at that – had little or no chance of success, while it had serious negative political consequences. Worse, the attack would telegraph the right wing's punch, and if Joffre had not been thinking about the threat to his left flank, the *attaque brusquée* on Liège would change all that. The Germans were also not going to be able to 'bounce' the Meuse bridges and the rail net near Liège was going to be rendered unusable for a considerable period. On 3 August the intelligence estimate reported that the garrison of Liège had been reinforced. Moltke ordered the attack to proceed anyway.

The attack was a fiasco. Only one brigade penetrated into the town, and had the Belgians been determined enough they could have destroyed it. The forts did not surrender, but were quickly and relatively easily reduced by German siege artillery. The Belgians executed all their demolitions, including the Meuse bridges, which the Germans had expected to capture intact. For this reason the Germans had not brought forward bridging material and the planned crossing of HKK 2 (*Heereskavalleriekorps* 2 – 2nd Cavalry Corps) to the west bank could not take place.

By scrapping the *attaque brusquée* and delaying the crossing of the border by five days (until the 8th) in favour of the planned attack on Liège on the tenth day, all manner of advantages might have accrued for the Germans. The British entry into the war may have been delayed and the French may have been confused concerning the German intentions. The attack would have been far better prepared and co-ordinated.

The *attaque brusquée* on Liège was Moltke's very own contribution to the German war plan and it is clear that he was not about to give it up. Moltke also seems to have inherited the elder Moltke's penchant for rigid thinking and adhering to preconceived ideas. This was merely the first in a long succession of unforced errors that the most senior German general staff officers would make during the Marne campaign.[19]

On 1 August the German Admiralty estimated that the British would land the BEF in Holland or Belgium as well as conduct a close blockade of the German coast.[20] This was both wrong on both counts and showed that the navy staff were no better than the army at abandoning preconceived ideas.

The same day, the Italians assured the Austrians that Italy would fulfil its treaty obligations.

The French ordered mobilisation at 1530 hours on 1 August. It is often asserted that the French were responding to German mobilisation or the German declaration of war against Russia. Neither can be true, because the Germans did not declare war on the Russians and mobilise until 1600 Paris time,[21] and the French did not learn that the Germans had declared war on Russia until 1900 hours.[22]

The French would complete their deployment of the combat troops (including the reserve brigade attached to each corps) and the supply trains by the tenth day of mobilisation. This was far ahead of the German army. The German troops that deployed first, the active army corps in Lorraine, would not be combat-ready until the evening of the eleventh day. The Germans did not complete their deployment in the west until 17 August. Due to the weak rail net in the Eifel, the 3rd Army would not be ready to march until 18 August. The 1st and 2nd Armies had to get around Liège. All four German right-wing armies then had a four- to six-day road march to reach the French border. The French therefore had about ten to twelve days to win a battle in Lorraine before the German right wing could be engaged.

As planned, the Franco-Russian armies attacked on 14 August, secured the initiative and forced the Germans on to the defensive both in the west and east. The initial battles, at Stallupönen and Tannenberg in the east, and Alsace and Lorraine in the west, were all fought on German territory. Of the four major land powers, the Germans were the last to begin major offensive operations, and then with only five of their eight armies: the German right wing did not begin its advance until 18 August.

Alsace & Lorraine

The French launched an attack with the VII CA towards Belfort on 7 August, which the Germans quickly threw back into France. The French attacked with their 1st and 2nd Armies into Lorraine on 14 August. Moltke initially believed that this was the French main attack, conducted with some thirty-eight to forty divisions, exactly as the French had done in his 1906 *Generalstabsreise West*. He therefore ordered the 5th Army to 'be prepared' to move south-west to counter-attack through Metz against the French left flank, while the 4th Army would also 'be prepared' to move south-west to cover the right flank and rear of the 5th Army. The six newly raised ersatz divisions were ordered to Lorraine to reinforce the 6th and 7th Armies.

Such a massive French attack in Lorraine would in fact have caused the Germans difficulties. The German 1st Army was already moving across the Meuse, and the 2nd Army too was moving west. Both armies would have been unable to participate in the main battle. The 3rd Army might have been shifted by rail to Alsace and Lorraine, as it was in many of Schlieffen's last exercises, but given the weak rail net in the Eifel, this would have consumed considerable time. On the other hand, the Germans were confident that they could still defeat this attack.[23]

Moltke soon discovered that the French were nowhere near as strong as he initially believed, and called off the 5th Army attack through Metz. On the French side, the German attack on Liège caused Joffre to move the French 5th Army by stages further to the north.

Moltke wanted to allow the French 1st and 2nd Armies to advance further into Lorraine, in order to give the German forces more time to redeploy for the counter-attack, as well as give the Germans more room to pursue before the retreating French reached the safety of their border fortifications. Moltke was

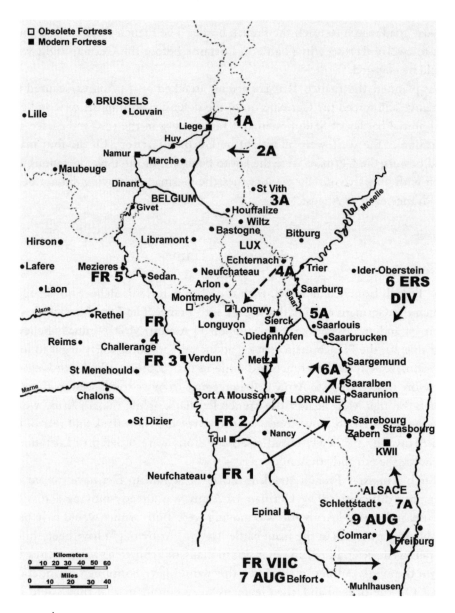

14–15 August

unable to impose his will on his subordinates, and finally granted the 6th Army chief of staff permission to counter-attack on 20 August. This was premature. Had the Germans waited, the French would have tried to continue the advance to the Saar. The 6th Army would have had the time to move its main attack to Metz against the French flank, and that attack would have hit French reserve divisions. Instead, the German 6th Army counter-attacked frontally against the French

2nd Army and drove it back with considerable loss, but the French were able to break contact and withdraw. The German 7th Army counter-attack against the French 1st Army met with much less success.

The Ardennes[24]

On 18 August the German 4th and 5th Armies began moving north-west. Based on their initial estimate that the Germans would deploy their mass of manoeuvre behind Metz, the French interpreted what little they could detect of this to mean that the German mass of manoeuvre was moving to join the forces that had attacked Liège. The German main attack would then be launched westward, along both the north and south banks of the Meuse. This would leave the German centre in the Ardennes weak, if not downright undefended. Joffre decided to launch his main attack with the 4th Army into the Ardennes, in order to cut off the German right wing. The 3rd Army would cover the 4th Army's right flank against Metz, and the 5th Army and the British Expeditionary Force would attack on the left.

Joffre ordered the 3rd and 4th Armies to begin advancing on the night of 20 August. This advance was detected by the German cavalry, which also blinded the French cavalry; aerial reconnaissance in the heavily forested Ardennes was difficult at best, and was further hampered by the weather. On the morning of 22 August the French 3rd and 4th Armies were convinced that any serious German forces were at least 30km to their front.

Moltke wanted the 5th Army to avoid contact until the 1st and 2nd Armies were in a position to engage the French left. As in Lorraine, he was unable to impose his will on the 5th Army chief of staff, who, like the 6th Army chief of staff, was determined to attack as soon as possible. The 5th Army therefore attacked in heavy fog on 22 August, even though there was a hole in the army centre that would not be filled by V RK until the afternoon. Nevertheless, the 5th Army gained complete operational surprise and won a tactical victory over the French 3rd Army. On the French 3rd Army left flank, the 8th Division was destroyed at Virton, as was most of the 7th Division at Ethe (both from IV CA). In the army centre, the V CA was in full retreat by noon, as was the VI CA on the army right by the afternoon.

German tactical success was not transformed into a decisive operational victory due to errors at the army and corps levels. Fear of a French counter-attack from Verdun deterred the 5th Army from turning the right flank of the French 3rd Army and penetrating the army position in depth: the French VI CA was merely pushed to the rear. The German XIII AK had half a day to penetrate

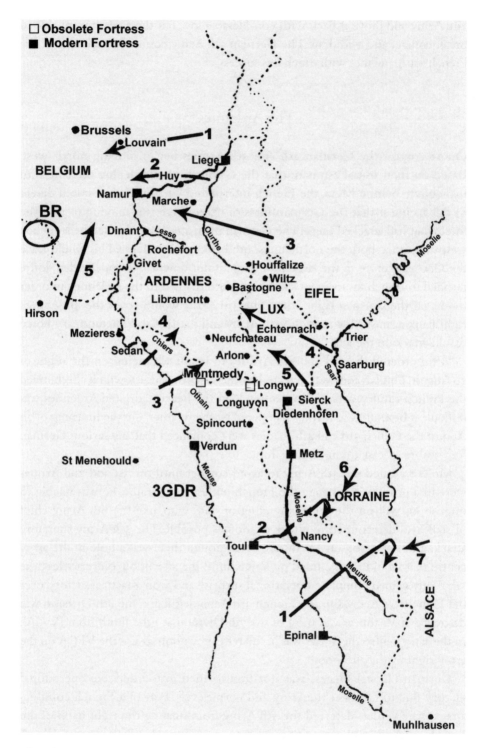

18-20 August

the French 3rd Army centre; it failed to do so, preferring 'safety first' – waiting until the situation had been 'clarified'.

The German 4th Army only learned of the German 5th Army's intent to attack early on the morning of 22 August, and then practically by accident, when a staff officer from the 5th Army's V AK requested 4th Army assistance in covering the V AK's open right flank. The 4th Army had only two active army and one reserve corps that could fight on 22 August; the other two corps were far to the north and east and could not arrive until 23 August.

Thanks in large part to the German 5th Army's premature attack, Joffre's plan had succeeded; he had concentrated five corps of the 4th Army, including the Colonial Corps, the best corps in the French army, in his main attack against the weak German centre – three German corps, one of which was a reserve corps. Nevertheless, the French 4th Army ran into a buzz saw. On the army right flank, the French II Corps was bottled up while marching on a single road in a deep valley and could not break through. This exposed the right flank of the 3rd Colonial Division which was surrounded and destroyed by the Germans at Rossignol. The German XVIII RK surrounded and destroyed the 5th Colonial Brigade at Neufchâteau, assisted by the inertia of the French XII CA, which uncovered the 5th Colonial left flank, while the defeat of the 3rd Colonial Division uncovered the brigade right. XII CA also exposed the right flank of the French 33rd Division (XVII CA), which was destroyed at Bertrix by the German 21st Division. On the French 4th Army left flank, the French XI CA failed to inflict a decisive defeat on the 50th Brigade of the German 25th Infantry Division; instead, the second brigade of the 25th Division, the 49th, turned the XI CA right flank and forced it to retreat. The outnumbered German 4th Army had decisively defeated the French 4th Army, which was conducting Joffre's main attack.

'Common knowledge' holds that the French lost in the Ardennes because they conducted bayonet charges against dug-in German positions. In fact, all of these battles on 20–22 August were meeting engagements: the opposing armies were in movement in converging directions. The Germans won because they had superior reconnaissance, command and control and combined-arms tactics. French bayonet charges and German trenches had nothing to do with it.

The Sambre–Meuse

Until the Germans' right wing could begin forward movement the German commanders remained on pins and needles, concerned that the British and French might occupy a line in central Belgium from Antwerp to Namur.

On 8 August the intelligence estimate speculated that the British might be in Brussels, and on 9 August that the French I and II Corps might be at Brussels–Namur. But by 15 August German cavalry reconnaissance showed that this area was unoccupied.[25]

The Belgian army in general and the fortress of Liège in particular posed no obstacle to German forward movement. On 13 August (a day earlier than planned) the 1st Army began to advance from its deployment assembly areas north-east of Aachen, through Aachen, to cross the Meuse on 14 August. On 15 and 16 August it occupied a forward assembly area on the west side of both the Meuse and Liège. On 18 August the German right wing began to move west, with the 1st and 2nd Armies to the north of the Meuse following an impenetrable screen of cavalry provided by HKK 2, and the 3rd Army following HKK 1 to the south of the Meuse. Hustled along by the German cavalry, the Belgian army quickly withdrew to Antwerp. With the exception of a short battle at Tirlemont, which served to demonstrate German tactical superiority over the Belgians, the advance of the two German armies was a pure foot-march.

The 1st and 2nd Armies were halfway through Belgium by 20 August, but Belgian and French intelligence were having great difficulty penetrating the German cavalry screen and forming a picture of German strengths and locations.

German air reconnaissance had detected seven corps near the Sambre–Meuse, but did not understand that two of these were the British Expeditionary Force. Rather, the pre-war intelligence estimate said that the BEF would probably assemble in north-east France, near Lille, and OHL as well as the 1st and 2nd Army HQ stayed with this estimate.

Bülow's concept on 20 August was to attack the French on the Sambre frontally with the 2nd Army, while the 3rd Army crossed the Meuse to attack the French right and the 1st Army enveloped the French left. This required the German right wing to conduct an enormous left wheel. The German cavalry was completely out of position to turn the French left: HKK 2 had been sent on a wild goose chase towards Lille to try to find the British; HKK 1 had been squeezed out by the converging 2nd and 3rd Armies and was moving west behind the 2nd Army. The 3rd Army would not be in position until 23 August, the 1st not until 24 or 25 August. The 2nd Army was to wait on the north side of the Sambre until at least the 3rd Army was in position. The 1st Army complied with Bülow's directive reluctantly; Kluck and Kuhl resented being under Bülow's operational control and were still convinced that they would win great glory by destroying the British when they appeared at Lille.

On 21 August the 2nd Guard Division (Guard Corps, 2nd Army) commander found the Sambre crossings lightly held and, encouraged by Ludendorff, seized a bridgehead. This set off a general fight on 22 August along the Sambre between

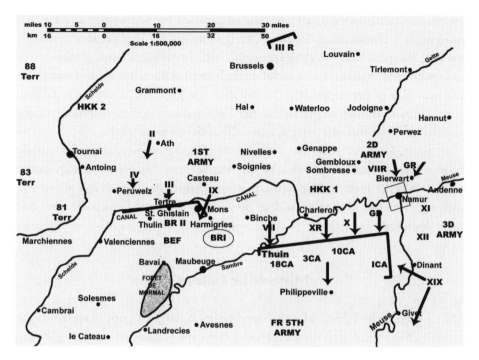

23 August

the German 2nd Army and the French 5th Army. Although the Germans enjoyed
tactical success almost everywhere, inflicting heavy casualties and throwing the
French back, Bülow was very concerned by the resistance his army had met.
Bülow now called for the 3rd Army to attack across the Meuse immediately on
22 August, which caught the 3rd Army unprepared and unable to comply. Bülow
was losing control of the battle.

By 22 August the BEF had closed up on the Canal du Centre. On 23 August it
was to swing north-east and attack on the left flank of the French 5th Army. On
learning near midnight of the French 5th Army's fight on 22 August, the attack
orders were cancelled, and Sir John French, the BEF commander, agreed to hold
his current position on 23 August, which was considerably north of the French
5th Army.

The fight between the German 2nd and French 5th Armies was renewed on
23 August, with the Germans pushing the French back. The 3rd Army's attack
across the Meuse, which was lined with cliffs, was unimaginative and made little
progress. Nevertheless, the 5th Army had been beaten and by that evening began
a general withdrawal.

The Germans defeated the French in the Battle of the Frontiers for
reinforcing reasons. The Germans benefited from superb cavalry reconnaissance/

counter-reconnaissance. Their doctrine emphasised fire superiority and fire and movement. German troops received excellent training at larger manoeuvre areas (MTAs). German troop-leading emphasised officer initiative (*Auftragstaktik*).

French reconnaissance was awful. French tactical doctrine did not recognise the necessity of fire superiority. In any case, the French did not have training areas adequate enough to practice tactics. French troop-leading emphasised rigid top-down command and control, especially at the division level.

In short, for forty years the German army had been preparing for mobile warfare. The French fancied they would win because they were naturally better soldiers and the heirs of Napoleon. In consequence, the French lost about five men for every two German casualties they inflicted. Several French divisions had been destroyed.

Mons & Le Cateau[26]

On 23 August the BEF held a V-shaped position, with I Corps oriented to the north behind the Canal du Centre and II Corps echeloned on its right rear, oriented north-east. This put the 3rd Division of I Corps at the apex of the V, which is where the German IX and III AK attacked. By the end of the day, the 3rd Division had been forced off the canal with heavy casualties. The BEF was saved from an even more serious defeat by the fact that the 1st Army leadership was still convinced they might be at Lille, and held up the III AK for four hours until Kluck and Kuhl could be absolutely sure that it was not. Tactically, the Germans had conducted an exemplary combined-arms battle. On the other hand, British cavalry, artillery and engineers failed to support the infantry. The British division, corps and army commanders and staffs were singularly ineffective: the British conducted a static defence based solely on rifle firepower. In spite of the strong British position behind a canal and in terrain offering plenty of cover, and of lurid British accounts of mowing the Germans down by rows, casualties were about equal, some 1,700 British and 2,000 German.

On 24 August the British defended a line 5km south of the Canal du Centre. Against a loss of 2,400 men, the Germans were able to inflict 2,600 further casualties on the British II Corps.

The subsequent British withdrawal was badly conducted. On 24 and 25 August the British failed to use effective rearguards: in two days' forced marching HKK 2 caught up with II Corps, as did the German 8 ID on the HKK 2 left.

II Corps was spared destruction only by an egregious error by Kluck and Kuhl, who convinced themselves that the BEF had withdrawn to the east, into the fortress of Maubeuge, a most unlikely course of action. On 25 August they therefore turned the 1st Army south-east, away from II Corps. Had Kluck and Kuhl merely continued the march in the only logical direction – south-west – then HKK 2 would have turned II Corps' left flank while IV AK and III AK (eight brigades) hit it in the front, and II Corps would have surely been destroyed. Instead, HKK 2 attacked the left side of II Corps, while one brigade of IV AK hit the II Corps centre and two brigades hit the right.

Nevertheless, II Corps took a fearful pounding. British tactical security was abysmal and the Germans appeared like a bolt from the blue directly in front of the British infantry. HKK 2 mauled the British 4th Division, while two regiments of German infantry and one of artillery crushed the II Corps right flank, destroying a British infantry brigade and capturing nearly half of the 3rd Division artillery.

Although the British enjoyed a significant superiority in men and guns, the Germans inflicted 7,800 British casualties at the cost of 2,900 German. In the withdrawal that afternoon and evening, II Corps units disintegrated down to platoon level. However, II Corps now got serious about retreating and, in two days and nights of almost continuous movement, broke contact. The BEF commander, Sir John French, was thoroughly shaken and began to consider withdrawing his army altogether.

The Moltke Plan

On the German side, the dreaded crisis in East Prussia seemed to have arrived. On 20 August the 8th Army reported that it had lost the Battle of Gumbinnen, and it appeared to Moltke by that evening that the 8th Army commander intended to abandon East Prussia and withdraw to the Vistula River. Moltke relieved the 8th Army commander on 22 August, replacing him with General von Hindenburg, and in addition sent Ludendorff to the east as Hindenburg's chief of staff. On the same day, the 8th Army operations officer, Colonel Hoffman, issued the orders that would lead to Tannenberg. On 24 August the 8th Army reported that it was engaged with the Russian 2nd Army. On the evening of 27 August the 8th Army reported that it had annihilated two Russian corps. The final victory at Tannenberg was not won until 29 August.

The original mission of the German 6th Army in Lorraine foresaw a follow-on attack between Toul and Verdun to begin the penetration of the fortress line. Instead, Moltke ordered the 6th Army to attempt to cut off the French 1st Army, a virtually hopeless undertaking. Beginning on 24 August, the French would succeed in stabilising the situation in Lorraine.

On 24 August Moltke knew that he had won the Battle of the Frontiers. The French army no longer had the ability to take the offensive. Moltke issued warning orders preparatory to transferring six corps east. But immediately Moltke had second thoughts. He reduced the force to be sent east to three corps, then only two: the Guard Reserve Corps from the 2nd Army and XI AK from the 3rd Army. The German armies continued to pursue the defeated French and British.

On 27 August Moltke issued his first general operations order.[27] It said that all the French active army corps had been engaged and had suffered heavy casualties and the French were withdrawing to the south and south-west, 'towards Paris'. As the German pre-war intelligence estimate had anticipated, and as Moltke expressly stated, the French strategy was to delay along successive river lines into the interior of France and hope that Russian pressure would force the Germans to shift forces to the east. The five armies on the German right wing were to pursue to the south-west in the general direction of Paris in order to occupy as much French territory as they could and prevent the reconstitution of the battered French units. The French would defend on the Aisne and Marne, which might force the Germans to turn south.

This order did not foresee a decisive result, such as forcing the French into Switzerland. Indeed, the 27 August order could be valid only for three or four days' advance at most, because Fortress Paris was far too strong to be simply overrun and was sure to force a change of mission and direction.

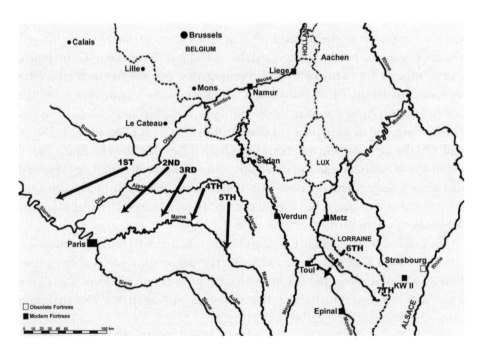

27 August OHL Operation Order

Since Moltke continued the advance in the west, transferring two corps to the east was a mistake. Pursuing the French further would obviously lengthen the German open right flank. Moltke needed every man for his campaign in the west.

Moltke had left all previous planning behind. The pre-war intelligence estimate said that the French would never withdraw towards Paris, as Moltke now assumed, but towards the south, which was in fact exactly what the French were doing. Moltke did not shift significant forces to the east, as Schlieffen would have done, and he had called off the 6th Army attack on the French fortress line, as Beseler would have done. We are now dealing with Moltke's very own planning, which was short term and purely opportunistic. In the next eight days his intent would dramatically change twice.

From Schlieffen's two-front war games, it would be safe to say that on 24 August Schlieffen would have transferred seven corps (if not more) to the east for a massive counter-attack. The German armies in the west would have halted, re-established their lines of communication, brought forward replacements and reduced Fortress Antwerp. The Germans won at Tannenberg with nine divisions. The forces Moltke sent east had to foot-march from Namur to the railheads at Aachen. Nevertheless, they arrived in East Prussia on 2 September. Had Moltke transferred forces from the left wing – which were in the immediate vicinity of the German railheads – they could have arrived even earlier. The Battle of the Masurian Lakes took place from 5 to 13 September. With twenty-three German divisions (instead of thirteen), the battle would have been a catastrophe for the Russians. It is easy to imagine that the Russian 1st Army would have been annihilated, as in Schlieffen's east front war games. Schlieffen would then have been free to once again use Germany's interior position and rail net to transfer the mass of the East Prussian forces back west, to conduct a renewed offensive, reinforced by six newly raised reserve corps that were available in October. This offensive probably would have resulted in a second defeat of the French armies, followed by a Beseler-style attack on the French fortress line between Verdun and Toul, from the front and rear, and the destruction of those forts which would link up the German left and right wings and encircle Verdun.

Allied Withdrawal, German Pursuit

In the centre, the successive river lines on the Franco-Belgian border facilitated French delaying tactics. However, the German 3rd, 4th and 5th Armies made steady progress. On the German right, the pursuit by the 1st and 2nd Armies was more effective.

The French 6th Army and Territorial divisions attempted to assemble on the German right flank. From 27 to 29 August they were roughly handled and pushed back by the German 1st Army. The French 5th Army counter-attacked on the Oise River on 29 August in order to cover the withdrawal of the BEF, and was thrown back by the German 2nd Army. On 31 August the German 1st Army had no serious enemy forces to the west, and turned south to conduct a 'parallel pursuit' of the French 5th Army, attempting to turn the French left flank. The 1st Army made prodigious forced marches, but was unable to catch the French and British, who could use the French rail net to assist and hasten their withdrawal. The French were also able to replace their casualties from depots that were now close at hand; German replacements would not begin to arrive until the second week of September.

Nevertheless, the entire Allied left was still in full retreat. The lead elements of the German 1st Army were now in front of the 2nd Army and reached the Marne on 2 September. Moltke was aware that the French were transferring forces from their right wing to Paris, and was concerned that the German right flank was vulnerable to a counter-attack from Paris. Moltke issued an order that day to the two right wing armies, instructing the 1st Army to act as flank guard, echeloned behind the 2nd Army. The 2nd Army was to turn the French left flank and push the French army into Switzerland.

This was the closest that Moltke ever got to the Schlieffen plan. From 2 to 5 September he tried to turn the French left flank. The 2nd Army was never remotely close to being able to do so. The 6th and 7th Armies in Lorraine had been stopped, the 5th Army in front of Verdun and the 4th and 3rd Armies, to its

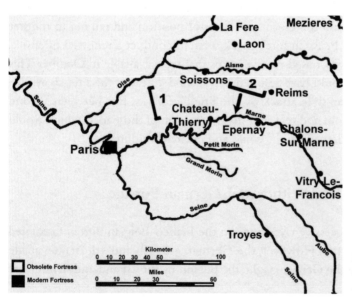

Moltke's 2 September Order to 1st and 2nd Armies

west, had been brought to a crawl. The Germans had an enormous open flank all the way to the English Channel.

The 1st Army ignored Moltke's order and left only a weak reserve corps (with three brigades) to guard against Paris. Kluck and Kuhl imagined that the French left flank was within their reach and pushed the 1st Army over the Marne and to the south-east of Paris. The French and British easily avoided the 1st Army's advance.

Even before the French began their Marne counter-attack, it had become clear not only to Moltke, but even to Kluck and Kuhl, that the German offensive had reached the *Clausewitzian* 'culmination point'; that is, it could proceed no further.

On 5 September Moltke issued his second general order of the campaign.[28] The 1st and 2nd Armies were to take up defensive positions facing west, the 1st between the Oise and the Marne, the 2nd between the Marne and the Seine. The 3rd, 4th and 5th Armies were to continue the attack south. But the principal attack would be delivered by the 5th Army, against the rear of the French fortress line between Verdun and Toul. This would open a corridor allowing the 6th Army to pass to the west of the French fortress line and give the German army a short and protected line of supply. In effect, Moltke had reverted to Beseler's 1900 plan.

In the real January–February 1906 Schlieffen plan the 5 September 1914 situation would never occur. In the real Schlieffen plan map the German centre stopped north of Paris while the 1st Army and the ersatz divisions swung to the west of Paris.

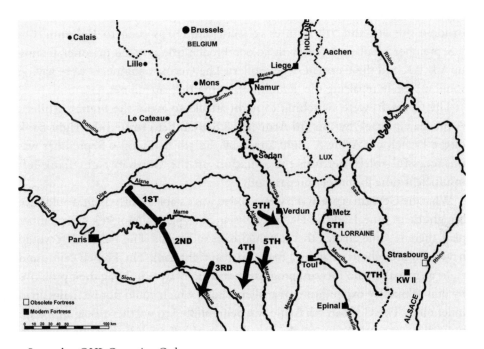

5 September OHL Operation Order

That Moltke's 5 September plan was stillborn was due to yet another act of insubordination by the 1st Army. On 6 September the French 6th Army advanced east from Paris and caught the 1st Army in the weak right flank. The 1st Army refused to fall back to its assigned defensive position and instead attacked the French. The 1st Army attack could not result in a decisive German victory because at any time the French 6th Army could simply withdraw behind the Paris fortifications. It would appear that the 1st Army leadership was willing to follow any course of action that might disguise the fact that it had been completely outmanoeuvred by the French.

The 1st Army attack left a gap between the left flank of the 1st Army and the right flank of the 2nd, allowing the French to push the 2nd Army east, further widening the gap between the two German armies. To add insult to injury, the BEF began to push into the gap, eventually forcing the 1st Army to retreat. The 1st Army's failure to destroy the BEF between 23 and 26 August was now fatal for the entire German right wing, which was forced to withdraw on 9 September.

The distinguishing characteristic of the French Marne 'offensive' was the prodigious quantity of artillery ammunition that the French were expending, smothering the German infantry and preventing it from advancing. Aside from the French and British advance into the gap between the 1st and 2nd Armies, the French attack was making no progress at all, indeed the French were hanging on to their positions for dear life.

Otherwise, the German situation was improving. On 5 September Moltke ordered the 6th and 7th Armies to send one corps each to Belgium. On 7 September Maubeuge fell, with 50,000 French troops taken prisoner, freeing up VII RK and the German siege artillery. The German engineers were having some success in repairing the demolitions to the Belgian rail net.

The Germans were switching to night attacks to avoid the French artillery. A pre-dawn attack by the 3rd Army on 8 September crushed the right flank of the French 9th Army. A night attack by the 5th Army on 9 September was unsuccessful solely because the situation on the German right flank left insufficient time for proper preparations.

What the German army in the west needed was a stable front, which would have bought them time. Had the 1st Army executed its part in Moltke's 5 September plan, there is some chance that it would have succeeded. The French left would have been brought to a halt by a firm German right flank. The French centre and right were making no forward progress; indeed, they were holding their positions by dint of massive expenditure of artillery shells, which could not be maintained indefinitely. The German 7th Army was being shifted to northern Belgium. With more time, the 5th Army might have broken the French fortress line. Verdun would have been surrounded and the mass of the 6th Army could have been brought forward. Even without such an optimistic scenario, it is certain that, had the 1st Army obeyed Moltke's 5 September orders, the German position would have been far stronger than it was after the Battle of the Marne.

After initial indecisive Austrian victories, the Russians crushed the Austrians on 11 September and forced them to retreat about 150km. The Central Powers' position in the east would only be saved by Ludendorff's manoeuvre in November at Lodz, which bears a striking similarity to Schlieffen's 1903 *Generalstabsreise Ost*.

Notes

1 B. Menning, *Bayonets Before Bullets: The Imperial Russian Army 1861–1914* (Bloomington and Indianapolis, IN, 1992), p. 242.

2 W.C. Fuller Jr, 'The Russian Empire' in *Knowing One's Enemies: Intelligence Assessment Before the Two World Wars*, E.R. May (ed.) (Princeton, 1984), p. 111.

3 J.J.C. Joffre, *Memoires* (Paris, 1932), I, p. 129.

4 D.N. Collins, 'The Franco-Russian Alliance and the Russian Railways' in *Historical Journal* 16 (1973), p. 782.

5 Joffre, *Memoires*, pp. 131–3; Fuller, 'Russian Empire', p. 104.

6 L.C.F. Fuller, 'The Russian Mobilization in 1914' in *The War Plans of the Great Powers*, P. Kennedy (ed.) (London, 1979), p. 257.

7 *Les Armées Françaises*, I, I, I, pp. 21–2.

8 Ministère de la Guerre, État-Major de la Armée, Service Historique, *Les Armées Françaises dans la Grande Guerre, Tome I, 1er Volume*.

9 Ibid., pp. 19ff, *Annexe*, pp. 21ff, *Cartes* 7, 8.

10 *Les Armées Françaises*, I, I, *Annexes*, pp. 21–31.

11 Joffre, *Memoires*, p. 129.

12 Ibid., p. 234.

13 *Les Armées Françaises*, I, I, I, pp. 86–7.

14 Greiner, 'Nachrichten' in Zuber, *German War Planning*, pp. 38–48.

15 Baare, *Hauptmann*, 'Neue taktische Anschauungen im französischen Heere' in *Vierteljahreshefte für Truppenführung und Heereskunde*, IX Jahrgang 3. Heft (1914), pp. 396–418; 'Taktische Fragen aus den französischen Armeemanöver 1913', IX Jahrgang 1. Heft (1914), pp. 390–5.

16 Generallandesarchiv Karlsruhe (hereafter GLA Karlsruhe), GLA 456/553 (XV Corps), *Nachrichten #2*. Also Haeften, 'Der deutsche Generalstabschef in der Zeit der Spannung Juli 1914' in *Deutsches Offizierblatt*, XXVIII Jahrgang Nr 24, 24 Juli 1924, pp. 185–8.

17 GLA Karlsruhe, GLA 456/553, *Nachrichten #3, 4, 6*.

18 Ibid., 4, 5.

19 Ibid., *Nachrichten #8*.

20 Ibid., *Nachrichten #6*.

21 *Weltkrieg* I, pp. 34, 103.

22 *Les Armées Françaises*, I, I, I, pp. 81–3.

23 GLA Karlsruhe, GLA 456/204, Stein to Krafft von Dellmensingen, 13 August 1914.

24 T. Zuber, *The Battle of the Frontiers: Ardennes 1914* (Tempus, 2007).

25 GLA Karlsruhe, GLA 456/553, *Nachrichten #13, 14, 20*.

26 T. Zuber, *The Mons Myth: A Reassessment of the Battle* (The History Press, 2010).

27 GLA Karlsruhe, GLA 456/659.

28 Ibid.

CONCLUSIONS

Document RH 61/v.96 (German War Planning 1893–1914) gives us the first real insight into the war planning of Schlieffen from 1904 to 1906 and the younger Moltke from 1906 to 1914. It may well give us the only information that we will ever possess concerning German war planning immediately prior to the Great War.

Both the German official history and the 'Schlieffen School' (Kuhl, Groener, Boetticher, Zoellner, et al.) maintained that the Schlieffen plan was the German war plan from 1906 to 1914. RH 61/v.96 shows that this was wrong. For example, in 1912/13 the sole German plan was the *Grosser Ostaufmarsch*, not the Schlieffen plan. RH 61/v.96 also confirms that the 1914/15 plan had practically nothing in common with the Schlieffen plan.

Deteriorating German Strategic Situation

From 1898 until 1913 the German national policy was to build a High Seas Fleet second only to the British Royal Fleet, obtain colonies and establish a say in world affairs. This led to an Anglo-German battleship-building race, which soon became an international naval arms race. The navy consumed Germany's disposable defence spending.

The mission of the German army during this period was to preserve the European military balance of power and status quo. Initially, the German force structure was adequate for that purpose. There was no strategic reason to increase the size of the German army and no financial resources available in any case. Therefore, the Germans were not going to launch a continental war. The proof of this proposition can be seen in German policy in 1904 and 1905, while Russia was involved in the Manchurian War with Japan. The Germans did not use this opportunity to attack either the Russians or the French, but rather to expand German international influence by asserting their rights in Morocco. Neither did the Germans use the Moroccan crisis as a pretext for a war against France.

The deterioration of the German military position between 1906 and 1914 is reflected in the German intelligence estimates and war plans. The odds against Germany became steadily worse. The number of enemies increased, those enemies became stronger, while the number of friends became fewer and the principal friend, Austria, weaker.

The Anglo-French Entente added six British divisions to the number the German army would have to face. Moreover, it was uncertain where these divisions would appear: the North Sea coast, Antwerp and northern France were equally possible. From 1906 to 1914 IX Reserve Corps would initially be deployed in coast defence in north Germany. The Anglo-French Entente also subtracted Italy from the list of Germany's possible allies. Italy was terrified of the damage that the British navy could wreak on her coastline, colonies, navy and trade. This meant that the Italian army would not be available to defend Alsace.

In 1915 the Italians began the war that they really wanted to fight – against Austria.

The Austrian annexation of Bosnia-Herzegovina in 1908 set in motion a chain of events that would involve Austria in a war with Serbia and Germany in a war with Russia. The German intelligence estimates recognised that the Austrians were faced with at least a two-front war, but the German war planners were unable to do anything about it. German foreign policy had attached Germany to Austria.

By 1912 the Germans acknowledged that they had lost the naval arms race with Britain, which was an advantage for the army. Spurred by the Balkan and Moroccan crises of 1911–13, the German Reichstag approved increases in the army budget in 1911 and 1912, which did little more than allow holes in the existing force structure to be filled in, such as the creation of MG companies. The defence bill of 1913 increased the German army by 58,500 men in October 1913 (and 58,500 in October 1914). This was too little, too late.

The Russian economy was booming. In June 1914 the Russian 'Great Programme' was approved, which would have increased the Russian standing army by 400,000 men (25 per cent) by 1917, making it twice as strong as the German 1914 army. More important, only two new corps would be created (about 60,000 men). The rest of these troops would bring the peacetime strength of the Russian army to wartime levels, obviating the need for mobilisation and increasing the speed of deployment. The French 1913 Three Years' Law kept three conscript classes under the colours instead of two. Again, the increased manpower went towards building up the existing active army units, not in creating new ones. This would speed French mobilisation and deployment appreciably.

The Austrian strategic position had deteriorated alarmingly. Due to the Balkan wars, Turkey was no longer a stabilising factor in the Balkans; Austria had to face the prospect of a two-front war against Russia and Serbia, and had changed its war plan correspondingly. Unfortunately, Colonel Redl betrayed this plan to the Russians.

The Russian deployment became steadily faster. From 1911 to 1914 the Russians and the French were both shifting from a defensive to an offensive strategy. By 1914 the Germans were faced with the certainty of a two-front war and on both fronts the German army would be seriously outnumbered. There were indicators that the French and Russians would launch near-simultaneous offensives. When the French attacked into Lorraine on the fifteenth day of mobilisation, the Germans were not surprised. Neither are there any indications that the Germans were surprised by the Russian attack into East Prussia on the fifteenth day of mobilisation: German intelligence estimates had been warning since 1911 that the Russians had speeded up their mobilisation and deployment. Assertions that the Germans did not expect the Russians to attack until weeks later have no basis in pre-war German planning or intelligence estimates. Given Austrian and German weakness in the east, a crisis on that front was predictable. The only benefit the Germans had to balance the odds was superior tactical doctrine and training.

The German concept was to use their interior position to mass against one enemy, and then use their tactical superiority to defeat him. This would allow the Germans to once again use their interior position and rail mobility to mass against a second enemy, and so on. As Schlieffen noted, the Germans could not repeat this procedure indefinitely; Germany needed decisive victories. These were most likely in the east.

The Russians and the French understood the German strategic situation fully. Their intent was to prevent the Germans from utilising their interior position by attacking simultaneously, before the Germans could attack. In the case of tactical defeat, both the French and the Russians would retreat into the interior of their countries, giving their ally time to attack the outnumbered Germans and draw them away from their railheads. There would be no strategic surprises on either side.

If War Had Not Come in 1914

Had war not broken out in 1914, the European military arms race would have continued with increased intensity. The Three Years' Law was the last gasp for the French army; no further French manpower increases were possible. In fact, there was significant opposition to the Three Years' Law and the German 1914 intelligence estimate speculated that the French might not be able to maintain it.

The Russian Great Programme would have increased the size of their peacetime army and its deployment speed.

The Austro-Germans had lost the arms race to this point, but there was every indication that they recognised the danger of their position, and the Austro-Germans had plenty of room for improvement. Between mid-August and mid-October 1914 the Germans had enough untrained manpower to easily raise six new reserve corps (about 180,000 men). What the Germans lacked was the time and cadres to train them adequately. If the Germans were given the opportunity in peacetime to add just six more trained corps to their order of battle – and the passing of the Russian Great Programme in June 1914 would surely have forced the Germans to do so (even the German socialists hated and feared the Tsarist government) – then the strategic situation would have been radically altered. The addition of even six corps (twelve divisions) would have fundamentally changed the German strategic calculus, which in 1914 was based on the fact that the Germans would be outnumbered on both fronts. The Germans would have been able to deploy eighty divisions in the west against some sixty-three French. The French would not have been able to convince themselves – as they did in 1914 – that they at least had numerical parity and that it was practical to launch an offensive.

The French might have been forced to adopt a strategic defensive outright; if the French had attacked, there was a good chance it would be a spectacular failure. A German attack would have had a far greater chance of quick success. Under these circumstances, the Russians would have been far from enthusiastic for an attack on East Prussia. Six more German corps would have derailed the Franco-Russian plan for simultaneous attacks on Germany. The Germans would have gained the strategic initiative. Due to Germany's interior position and rail net, they would have been free to mass on one front or the other, at the time and place of their own choosing. Giving the German army the initiative was the recipe for a Franco-Russian catastrophe.

The strategic situation in 1914 was optimal for the Entente. The German strategic position was nearing a 'worst possible case' scenario. It was very much in the Franco-Russian interest to fight in 1914, when Germany was still faced with the prospect of being outnumbered on both fronts. In the near future that might no longer have been true.

German War Planning 1904–06

In midsummer 1904 it appeared to German intelligence that the Manchurian War would cause the French to assume a defensive posture and extend their left flank further north (which was erroneous). Therefore, the German 1905/06 *Aufmarsch* I extended the right flank as far as the Dutch border.

The only major innovation in Schlieffen's 1906/07 actual planning was his recognition that the British would probably send troops to assist the French. There is no evidence of a radically different Schlieffen plan in the 1906/07 *Aufmarschanweisung*.

Based on the Schlieffen plan dogma, it is 'common knowledge' that Schlieffen had an offensive war plan. This assertion is not supported by Schlieffen's actual war plans or war games. Schlieffen held two *Generalstabsreisen West* in 1904 and one in 1905; in all three exercises the French were attacking. In his 1905 *Kriegsspiel*, his last and greatest exercise, both the French and the Russians were attacking. In all four exercises the initial battles took place in German or Belgian territory. There is no evidence that Schlieffen ever played an outright offensive into France or Russia. In all of Schlieffen's exercises the Germans counter-attacked against French and Russian offensives. This would be very curious if, as 'common knowledge' maintains, Schlieffen had spent fifteen years perfecting the Schlieffen plan for an offensive against France.

In the 1905/06 *Aufmarsch* I, for a war against France alone the Germans could deploy seventy-two divisions against an estimated fifty-five French. This would seem to be a great enough numerical superiority for the Germans to have launched a preventive war against France. The Germans did nothing of the kind.

If Germans in general, and Schlieffen in particular, were congenital aggressors, and the Russians were completely defenceless in the west due to their war in Manchuria, as 'common knowledge' and the German war guilt school maintains, it follows that the Germans should have launched a preventive war in the east (as the elder Moltke had wanted to do in 1887). This was so far from German intentions that, though Schlieffen had an *Ostaufmarsch* II in 1900/01 and 1901/02 with forty-four divisions in the east, he did not even have a plan for an *Ostaufmarsch* against Russia in 1905/06 and 1906/07. Instead, Schlieffen once again in 1905 played both an operational study and a war game with the scenario of a Russian attack into East Prussia.

The remarkable thing about the Schlieffen plan was that Schlieffen maintained that in a one-front war against France alone the Germans needed ninety-six divisions – twenty-four divisions that they did not have – and even this might not be enough. Even if Schlieffen wanted to conduct a war of aggression against France, the Schlieffen plan was an open admission that he was one-third short of the force he needed to do so.

Moltke's War Planning 1907–14

In 1907/08 to 1908/09 Moltke only tinkered with Schlieffen's real planning. Moltke's 1906 and 1908 *Generalstabsreisen West* are firmly in line with Schlieffen's actual planning and exercises. Nothing during this period shows any influence of the 'Schlieffen plan'. Moltke's major innovation was the inclusion in the 1908/09 plan of the requirement to take Liège 'quickly'.

The crisis from October 1908 to March 1909, caused by the Austrian annexation of Bosnia-Herzegovina, resulted in major changes in Moltke's war planning. Germany was faced with the possibility that the war would start in the east or the west, either of which could immediately develop into a two-front war which Britain would join. In 1909/10 there was now an *Aufmarsch* I for a war in which all seventy-four divisions deployed against France, and an *Aufmarsch* Ia in which sixty-four divisions deployed in the west and ten in the east. Moltke revived Schlieffen's *Grosser Ostaufmarsch* with forty-two divisions deploying in the east. The 1910/11 and 1911/12 deployment plans were essentially the same.

Moltke's *Ostaufmarsch* puts paid to all manner of myths concerning German war planning. It is now clear that the Schlieffen plan was not the single perfect war plan: Moltke massively modified German planning to conform to the changing political situation. In addition, it has been 'common knowledge' that the elder Moltke originated the *Ostaufmarsch*, and the fact that the younger Moltke cancelled it is proof that the younger Moltke wanted to launch an aggressive war in the west. In fact, the elder Moltke, Schlieffen and the younger Moltke all adopted and then rejected the *Ostaufmarsch* for reasons unrelated to an aggressive war in the west.

Beginning in 1910, the Austro-German position in the east deteriorated. The Russian army was rapidly improving. The 1910/11 plan stated that in case of *Aufmarsch* I, the thirteen divisions in East Prussia might not be able to defend the province. On the other hand, although the German army had risen to seventy-nine divisions by forming new reserve divisions, the Austrian army stagnated.

The second Moroccan crisis lasted from June to November 1911. That year, the French and Russians agreed to conduct a joint offensive against Germany on the sixteenth day of mobilisation. While the Germans had no direct knowledge of this, the German 1911 west front intelligence estimate said that the Russian army had completely recovered, that the British would support the French and, in consequence, French confidence had increased dramatically. The 1911/12 German war plan said that it might be necessary to fortify Berlin. It was suspected that in a crisis the Russians would conduct a secret mobilisation in order to speed up their deployment.

The German 1912 intelligence estimates continued to show deterioration in the German strategic situation. Russian industry was booming and their military capabilities were improving. The French were beginning to switch from a defensive-offensive doctrine to one of outright offence. A 'new school' of French officers expected the Germans to attack through Belgium.

This intelligence estimate was still in force in August 1914. It is clear that the Germans did not expect a quick, decisive victory in the west. The French were prepared to retreat far into their interior, drawing the Germans after them and giving the Russians the opportunity to overwhelm the Germans in the east.

The First Balkan War Crisis lasted throughout the winter of 1912/13. The Germans decided that the Russians were secretly mobilising. The German war plan was again hastily revised to provide for a war that began in the east, with France at least initially being neutral. There was no concept of the operation in the east, probably because the Russian mobilisation was already far advanced. In the west, the Germans would deploy from their mobilisation stations to counter-attack against the French offensive. According to the 'Schlieffen plan' dogma, the Germans should have responded to any crisis by preparing to conduct an aggressive war against France. That was obviously not the case. In the 1913/14 plan any illusions that Germany might be able to fight a one-front 'Schlieffen plan' war were abandoned. In the next war, Germany would have to face France, Russia and Britain.

The Austro-Germans would be outnumbered on both fronts. The Germans expected that sixty-eight German divisions in the west would be opposed by seventy-five French, British and Belgian divisions. The nine German divisions in East Prussia and forty-nine Austrian divisions would be opposed by a hundred Russian and twelve Serbian divisions: in total 128 Austro-German divisions against 187 Entente. While the German divisions may have been of the highest quality, the Austrian divisions were the weakest.

'Common Knowledge' & the Survival of the Schlieffen Plan

'The Schlieffen Plan Reconsidered', which set off the Schlieffen plan debate, was published in *War in History* in the autumn of 1999. *Inventing the Schlieffen Plan* was published in 2002. It received numerous reviews, including *The Times* Literary Supplement. The historical section of the German army called an international Schlieffen Plan conference at Potsdam in 2004. Schlieffen's planning documents were published in *German War Planning 1891–1914: Sources and Interpretations*. The Schlieffen plan debate continues in *War in History* and is the subject of about fourteen articles to date.

None of this is reflected in that repository of 'common knowledge', Wikipedia. The author of the Schlieffen plan Wikipedia entry recites every Schlieffen plan cliché; indeed, he agrees that 'this article seems like tired conventional wisdom rather than a reflection of modern scholarship'.[1]

The article naturally features the *West Point Atlas* map. According to the Wikipedia author, the Schlieffen plan was written for a two-front war, even though the first line of the original document says 'War against France', that is, a one-front war. He seems unaware that Paris was a huge fortress and says that the plan provided for the capture of Paris in thirty-nine days. The French army was to be annihilated near Paris in exactly forty-two days. This was supposedly the length of time the Germans thought it would take the Russians to mobilise their army. He relies on his own imagination and old secondary literature and there is no indication that he has ever even read the Schlieffen plan *Denkschrift*, much less the rest of the German and French planning documents.

Indeed, 'common knowledge' experts on the Schlieffen plan always feel free to embellish the story without the need for evidence. The Wikipedia author says that after the Franco-British Entente was signed in 1904, Kaiser Wilhelm ordered Schlieffen to prepare a plan for a two-front war. One wonders what the Wikipedia author thinks the German war plan had been in the ten years since 1894, when the French and Russians finalised their alliance and a two-front war was a certainty.

Wikipedia is not alone in relying exclusively on 'common knowledge' concerning German war planning. Holger Herwig has a long history of repeating the entire Schlieffen plan dogma.[2] He wrote in 2002 that the Schlieffen plan depended on a rigid timetable, which would end in complete victory on the forty-second day of mobilisation.[3] This drew the attention of Terence Holmes, who said:

> He [Herwig] gives his background summary of the Schlieffen plan 'at the risk of overkill', implying that the details are so well known and so firmly established that they hardly need to be gone over yet again. What he offers is indeed a familiar and widely accepted reading, but it is nevertheless one that ought to be reexamined rather than simply restated ... Of course, if something could become true by dint of mere repetition, then the six-week theory would now be incontrovertible, so often has it been reiterated.[4]

Holmes easily shows that no such timetable was actually in the Schlieffen plan *Denkschrift*. The six-week figure was grafted on later, and Holmes notes that where the six-week figure came from at all is murky.

In 1997 Herwig said that the Schlieffen plan provided for 'a single army' to be deployed in East Prussia. In 2002 Herwig reduced this to 'a single corps'. Holmes makes two apposite observations. First, there is a significant difference between a corps and an army. Second:

> In the end, though, this is not really an issue. Neither alternative is compatible with the Schlieffen plan of December 1905, which makes no reference whatever to an eastern deployment ... the Schlieffen plan not only used the whole of the German field army in the west, it also called for a considerable expansion of that force to make it strong enough for the task of annihilating the French army. There was no question of having any units left over as spare capacity for deployment in the east.

Holmes notes that the Schlieffen plan was based on *Aufmarsch* I for a one-front war in the west:

> The plan was predicated on a situation when there would be no enemy in the east. It also explains why there was no six-week deadline for completing the western offensive: the speed of the Russian advance was irrelevant to a plan devised for a war scenario excluding Russia.

Herwig introduced his 2009 book, *The Marne 1914*, by trumpeting that 'a massive research effort' would allow him to take a 'fresh and revealing look at the Marne'.[5] That fresh look did not extend to the Schlieffen plan. Herwig repeats the Schlieffen plan myth *in toto*:

> The Germans gambled all on a brilliant operational concept devised by Chief of the General Staff Alfred von Schlieffen in 1905 and carried out (in revised form) by his successor, Helmuth von Moltke, in 1914: a lightning forty-day wheel through Belgium and northern France ending in a victorious entry march into Paris, followed by a redeployment of German armies to the east to halt the Russian steamroller. It was a single roll of the dice.[6]

Herwig is now back to 'a single army ... would hold off the Russians' in East Prussia.[7] He still uses the *West Point Atlas* Schlieffen plan map. Herwig does not cite any source to support this assertion, which, like the Wikipedia article, is based on 'common knowledge' and not the Schlieffen plan *Denkschrift* or Moltke's plans and orders.

Herwig has ignored Holmes' arguments completely: Holmes isn't mentioned in Herwig's footnotes or bibliography, not even Holmes' two 'Schlieffen Plan' debate articles in *War in History*. (Full disclosure: Herwig gives *Inventing the*

Schlieffen Plan one line, so that he can summarily dismiss it.) Herwig has changed nothing from his 1997 and 2002 descriptions of the Schlieffen plan; even the verbiage is repeated ('a single roll of the dice'). Herwig's manner of proving his case – simply ignoring the opposition – would not be permitted in a high school debate tournament.

Herwig has good reason to ignore Holmes. Holmes' case is airtight. Herwig is on record for over a decade as having presented a demonstrably and fundamentally erroneous description of German war planning.

Prior to 1999 it was 'common knowledge' to simultaneously maintain that the Schlieffen plan was the German war plan while being mildly puzzled by the numerous glaring inconsistencies this proposition entailed. But, as Herwig himself notes, the fall of the Wall made a mass of new documentation available, which forces serious historians to conduct a fundamental reappraisal of German war planning. This new documentation was not presented by Herwig, who relies solely on outdated 'common knowledge', but is in *Inventing the Schlieffen Plan*.

War Plans & War Guilt

It is also 'common knowledge' that the Germans had an aggressive war plan, which proves German guilt for starting the First World War. This 'common knowledge' is directly contradicted by both the French and Russian war plans, which provided for a co-ordinated offensive against Germany, and by the fact that it was the French and Russians that attacked first. The first battles, at Stallupönen and Tannenberg in East Prussia and in Alsace and Lorraine in the west, were all fought on German territory. If aggressive war planning and conducting the first attack are proof of war guilt, then it was the French and Russians who were guilty, not the Germans. In fact, the Russians and the French attacked because it was militarily advantageous to do so; the Germans defended on interior lines because it was militarily advantageous for them to do so. Neither strategy is intrinsically 'moral' or 'immoral'.

The decision to go to war is *political*. Whether international politics are moral or immoral – indeed, whether the idea of 'war guilt' makes any political or ethical sense at all – is not a problem for military history.

Alternatively, the German war guilt school maintains that the Germans recognised the deterioration of their military position and launched an aggressive war while they still had a chance of winning. The most recent representative of this school is Mark Hewitson's *Germany and the Causes of the First World War*.[8] Hewitson's knowledge of German war planning goes no further than a firm conviction that there was an aggressive Schlieffen plan, the features of which were 'common knowledge' which did not require further explanation. He notes that the Germans knew they would be outnumbered. Nevertheless, he is convinced that the only way the Germans thought they could win a decisive victory was by a Schlieffen plan attack into France. He does not consult the actual German war plans; instead, Hewitson cites secondary literature, some of it quite old. I maintain that there never was a Schlieffen plan, which Hewitson somehow transforms into an assertion that 'there never was a single Schlieffen plan', whatever that means (multiple Schlieffen plans?).[9]

Hewitson thinks that the Germans had offensive tactics, which proves that they alone had an offensive strategy. Hewitson is evidently unaware that 'the cult of the offensive' in all pre-Great War European armies is an old and established theme of military history. He has apparently never heard of the French *offensive à outrance.*[10]

Hewitson does not address French and Russian strategy. Neither does he consider the actual conduct of the first month of the war. For Hewitson and the rest of the German war guilt school it's much better not to look at the military details. In fact, the Russians mobilised first, which started the clock ticking on the Russo-French co-ordinated attack, which would begin on the fifteenth day of mobilisation. There was no such timetable in the German war plan – ever. If there was, as A.J.P. Taylor thought, a 'War by Timetable', then that timetable was Franco-Russian.

If the Germans had an aggressive war plan, they did not get an opportunity to use it. The initial battles of the war were fought on German territory, with the French and Russians attacking and the Germans counter-attacking. By Hewitson's own strategic, political, tactical and moral standards, the French and Russians were blatant aggressors.

German Force Structure & the Schlieffen Plan

I contend that the 1906 Schlieffen plan *Denkschrift* required ninety-six divisions in a one-front war, but that only seventy-two were available in 1905, 1906 or 1907 – years in which the various fanciers of the Schlieffen plan have said it was implemented as the real German war plan.[11] The Schlieffen plan was short by one active, seven reserve divisions and sixteen ersatz divisions, a total of twenty-four divisions, which I call 'ghost divisions'. Indeed, ten of these ersatz divisions never existed. In 1914 the Germans were initially able to deploy sixty-eight divisions in the west, twelve short of the eighty required, and six ersatz divisions, ten short of the sixteen required. In 1914 the Germans were twenty-two divisions short of a Schlieffen plan-sized army.[12]

Some advocates of the Schlieffen plan, such as Herwig and Hewitson, simply refuse to address the problem, even though the Reichsarchiv said in 1925 that the need to raise the additional forces was an integral part of the plan.

Terence Holmes said:

> Schlieffen took the question of numbers very seriously because it was inseparable from his war planning. I will try to examine this question just as seriously … Anyone who finds this sort of thing tedious beyond words can skip the following discussion and refrain from taking a view of the Schlieffen plan.[13]

Holmes easily disposes of the opinions of Gross, Robert Foley and Annika Mombauer concerning the Schlieffen plan's missing divisions. He gives no credence to Gross' argument that, because Schlieffen allegedly used an unspecified number of non-existent heavy artillery batteries in 1893/94, it is perfectly plausible that he wrote twenty-four non-existent divisions into the Schlieffen plan. Neither does Holmes find Foley's argument that Schlieffen planned to use extra active army units to create the ersatz divisions very helpful. Foley, Holmes says, is mixing apples and oranges: active army and ersatz units were two different things. 'Mombauer offers no opinion on the subject of troop numbers in the Schlieffen plan, perhaps because it belongs to what she rather disdainfully calls the "minutiae" of the debate between Zuber and me.'[14] I agree wholeheartedly.[15]

The Real German War Plan

For diametrically different purposes both the Schlieffen School and Gerhard Ritter contended that the January–February 1906 Schlieffen plan *Denkschrift* provided Germany with the 'perfect plan'. The discovery of the RH 61/v.96 summary of the German deployment plans from 1893 to 1914 puts the final nails in the coffin of the Schlieffen plan dogma. It is now evident that after 1906, the Schlieffen plan *Aufmarsch* I was only one of several possible plans, one being for a far more probable two-front war. From 1909/10 to 1912/13 there were multiple plans, including the *Ostaufmarsch*. Far from being the 'perfect plan', the plan that survived to 1914 was not the one-front Schlieffen plan but the two-front *Aufmarsch* I *West und Ost*.

The central theme of German war planning from 1891 onwards was that the Germans would have to fight a two-front war and that in this war they would be seriously outnumbered. It is evident from Schlieffen's war plans and war games that an offensive into France was infeasible: the French army was just as strong (or stronger) as the German forces in the west, the French border fortifications were too formidable and even if the French were defeated, they could withdraw into the interior of the country. An all-out offensive on one front would not be decisive and would only ensure a quick crisis on the other front. Schlieffen's solution to the two-front war problem was to use Germany's interior position and rail mobility as force multipliers to counter-attack against the Franco-Russian offensive.

In 1914 the Russians mobilised first and the French and Russians attacked into Germany. They were defeated by German counter-attacks. In the east, Tannenberg was everything Schlieffen could have asked for – indeed, it was a replay of Schlieffen's 1894 *Generalstabsreise Ost*. In the west, Moltke could not impose a unified strategy on the army chiefs of staff (Kuhl, for one, was completely out of control). They were, in Schlieffen's words, content to conduct frontal attacks and win 'ordinary victories'. As Schlieffen had foreseen, the defeated French were able to withdraw into the interior of the country. The only real prospect for German victory at this point would have been the transfer of at least seven corps from the west to the east. This was the strategy in all of Schlieffen's *Generalstabsreisen Ost*. Had Moltke done so, it is hard to imagine how the Russian forces in East Prussia could have escaped total destruction. Instead, Moltke pursued the French, a course of action Schlieffen never recommended. Moltke had no firm concept of the operation: from 27 August to 5 September he would issue three fundamentally different operations orders. As Schlieffen had foretold, on 5 September, even before the French Marne offensive, the German advance had ground to a halt. The result was stalemate. Schlieffen had warned that a long war would be ruinous for European civilisation. The old master strategist was right for one last time.

Notes

1 http://en.wikipedia.org/wiki/Schlieffen_Plan, 20 October 2010.
2 Holger Herwig, *The First World War: Germany and Austria-Hungary 1914–1918* (London, 1997), pp. 46–50.
3 Holger Herwig, 'Germany and the "Short War" Illusion: Toward a New Interpretation?' in *Journal of Military History* 66 (July 2002), pp. 681–93.
4 Terence Holmes, '"One Throw of the Gambler's Dice": A Comment on Holger Herwig's View of the Schlieffen Plan' in *War in History* 67 (April 2003), pp. 513–6.
5 Holger Herwig, *The Marne 1914* (New York, 2009), p. xiv.
6 Ibid., pp. xii–xiii.
7 Ibid., p. 36.
8 Mark Hewitson, *Germany and the Causes of the First World War* (Oxford, 2004).
9 Ibid., p. 124.
10 Ibid., pp. 124–5.
11 It must be noted that at no point in the 1906 Schlieffen plan *Denkschrift* is there a concise summary of the force required. Coming up with this total involves some complicated searching. The usual Schlieffen plan force structure is given as twenty-six active corps

(fifty-two divisions), fourteen reserve corps (twenty-eight divisions, a total of eighty active and reserve divisions) and eight ersatz corps (sixteen divisions), for a grand total of forty-eight corps (ninety-six divisions).

12 IX Reserve Corps was sent west from coastal defence duty in Schleswig-Holstein to blockade Antwerp, while the Guard Reserve Corps (2nd Army) and XI Corps (3rd Army) were sent to East Prussia.

13 Terence Holmes, 'All Present and Correct: The Verifiable Army of the Schlieffen Plan' in *War in History* (2009), 16 (1), pp. 98–115.

14 Ibid., pp. 99–101.

15 As Terence Holmes has pointed out, Annika Mombauer hates attention to military detail, and with good reason. I said (in German) that German intelligence had been made aware by an agent report of the secret Anglo-French military conversations. Mombauer, who speaks fluent German, interpreted this to mean that 'the German Secret Service (!) had decided to take Liège', by which I assume she means that German spies were going to capture the fortress (Mombauer, 'German War Plans' in *War Planning 1914*, R. Hamilton and H. Herwig (eds), p. 61). The problem is not Mombauer's German, but the fact that she knows nothing about intelligence operations. She translates 'Joffre's *plan de renseignements*', which means 'intelligence collection plan', as 'the so-called [?] Plan XVII'; that is, the operations plan (p. 69). She says, 'according to Zuber, it was not the Germans who had the offensive war plan, but the Franco-Russian alliance' (p. 62). Presumably she does not believe this to be true. In the same book, Bruce Menning (p. 127) says that the Russians had an offensive war plan and Robert Doughty (p. 157) that the French did too, that they executed these plans, and that the first battles were fought on German territory. That would seem to me to constitute offensive French and Russian war plans. The problem is that for Mombauer German aggression is an article of faith, and any other conclusion is literally unthinkable.

INDEX